Be a Fodor's Correspondent

‖‖‖‖‖‖‖‖‖‖‖‖‖‖‖‖‖‖‖‖‖‖‖‖‖
☑ **W9-APT-686**

Your opinion matters. It matters to us. It matters to your fellow Fodor's travelers, too. And we'd like to hear it. In fact, we *need* to hear it. When you share your experiences and opinions, you become an active member of the Fodor's community. Here's how you can help improve Fodor's for all of us.

Tell us when we're right. We rely on local writers to give you an insider's perspective. But our writers and staff editors also depend on you. Your positive feedback is a vote to renew our recommendations for the next edition.

Tell us when we're wrong. We update most of our guides every year. But things change. If any of our descriptions are inaccurate or inadequate, we'll incorporate your changes in the next edition and will correct factual errors at fodors.com *immediately*.

Tell us what to include. You probably have had fantastic travel experiences that aren't yet in Fodor's. Why not share them with a community of like-minded travelers? Share your discoveries and experiences with everyone directly at fodors.com. Your input may lead us to add a new listing or a higher recommendation.

Give us your opinion instantly at our feedback center at www.fodors.com/feedback. You may also e-mail editors@fodors.com with the subject line "St. Maarten, St. Barth & Anguilla Editor." Or send your nominations, comments, and complaints by mail to St. Maarten, St. Barth & Anguilla Editor, Fodor's, 1745 Broadway, New York, NY 10019.

Happy Traveling!

Tim Jarrell

Tim Jarrell, Publisher

FODOR'S IN FOCUS ST. MAARTEN, ST. BARTH & ANGUILLA

Series Editor: Douglas Stallings

Editor: Douglas Stallings
Editorial Contributors: Elise Meyer, Roberta Sotonoff

Production Editor: Carolyn Roth
Maps & Illustrations: David Lindroth, *cartographer*; Bob Blake and Rebecca Baer, *map editors;* William Wu, *information graphics*
Design: Fabrizio La Rocca, *creative director*; Guido Caroti, *art director*; Ann McBride, *designer*; Melanie Marin, *senior picture editor*
Cover Photo: Big Bay, Philipsburg, Saint Maarten: Dennis Cox/WorldViews
Production Manager: Angela McLean

2nd Edition

ISBN 978-1-4000-0467-6
ISSN 1942-7344

SPECIAL SALES

This book is available for special discounts for bulk purchases for sales promotions or premiums. Special editions, including personalized covers, excerpts of existing books, and corporate imprints, can be created in large quantities for special needs. For more information, write to Special Markets/Premium Sales, 1745 Broadway, MD 6-2, New York, NY 10019, or e-mail specialmarkets@randomhouse.com.

AN IMPORTANT TIP & AN INVITATION

Although all prices, opening times, and other details in this book are based on information supplied to us at press time, changes occur all the time in the travel world, and Fodor's cannot accept responsibility for facts that become outdated or for inadvertent errors or omissions. **So always confirm information when it matters,** especially if you're making a detour to visit a specific place. Your experiences—positive and negative—matter to us. If we have missed or misstated something, **please write to us.** We follow up on all suggestions. Contact the St. Maarten, St. Barth & Anguilla editor at editors@fodors.com or c/o Fodor's at 1745 Broadway, New York, NY 10019.

PRINTED IN CHINA
10 9 8 7 6 5 4 3 2 1

CONTENTS

MAPS

DID YOU KNOW?

Anguilla, an island only 16 miles long and 3 miles wide, has over 30 white-sand beaches.

ABOUT THIS BOOK

Our Ratings

We wouldn't recommend a place that wasn't worth your time, but sometimes a place is so experiential that superlatives don't do it justice: you just have to be there to know. These sights, properties, and experiences get our highest rating, **Fodor's Choice** indicated by orange stars throughout this book. Black stars highlight sights and properties we deem **Highly Recommended** places that our writers, editors, and readers praise again and again for consistency and excellence.

Credit Cards

AE, D, DC, MC, V following restaurant and hotel listings indicate whether American Express, Discover, Diners Club, MasterCard, and Visa are accepted.

Restaurants

Unless we state otherwise, restaurants are open for lunch and dinner daily. We mention dress only when there's a specific requirement and reservations only when they're essential or not accepted.

Hotels

Unless we tell you otherwise, you can assume that the hotels have private bath, phone, TV, and air-conditioning. We always list facilities but not whether you'll be charged an extra fee to use them, so when pricing accommodations, find out what's included.

Many Listings
★	Fodor's Choice
★	Highly recommended
✉	Physical address
⊕	Directions
🕮	Mailing address
☎	Telephone
🖷	Fax
⊕	On the Web
✆	E-mail
🎫	Admission fee
⊙	Open/closed times
Ⓜ	Metro stations
⊟	Credit cards

Hotels & Restaurants
🏨	Hotel
➟	Number of rooms
⚭	Facilities
⭐	Meal plans
✕	Restaurant
⚏	Reservations
⭘	Smoking
🆈	BYOB
✕🏨	Hotel with restaurant that warrants a visit

Outdoors
🏌	Golf
⛺	Camping

Other
⊕	Family-friendly
⇨	See also
✉	Branch address
☞	Take note

Experience
St. Maarten, St. Barth,
and Anguilla

WHAT'S WHERE

1 St. Maarten/St. Martin. Two nations (Dutch and French), many nationalities, one small island, a lot of development. But there are also more white, sandy beaches than days in a month. Go for the awesome restaurants, extensive shopping, and wide range of activities. Don't go if you're not willing to get out and search for the really good stuff.

2 St. Barthélemy. If you come to St. Barth for a taste of European village life, not for a conventional full-service resort experience, you will be richly rewarded. Go for excellent dining and wine, great boutiques with the latest hip fashions, and an active, on-the-go vacation. Don't go for big resorts, and make sure your credit card is platinum-plated.

3 Anguilla. With miles of brilliant beaches and a range of luxurious resorts (even some that mere mortals can afford), Anguilla is where the rich, powerful, and famous go to chill out. Go for the fine cuisine in elegant surroundings, great snorkeling, and funky late-night music scene. Don't go for shopping and sightseeing. This island is all about relaxing and reviving.

ST. MAARTEN, ST. BARTH, AND ANGUILLA PLANNER

Island Activities	Logistics
All three islands have beautiful **beaches**, but those on Anguilla are probably the best. Baie Orientale on St. Martin is one of the Caribbean's most beautiful beaches, but it's very busy. St. Barth has a wide range of lovely, relatively small beaches.	**Getting to the Islands:** Only Queen Julianna International Airport (SXM) in St. Maarten has nonstop flights from the U.S. But you can get a small plane or ferry to Anguilla (AXA) or St. Barth (SBJ).
Anguilla has a good **golf course**, but these islands are not a major golfing destination.	**Hassle Factor:** Low for St. Maarten, medium to high for Anguilla or St. Barth.
Water sports, including windsurfing, are popular, especially on St. Barth and St. Maarten/St. Martin. **Diving** is good but not great in the area. St. Maarten in particular also has many **land activities** and attractions.	**Nonstops:** There are nonstop flights to St. Maarten from Atlanta (Delta), Charlotte (US Airways), Chicago (United—seasonal), Fort Lauderdale (Spirit), Miami (American), New York–JFK (American, JetBlue), New York–Newark (Continental), Philadelphia (US Airways), and Boston (JetBlue). There are also some nonstop charter flights (including GWV/Apple Vacations from Boston).
Shopping is great on both St. Barth and St. Maarten/St. Martin.	**On the Ground:** Taxis are available on all three islands, but many hotels in St. Barth offer free airport transfers since they own and rent out cars themselves.
Fine dining is a popular activity on all three islands. Grand Case in St. Martin is renowned across the Caribbean for its great restaurants. But dining on any of these islands can be quite expensive.	**Renting a Car:** Most visitors to St. Maarten/St. Martin and St. Barth rent cars (taxis are particularly expensive on St. Barth). Driving is on the right on both islands. Visitors to Anguilla often rent cars, but it's possible to do without if you choose your accommodation carefully; taxis, however, are expensive. Driving is on the left in Anguilla. Gas is generally more expensive than in the U.S.

Where to Stay

Time-Shares: Only Dutch St. Maarten has a large number of time-share resorts.

Large Resorts: Both Dutch St. Maarten and Anguilla have several fairly large resorts, and especially on Anguilla, many of the resorts can be quite luxurious and expensive. Some resorts in St. Maarten offer all-inclusive (AI) plans as add-ons, but there are no AI resorts on the island.

Small Hotels: All three islands have their share of small hotels (all the hotels and resorts on St. Barth are quite small, and most are exceedingly expensive); in French St. Martin, small hotels predominate, but there are a few larger resorts.

Villas: Most accommodations in St. Barth are in villas. Anguilla and St. Maarten/St. Martin also have many private villas for rent.

Hotel and Restaurant Costs

Restaurant prices are for a main course at dinner, and include any taxes or service charges. Hotel prices are per night for a double room in high season, excluding taxes, service charges, and meal plans.

Tips for Travelers

English is widely understood by most people involved in the tourism industry on all three islands; French is spoken in St. Barth and French St. Martin.

The minimum legal drinking ages: 18 in St. Maarten/St. Martin and St. Barth, 16 in Anguilla.

Electricity is 110 volts, just as in the U.S., on both St. Maarten and Anguilla; the standard in French St. Martin and St. Barth is the European, at 220 volts AC (60-cycle), requiring a plug adaptor and, for some appliances, a voltage converter.

U.S. currency is accepted almost everywhere in the islands, though the standard currency in French St. Martin and St. Barth is the euro.

What It Costs in U.S. Dollars

	$$$$	$$$	$$	$	¢
Restaurants	over $30	$20–$30	$12–$20	$8–$12	under $8
Hotels*	over $350	$250–$350	$150–$250	$80–$150	under $80
Hotels**	over $450	$350–$450	$250–$350	$125–$250	under $125

* Indicates hotels on the European Plan (EP—with no meals), Continental Plan (CP—with a continental breakfast), or Breakfast Plan (BP—with full breakfast), ** Indicates hotels on the Modified American Plan (MAP—with breakfast and dinner), Full American Plan (FAP—including all meals but no drinks), or All-Inclusive (AI—with all meals, drinks, and most activities).

TOP EXPERIENCES

Have lunch at the "lolos" in Grand Case, St. Maarten/ St. Martin

(A) Longtime visitors to St. Maarten/ St. Martin know that some of the best dining bargains can be found at one of several "lolos," roadside barbecue stands in Grand Case, the island's culinary capital. Though they're open from lunch until early evening, the best time to go is earlier in the day, when you can have your pick of delicious fare in ultracasual surroundings.

Taking the temperature of Baie Orientale, St. Maarten/ St. Martin

(B) Many consider this 2-mi-long wonder the island's most beautiful beach, and it's always buzzing with a variety of water-sports outfitters, beach clubs, and hotels. This is not the beach to visit to escape the crowds, but you will have fun here. Come and spend the day: have an open-air massage, try any sea toy you fancy, and stay until dark.

Play a round of golf at Temenos, Anguilla

(C) Now that Cap Juluca has taken over the management of the wonderful $50-million course designed by Greg Norman (where 13 of the 18 holes are directly on the water), you can once again thrill to the spectacular vistas of St. Maarten and blue sea at the tee box of the 390-yard starting hole. This is Anguilla's best (and only) golf course.

Shopping in Gustavia, St. Barth

(D) Whether you are shopping for fashionable clothing, accessories, or beautiful items for the home, it is fair to say that you will find

no better place in all the Caribbean than St. Barth. And most of the best stores line three streets in the island's capital, Gustavia. The best of the boutiques line Quai de la République, along the town's picturesque harborfront.

Luxuriate at the Eden Rock, St. Barth

(E) St. Barth's first hotel opened in the 1950s on the craggy bluff that splits Baie de St-Jean. Extensive renovations and an expansion in 2005 raised it into the top category of St. Barth properties, where it has remained. It's a chic yet comfortable beachside mini-resort and the ideal retreat from harsh northern winters. Bring your platinum card, because all this pampering doesn't come cheap.

Have the Caribbean's best rum punch at Elvis' Beach Bar, Anguilla

You can visit this bar (well, it's actually a boat) at Sandy Ground every day but Tuesday, when it's closed. Come to have one of the best rum punches in the Caribbean, to dance the night away, or to have a bite to eat until late. And be sure to come for one of the famous Lunasea parties if you're on the island during a full moon.

Relax and restore your soul at The Spa, St. Maarten/St. Martin

One of the best places in St. Maarten to relax and rejuvenate is this spa in the shopping center at Maho Village, one of the island's busiest resort areas. In addition to a huge hydrotherapy pool with seating that resembles lounge chairs,

TOP EXPERIENCES

you can have any of a number of treatments in chic surroundings.

Have dinner at KoalKeel, Anguilla

(F) Dinner at KoalKeel is a unique culinary and historic treat not to be missed on Anguilla. Originally part of a sugar and cotton plantation, the restaurant, with its beautiful dining verandah, is owned and lovingly overseen by Lisa Gumbs, a descendent of the slaves once housed here. A tour of the history-rich buildings is a must.

Hang out in Marigot, St. Maarten/St. Martin

(G) St. Martin's lovely seaside capital is a must-see destination. Everyone coming to St. Maarten/ St. Martin should spend at least a few hours exploring the bustling harbor, shopping stalls, open-air cafés, and boutiques of French St. Martin's biggest town.

Stroll the powdery sands of Shoal Bay, Anguilla

(H) This 2-mi-long beach is covered with sand as fine and white as powdered sugar, making it one of the best of many excellent beaches on this tiny island. Park yourself at one of the multitude of restaurants that offer food and umbrella rentals, and relax with a view of the turquoise water.

Let it all hang out at Anse de Grande Saline, St. Barth

(I) Secluded, with its sandy ocean bottom, this is just about everyone's favorite beach, and is great for swimmers, too. Best of all, there's no major development here. What you will find is a bit of wind, so you can enjoy yourself more if you go on a calm day. And

despite the official prohibition, this is St. Barth's de facto nude beach, enjoyed by young and old alike.

Meet some new friends at the Butterfly Farm, St. Maarten/ St. Martin

(J) This quiet, shady haven will mesmerize you with hundreds of beautiful tropical butterflies flitting about in a large, screened enclosure. There's also a cute gift shop. But come soon after your arrival on St. Maarten/St. Martin, because your entry ticket allows you to come back as many times as you want during your stay.

Find "paradis" at Loterie Farm, St. Maarten/St. Martin

On the slopes of Pic du Paradis, the highest mountain on St. Maarten/ St. Martin, Loterie Farm is a family-friendly, family-run private nature reserve with hiking trails, restaurants, and a zip line. It's a must-see attraction if you have kids (or even if you don't).

Throw caution (and credit cards) to the wind at Le Gaïac, St. Barth

Chef Stéphane Mazières' restaurant at Le Toiny features a dramatic, tasteful cliff-side dining porch and showcases his gastronomic art. This is one ultra-expensive dinner that you will certainly want to budget for in St. Barth. The French cuisine is notable for its innovation and extraordinary presentation. The restaurant even produces much of its own organic produce.

WHEN TO GO

The Caribbean high season is traditionally from December 15 through April 15—when northern weather is at its worst. During this season you're guaranteed that all hotels and restaurants will be open and busy. It's also the most fashionable, the most expensive, and the most popular time to visit. The Christmas holiday season is an especially expensive time to visit Anguilla and St. Barth, and you may very well pay double during this period, not to mention have a one- to two-week minimum rental requirement for villas and even some hotels. If you wait until mid-May or June, prices may be 20% to 50% less, and this is particularly true of St. Barth and Anguilla; however, some hotels close, particularly later in summer and early fall. The period from mid-August through late November is typically the least busy time in all three islands, when many of the major resorts on Anguilla and restaurants on St. Barth close.

Climate

The Caribbean climate is fairly constant. Summer, however, can bring somewhat higher temperatures and more humidity because the trade winds blow. The Atlantic hurricane season begins on June 1 and stretches all the way through November 30. While heavy rains can happen anytime throughout the year, it's during this six-month period when tropical fronts are most likely. Major hurricanes are possible but a relatively rare occurrence, and in recent years building standards have been raised to a much higher level to avoid some of the devastating damage such as that caused in St. Maarten by Hurricane Louis in 1995.

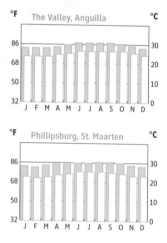

GREAT ITINERARIES

Here are some suggestions for how to make the most of your trip to the islands, whichever one you choose.

A Perfect Day in St. Maarten/St. Martin

In the morning head out to Loterie Farm on the slopes of Pic du Paradis and take advantage of some of the hiking trails or try the zip line. You can stay and have lunch in the Hidden Forest Café, but if you are hot, head right to Baie Orientale, where you can rent some chairs and umbrellas from one of the beach clubs and take advantage of the lovely surf. If you get hungry, you can have lunch there, too. The afternoon is a good time to stroll along Front Street in Philipsburg, because you can duck into one of the many air-conditioned stores to escape the heat. In the late afternoon, a nap is in order, but you have to be awake before sunset. For a splurge, have your sunset cocktail at the bar of La Samanna before heading to one of the restaurants in Grand Case for a perfect dinner.

A Perfect Day in Anguilla

The perfect day in Anguilla often involves the least activity. After breakfast, head to powdery Shoal Bay. If you get tired of sunning and dozing, take a ride on Junior's Glass Bottom Boat, or arrange a wreck dive at Shoal Bay Scuba.

Have lunch at one of the beachside restaurants and relax a little more. In the late afternoon, head back to your hotel room to shower and change before going to Elvis' Beach Bar to watch the sunset with a cold rum punch. Have dinner at one of the island's great restaurants.

A Perfect Day in St. Barth

Have your café au lait and croissant in a harbor-side café in Gustavia, and then explore some of the many boutiques on Quai de la République. If you tire of the relative hubbub, have lunch in quieter St-Jean and then shop and stroll some more. If you're not a shopper, take a snorkeling excursion or go deep-sea fishing. Be sure to get a late-afternoon nap, because the nightlife in St. Barth doesn't get going until late. After a sunset cocktail, have dinner at one of the island's many great restaurants. Perhaps you'll choose Le Ti St. Barth Caribbean Tavern, which is as much a gathering spot as a restaurant. By the time dessert comes, someone is sure to be dancing on the tables; perhaps it will be you.

WEDDINGS AND HONEYMOONS

There's no question that St. Maarten/St. Martin, St. Barth, and Anguilla are three of the Caribbean's foremost honeymoon destinations. Romance is in the air here, and the white, sandy beaches and turquoise water and swaying palm trees and balmy tropical breezes and perpetual summer sunshine put people in the mood for love. Destination weddings—no longer exclusive to celebrities and the super rich—are also popular on Anguilla and St. Maarten, but French laws make getting married in French St. Martin or St. Barth too difficult. All the larger resorts in Anguilla and St. Maarten have wedding planners to help you with the paperwork and details.

The Big Day

Choosing the Perfect Place. When choosing a location, remember that you really have two choices to make: the ceremony location and where to have the reception, if you're having one. For the former, there are beaches, bluffs overlooking beaches, gardens, private residences, resort lawns, and, of course, places of worship. As for the reception, there are these same choices, as well as restaurants. If you decide to go outdoors, remember the seasons—yes, the Caribbean has seasons. If you're planning a wedding outdoors, be sure you have a backup plan in case it rains. Also, if you're planning an outdoor

wedding at sunset—which is very popular—be sure you match the time of your ceremony to the time the sun sets at that time of year.

Finding a Wedding Planner. If you're planning to invite more than a minister and your loved one to your wedding ceremony, seriously consider an on-island wedding planner who can help select a location, help design the floral scheme and recommend a florist as well as a photographer, help plan the menu, and suggest any local traditions to incorporate into your ceremony.

Of course, all the larger resorts have their own wedding planners on-site. If you're planning a resort wedding, work with the on-site wedding coordinator to prepare a detailed list of the exact services they'll provide. If your idea of your wedding doesn't match their services, try a different resort. Or look for an independent wedding planner. Both Anguilla and St. Maarten have independent wedding planners who do not work directly for resorts.

Legal Requirements. There are minimal residency requirements on both Anguilla and St. Maarten, and no blood tests or shots are required on either island. On Anguilla, you can get a wedding license in two working days; paperwork in St. Maarten has to be submitted 14 days in advance, but there is no residency requirement there. You need

to supply proof of identity (a passport or certified copy of your birth certificate signed by a notary public, though in Anguilla even a driver's license with a photo will do). If you've been married before, then you must provide proof of divorce with the original or certified copy of the divorce decree if divorced, or copy of the death certificate if you are a widow or widower.

Wedding Attire. In the Caribbean, basically anything goes, from long, formal dresses with trains to white bikinis. Floral sundresses are fine, too. Men can wear tuxedos or a simple pair of solid-color slacks with a nice white linen shirt. If you want formal dress and a tuxedo, it's usually better to bring your formal attire with you.

Photographs. Deciding whether to use the photographer supplied by your resort or an independent photographer is an important choice. Resorts that host a lot of weddings usually have their own photographers, but you can also find independent, professional island-based photographers, and an independent wedding planner will know the best in the area. Look at the portfolio (many photographers now have Web sites), and decide whether this person can give you the kind of memories you are looking for. If you're satisfied with the photographer that

your resort uses, then make sure you see proofs and order prints before you leave the island.

The Honeymoon

Do you want champagne and strawberries delivered to your room each morning? An infinity-edged swimming pool in which to float? A five-star restaurant in which to dine? Then a resort is the way to go, and both Anguilla and St. Maarten have options in different price ranges (though Anguilla resorts are more luxurious and expensive as a rule). Whether you want a luxurious experience or a more modest one, you'll certainly find someplace romantic to which you can escape. You can usually stay on at the resort where your wedding was held. On the other hand, maybe you want your own private home in which to romp naked—or your own kitchen in which to whip up a gourmet meal for your loved one. In that case, a private vacation-rental home or condo is the answer.

DID YOU KNOW?

Not counting Trinidad, the Caribbean has about 300 native species of butterflies, far fewer than in Central America, which has over 2,000.

St. Maarten/
St. Martin

WORD OF MOUTH

"St. Maarten is very small and there are excellent restaurants on both sides of the island. I would never recommend one side over the other and it is meaningless anyway because it is so easy to get from one side to the other."

—Barbara1

Updated
by Elise
Meyer and
Roberta
Sotonoff

ST. MAARTEN/ST. MARTIN IS VIRTUALLY unique among Caribbean destinations. The 37-square-mi (96-square-km) island is a seamless place (there are no border gates), but it is governed by two nations—the Netherlands and France—and has residents from 70-some different countries. A call from the Dutch side to the French is an international call, currencies are different, and the vibe is even different. Only the island of Hispaniola, which encompasses two distinct countries, Haiti and the Dominican Republic, is in a similar position in the Caribbean.

Happily for Americans, who make up the majority of visitors to St. Maarten/St. Martin, English works in both nations. Dutch St. Maarten might feel particularly comfortable for Americans, the prices are lower (not to mention in U.S. dollars), the big hotels have casinos, and there is more nightlife. Huge cruise ships disgorge masses of shoppers into the Philipsburg shopping area at mid-morning, when roads can quickly become overly congested. But once you pass the meandering, unmarked border into the French side, you will find a bit of the ambience of the south of France: quiet countryside, fine cuisine, and in Marigot a walkable harbor area with outdoor cafés, outdoor markets, and plenty of shopping and cultural activities.

HISTORY AND CULTURE

Almost 4,000 years ago it was salt and not tourism that drove the little island's economy. Arawak Indians, the island's first known inhabitants, prospered until the warring Caribs invaded, adding the peaceful Arawaks to their list of conquests. Columbus spotted the isle on November 11, 1493, and named it after St. Martin (whose feast day is November 11), but it wasn't populated by Europeans until the 17th century, when it was claimed by the Dutch, French, and Spanish. The Dutch and French finally joined forces to claim the island in 1644, and the Treaty of Concordia partitioned the territory in 1648. According to legend, the border was drawn along the line where a French man and a Dutch man, running from opposite coasts, met.

Both sides of the island offer a touch of European culture along with a lot of laid-back Caribbean ambience. Water sports abound—diving, snorkeling, scuba, sailing, windsurfing, and in early March, the Heineken Regatta.

With soft trade winds cooling the subtropical climate, it's easy to while away the day relaxing on one of the 37 beaches, strolling Philipsburg's boardwalk, and perusing the

Oyster Pond, St. Maarten

shops on Philipsburg's Front Street or the *rues* (streets) of the very French town of Marigot. While luck is an important commodity at St. Maarten's 13 casinos, chance plays no part in finding a good meal at the excellent eateries or after-dark fun in the subtle to sizzling nightlife. Still, the isle's biggest assets are its friendly residents.

Although the island has been heavily developed—especially on the Dutch side—somehow the winding, unmarked roads escaped improvement. When cruise ships are in port (and there can be as many as seven at once), shopping areas are crowded and traffic moves at a snail's pace. We suggest spending the days on the beach or the water, and plan shopping excursions for the early morning or at cocktail hour, after "rush hour" traffic calms down. Still, these are minor inconveniences compared to the feel of the sand between your toes or the breeze through your hair, gourmet food sating your appetite, or having the ability to crisscross between two nations on one island.

EXPLORING ST. MAARTEN/ ST. MARTIN

The best way to explore St. Maarten/St. Martin is by car. Though often congested, especially around Philipsburg and Marigot, the roads are fairly good, though narrow and winding, with some speed bumps, potholes, roundabouts,

TOP REASONS TO GO

A two-nation vacation is what you get with St. Maarten/ St. Martin. But the island has much more going for it than that.

■ Philipsburg is one of the best shopping spots in the Caribbean; though it has fewer bargains these days with the growing strength of the euro, Marigot (the capital of French St. Martin) is still chock-full of interesting stores.

■ Grand Case is the island's gastronomic capital, but there are good restaurants all over the French side. You'll find plenty of great restaurants in

Philipsburg and Simpson Bay as well.

■ Thirty-seven perfect beaches are spread out all over the island (and most of the island's hotels are not on the best beaches, one reason so many people choose to rent a car). Whether you are looking for the busy scene at Baie Orientale or the deserted stretches of sand at Simpson Bay, each is unique.

■ The wide range of water sports—from sailing to water-skiing, snorkeling to deep-sea fishing—will meet almost any need.

and an occasional wandering herd of goats. Few roads are marked with their names, but destination signs are common. Besides, the island is so small that it's hard to get really lost—at least that is what locals tell you.

A scenic "loop" around the island can take most of a day, but gives you time to take plenty of stops. If you head up the east shoreline from Philipsburg, follow the signs to Dawn Beach and Oyster Pond. The road winds past soaring hills, turquoise waters, quaint West Indian houses, and wonderful views of St. Barth. As you cross over to the French side, turn into Le Galion for a stop at the beach, the stables, the butterflies, or the windsurf school, then keep following the road around Orient Bay, the St-Tropez of the Caribbean. Continue to Anse Marcel, Grand Case, Marigot, and Sandy Ground. From Marigot, the flat island of Anguilla is visible. Completing the loop brings you past Cupecoy Beach, through Maho and Simpson Bay, where Saba looms on the horizon, and back over the mountain road into Philipsburg.

DUTCH SIDE

Guana Bay Point. On the rugged, windswept east coast about 10 minutes north of Philipsburg, Guana Bay Point is an isolated, untended beach with a spectacular view of St. Barth. Undercurrents make it more a turf than a surf destination, and locals favor the area for hiking.

Philipsburg. The capital of Dutch St. Maarten stretches about a mile (1½ km) along an isthmus between Great Bay and the Salt Pond and has five parallel streets. Most of the village's dozens of shops and restaurants are on narrow and cobblestoned Front Street, closest to Great Bay. It's generally congested when cruise ships are in port, because of its many duty-free shops and several casinos. Little lanes called *steegjes* connect Front Street with Back Street, which has fewer shops and considerably less congestion. Along the beach is a ½-mi-long boardwalk with restaurants and several Wi-Fi hotspots.

Wathey Square (pronounced *watty*) is in the heart of the village. Directly across from the square are the town hall and the courthouse, in the striking white building with the cupola. The structure was built in 1793, and has served as the commander's home, a fire station, a jail, and a post office. The streets surrounding the square are lined with hotels, duty-free shops, fine restaurants, and cafés. The **Captain Hodge Pier,** just off the square, is a good spot to view Great Bay and the beach that stretches alongside.

The **Sint Maarten Museum** hosts rotating cultural exhibits and a permanent historical display called Forts of St. Maarten–St. Martin. Artifacts range from Arawak pottery shards to objects salvaged from the wreck of the HMS *Proselyte.* ⊠ *7 Front St., Philipsburg* ☎ *599/542–4917* ⊡ *Free* ⊙ *Weekdays 10–4*

St. Maarten Park. This delightful little enclave houses animals and plants indigenous to the Caribbean and South America, including many birds that were inherited from a former aviary. There are also a few strays from other parts of the world and a snake house with boa constrictors and other slithery creatures. The zoo's lone male collared peccary now has a female to keep him company. A family of cotton-topped tamarins also have taken residence at the zoo. All the animals live among more than 100 different plant species. The Monkey Bar is the zoo's charming souvenir shop, and sells Caribbean and zoo mementos. This is a

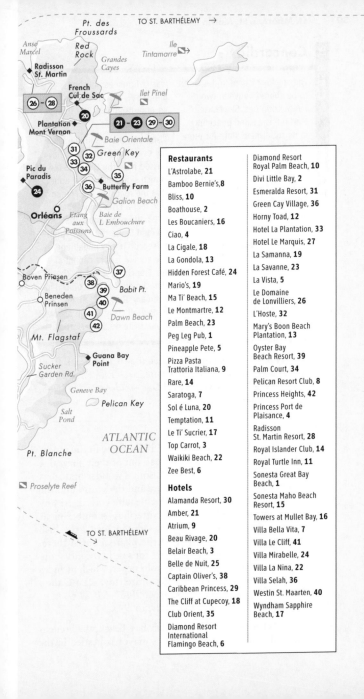

Pt. des Froussards

TO ST. BARTHÉLEMY →

Anse Marcel
Red Rock
Grandes Cayes
Ile Tintamarre

Radisson St. Martin

French Cul de Sac
Ilet Pinel

26 – 28
20
21 – 23 29 30

Plantation Mont Vernon
Baie Orientale
31 32
Green Key
33 34
35
Pic du Paradis
36 Butterfly Farm
24
Galion Beach
Orléans
Etang aux Poissons
Baie de L'Embouchure

Boven Prinsen
37
38 39 Babit Pt.
Beneden Prinsen
40
41 Dawn Beach
42

Mt. Flagstaf

Guana Bay Point
Sucker Garden Rd.

Geneve Bay
Pelican Key
Salt Pond
ATLANTIC OCEAN

Pt. Blanche

Proselyte Reef

TO ST. BARTHÉLEMY →

Restaurants
L'Astrolabe, **21**
Bamboo Bernie's, **8**
Bliss, **10**
Boathouse, **2**
Les Boucaniers, **16**
Ciao, **4**
La Cigale, **18**
La Gondola, **13**
Hidden Forest Café, **24**
Mario's, **19**
Ma Ti' Beach, **15**
Le Montmartre, **12**
Palm Beach, **23**
Peg Leg Pub, **1**
Pineapple Pete, **5**
Pizza Pasta Trattoria Italiana, **9**
Rare, **14**
Saratoga, **7**
Sol é Luna, **20**
Temptation, **11**
Le Ti' Sucrier, **17**
Top Carrot, **3**
Waikiki Beach, **22**
Zee Best, **6**

Hotels
Alamanda Resort, **30**
Amber, **21**
Atrium, **9**
Beau Rivage, **20**
Belair Beach, **3**
Belle de Nuit, **25**
Captain Oliver's, **38**
Caribbean Princess, **29**
The Cliff at Cupecoy, **18**
Club Orient, **35**
Diamond Resort International Flamingo Beach, **6**
Diamond Resort Royal Palm Beach, **10**
Divi Little Bay, **2**
Esmeralda Resort, **31**
Green Cay Village, **36**
Horny Toad, **12**
Hotel La Plantation, **33**
Hotel Le Marquis, **27**
La Samanna, **19**
La Savanne, **23**
La Vista, **5**
Le Domaine de Lonvilliers, **26**
L'Hoste, **32**
Mary's Boon Beach Plantation, **13**
Oyster Bay Beach Resort, **39**
Palm Court, **34**
Pelican Resort Club, **8**
Princess Heights, **42**
Princess Port de Plaisance, **4**
Radisson St. Martin Resort, **28**
Royal Islander Club, **14**
Royal Turtle Inn, **11**
Sonesta Great Bay Beach, **1**
Sonesta Maho Beach Resort, **15**
Towers at Mullet Bay, **16**
Villa Bella Vita, **7**
Villa Le Cliff, **41**
Villa Mirabelle, **24**
Villa La Nina, **22**
Villa Selah, **36**
Westin St. Maarten, **40**
Wyndham Sapphire Beach, **17**

Concordia

The smallest island in the world to be shared between two different countries, St. Maarten/St. Martin has existed peacefully in its subdivided state for more than 360 years. The Treaty of Concordia, which subdivided the island, was signed in 1648, and was really inspired by the two resident colonies of French and Dutch settlers' (not to mention their respective governments') having joined forces to repel a common enemy, the Spanish, in 1644. Although the French were promised the side of the island facing Anguilla and the Dutch the south side of the island, the boundary itself wasn't firmly established until 1817, and then after several disputes (16 of them, to be exact).

Visitors to the island will likely not even notice that they have passed from the Dutch to the French side unless they notice that the roads on the French side feel a little smoother. In 2003, the population of St. Martin (and St. Barthélemy) voted to secede from Guadeloupe, the administrative capital of the French West Indies. That detachment became official in February 2007, and St. Martin is now officially known as the Collectivité de Saint-Martin.

---

perfect place to take the kids when they need a break from the sand and sea. ⊠ *Madame Estate, Arch Rd., Philipsburg* ☎ *599/543–2030* ⊇ *$10* ☉ *Mid-Dec.–mid-Apr., daily 9–5; mid-Apr.–mid-Dec., daily 9:30–6.*

FRENCH SIDE

★ Fodor'sChoice **Butterfly Farm.** If you arrive early in the morn-
☾ ing when the butterflies first break out of their chrysalis, you'll be able to marvel at the absolute wonder of dozens of butterflies and moths from around the world and the particular host plants with which each evolved. At any given time, some 40 species of butterflies—numbering as many as 600 individual insects—flutter inside the lush screened garden and hatch on the plants housed there. Butterfly art and knickknacks are for sale in the gift shop. In case you want to come back, your ticket, which includes a guided tour, is good for your entire stay. ⊠ *Le Galion Beach Rd., Quartier d'Orléans* ☎ *590/87–31–21* ⊕ *www. thebutterflyfarm.com* ⊇ *$12* ☉ *Daily 9–3:30.*

French Cul de Sac. North of Orient Bay Beach, the French-colonial mansion of St. Martin's mayor is nestled in the hills. Little, red-roof houses look like open umbrellas tumbling down the green hillside. The area is peaceful and good for hiking. From the beach here, shuttle boats make the five-minute trip to **Ilêt Pinel,** an uninhabited island that's fine for picnicking, sunning, and swimming. There are full-service beach clubs there, so just pack the sunscreen and head over.

Grand Case. The Caribbean's own Restaurant Row is the heart of this French side town, a ten-minute drive from either Orient Bay or Marigot, stretching along a narrow beach overlooking Anguilla. You'll find a first-rate restaurant for every palate, mood, and wallet. At lunchtime, or with kids, head to the casual *lolos* (open-air barbecue stands) and feet-in-the sand beach bars. Twilight drinks and tapas are fun. At night, stroll the strip and preview the sophisticated offerings on the menus posted outside before you settle in for a long and sumptuous meal. If you still have the energy, there are lounges with music (usually a DJ) that get going after 11 PM.

★ Fodor'sChoice **Marigot.** It is great fun to spend a few hours exploring the bustling harbor, shopping stalls, open-air cafés, and boutiques of St. Martin's biggest town, especially on Wednesday and Saturday, when the daily open-air craft markets expand to include fresh fruits and veggies, spices, and all manner of seafood. The market might remind you of Provence, especially when aromas of delicious cooking waft by. Be sure to climb up to the fort for the panoramic view, stopping at the Museum for an overview of the Island. Marina Royale is the shopping/lunch spot central to the port, but rue de la République and rue de la Liberté, which border the bay, have duty-free shops, boutiques, and bistros. The West Indies Mall offers a deluxe (and air-conditioned) shopping experience, with such shops as Lacoste. There's less bustle here than in Philipsburg, but the open-air cafés are still tempting places to sit and people-watch. Marigot is fun into the night, so you might wish to linger through dinnertime. From the harborfront you can catch ferries for Anguilla and St. Barth. Parking can be a real challenge during the business day, and even at night during the high season.

Though not much remains of the structure itself, **Fort Louis,** which was completed by the French in 1789, is great fun if you want to climb the 92 steps to the top for the wonderful views of the island and neighboring Anguilla. On

DID YOU KNOW?

Le Fort Louis sits high above Marigot, St. Martin. It was completed by the French in 1789.

Wednesdays and Saturdays there is a market in the square at the bottom. ⊠ *Marigot*.

Ⓒ The **Saint Martin Museum** is a model example of how a small museum can make an impact. This historic building (near the Catholic Church) explores the archaeology, anthropology, geology, marine life, and history of St. Martin in attractive displays that offer explanations in both French and English. ⊠ *7 Fichot St., Marigot* ☎ *0690/56–78–92* ⌨ *$5* ☉ *Daily 9–1 and 3–5.*

Orléans. North of Oyster Pond and the Étang aux Poissons (Fish Lake) is the island's oldest settlement, also known as the French Quarter. You can find classic, vibrantly painted West Indian–style homes with the original gingerbread fretwork, and large areas of the nature and marine preserve that is actively working to save the fragile ecosystem of the island.

★ Fodor'sChoice **Pic du Paradis.** Between Marigot and Grand Case, "Paradise Peak," at 1,492 feet, is the island's highest point. There are two observation areas. From them, the tropical forest unfolds below, and the vistas are breathtaking. The road is quite isolated and steep, best suited to a four-wheel-drive vehicle, so don't head up here unless you are prepared for the climb. There have also been some problems with crime in this area, so it might be best to go with an experienced local guide.

Halfway up the road to Pic du Paradis is **Loterie Farm**, a peaceful 150-acre private nature preserve opened to the public in 1999 by American expat B. J. Welch. There are hiking trails and maps, so you can go on your own (€5) or arrange a guide for a group (€25 for six people). Along the marked trails you will see native forest with tamarind, gum, mango, and mahogany trees, and wildlife including greenback monkeys if you are lucky. Don't miss a treetop lunch or dinner at **Hidden Forest Café** (⇨ *Where to Eat, below*), Loterie Farm's restaurant, where Julie, B. J.'s wife, cooks. If you are brave—and over 4 feet 5 inches tall—try soaring over trees on one of the longest zip lines in the Western Hemisphere. ⊠ *Rte. de Pic du Paradis* ☎ *590/87–86–16 or 590/57–28–55* ⌨ *€35–€55* ☉ *Daily sunrise–sunset.*

Plantation Mont Vernon. Wander past indigenous flora, a renovated 1786 cotton plantation, and an old-fashioned rum distillery at a unique outdoor history and eco-museum. Along the rambling paths of this former wooded estate,

BEST BETS FOR DINING

Fodor's Choice ★

Bacchus, La Cigale, L'Astrolabe, Le Pressoir, Le Tastevin, Mario's Bistro, Ocean Lounge, Talk of the Town, Temptation

MOST ROMANTIC

Antoine, Le Pressoir, Sol é Luna, Temptation

BEST VIEW

Antoine, Le Cigale, Sol é Luna, Taloulah Mango's

BEST LOCAL FOOD

Chesterfield's, Claude Mini-Club, Les Boucaniers

BEST FOR FAMILIES

Kangaroo Court Café, Pineapple Pete, Taloulah Mango's

HIP AND YOUNG

Hidden Forest Café, La Gondola, Palm Beach, Temptation, Waïkiki Beach

bilingual signs give detailed explanations of the island's agricultural history when its economy was dependent on salt, rum, coffee, sugar, and indigo. There's a complimentary coffee bar along the way and a delightful gift shop at the entrance. Sadly, the sight has seen better days and is no longer a must-visit. ⊠ *Rte. d'Orient-Baie* ☎ *590/29–50–62* ⊕ *www.plantationmontvernon.com* ☎ *€12* ☉ *Daily 9–5.*

WHERE TO EAT

Although most people come to St. Maarten/St. Martin for sun and fun, they leave praising the cuisine. On an island that covers only 37 square miles, there are more than 400 restaurants from which to choose. You can sample the best dishes from France, Thailand, Italy, Vietnam, India, Japan, and, of course, the Caribbean.

Many of the best restaurants are in Grand Case (on the French side), but you should not limit your culinary adventures to that village. Great dining thrives throughout the island, from the bistros of Marigot to the hopping restaurants of Cupecoy to the low-key eateries of Simpson Bay. Whether you enjoy dining on fine china in one of the upscale restaurants or off a paper plate at the island's many lolos (roadside barbecue stands), St. Maarten/St. Martin's culinary options are sure to appeal to every palate.

ABOUT THE RESTAURANTS

During high season, it's essential to make reservations, and making them a month in advance is advisable for some of the best places. Dutch-side restaurants sometimes include a 15% service charge, so check your bill before tipping. On the French side service is always included, but it is customary to leave 5% to 10% extra in cash for the server. Keep in mind that you can't always leave tips on your credit card (and it's customary to tip in cash, anyway), so carry enough cash. A taxi is probably the easiest solution to the parking problems in Grand Case, Marigot, and Philipsburg. Grand Case has two lots—each costs $4—at each end of the main boulevard, but they're often packed.

WHAT TO WEAR

Although appropriate dining attire ranges from swimsuits to sport jackets, casual dress is usually appropriate throughout restaurants on the island. For men, a jacket and khakis or jeans will take you anywhere; for women, dressy pants, a skirt, or even fancy shorts are usually acceptable. Jeans are fine in the less formal eateries. In the listings below dress is casual (albeit chic) unless otherwise noted, but ask when making reservations if you're unsure.

WHAT IT COSTS IN DOLLARS AND EUROS				
¢	$	$$	$$$	$$$$
RESTAURANTS				
Under $8	$8–$12	$12–$20	$20–$30	Over $30
Under €6	€6–€9	€9–€15	€15–€22	Over €22

Restaurant prices are per person for a main course at dinner and do not include taxes and service charges. Prices on restaurant menus in Dutch St. Maarten are usually listed in dollars; prices in French St. Martin are usually listed in euros.

DUTCH SIDE

COLE BAY

$$$ Fodor's Choice ✕ **Peg Leg Pub.** *Steak.* This place is a cross between your typical beach bar and an English pub, albeit one where steaks make up the heart of the menu. Lunch options include deli-style sandwich platters at much more moderate prices than what you'll find at dinner (most options are under $10). By night, red meat rules the menu, though seafood, kebabs, and pastas shouldn't be over-

looked. Good news for beer lovers: Peg Leg Pub serves more than 35 different brews. Best of all, appetizers are half-price during happy hour; try the bacon-wrapped shrimp, jalapeño cheese poppers, or the coconut shrimp. There's entertainment on Wednesday and Friday nights. ⊠ *Port de Plaisance, Cole Bay* ☎ *599/544–5859* ⊕ *www.peglegpub. com* ⊟ *AE, D, MC, V* ⊗ *No lunch Sun.*

CUPECOY

$$$ ✕ **La Gondola.** *Italian.* Owner Davide Foini started out by selling just his homemade pasta, which proved to be so popular that he opened this authentic trattoria that has found its way onto many "best bets" lists of island regulars. The kitchen still rolls out the dough for the dozens of pasta dishes on the encyclopedic Italian menu, which also includes favorites like veal parmigiana, chicken piccata in marsala sauce, and osso buco Milanese. Save room for desserts like the *fantasia di dessert del Carnevale di Venezia* (a warm chocolate tart and frozen nougat served with raspberry sauce) or tiramisu. The service is professional and high-tech—the waiters take orders with earpieces and handheld computers. ⊠ *Atlantis World Casino, Rhine Rd. 106, Cupecoy* ☎ *599/544–3938* ⊕ *www.lagondola-sxm. com* ⊟ *AE, MC, V* ⊗ *No lunch.*

$$$ ✕ **Le Montmartre.** *French.* Newly refurbished, Montmarte has a new look and a whole new menu. Cane-back chairs, white tablecloths, and mirrored white walls have a cozy look about them. Four French chefs prepare tasty morsels like foie gras, frogs' legs, and profiteroles with hazelnut whipped cream, but also stray from their heritage to offer up entrées like Chinese-style ribs and "paella-style" calamari with risotto and mussels. The lounge stays open well past 11, when the kitchen closes. ⊠ *Atlantis World Casino, Rhine Rd. 106, Cupecoy* ☎ *599/544–3939* ⊕ *www. lemontmartre.com* ⊟ *AE, MC, V* ⊗ *No lunch.*

$$$$ ✕ **Rare.** *Steak.* Within an intimate, clubby setting, a guitarist provides background music while carnivores delight in Chef Dino Jagtiani's creative menu. The focus is steak: certified Angus Prime cuts topped with chimichurri, béarnaise, horseradish, peppercorn, or mushroom sauce. Not into red meat? You can also choose from seafood, pork, lamb, or veal. Sample some delicious sides like truffled mashed potatoes or cultivated mushroom sauté (a tasty fungi variety). Luscious desserts will make you forget that you will want to look good in your bathing suit tomorrow morning. ⊠ *Atlantis World Casino, Rhine Rd. 106, Cupecoy*

☎599/545–5714 ⊕*www.dare-to-be-rare.com* ▭ AE, D, MC, V ☺*Closed Sept. and Mon. June–Oct. No lunch.*

★ Fodor'sChoice ✕**Temptation.** *Eclectic.* Super, creative Chef Dino

$$$$ Jagtiani, who trained at the Culinary Institute of America, is the mastermind behind dishes like seared foie gras PB and J (melted foie gras accented with peanut butter and homemade port-wine fig jam) and herb-crusted Chilean sea bass. The chef, who compares dessert to lovemaking ("both intimate, and not to be indulged in lightly"), offers a crème brûlée tasting, as well as Granny Smith apple tempura with cinnamon ice cream and caramel sauce for the sweet tooth. The wine list is extensive, and features a number of reasonably priced selections. There are also many inventive cocktails, such as the St. Maartini—a refreshing blend of coconut rum, guava puree, passion-fruit juice, and peach schnapps. The dining room is pretty and intimate, in spite of its location behind the casino. There's outdoor seating as well. ⊠ *Atlantis World Casino, Rhine Rd. 106, Cupecoy* ☎599/545–5741 ▭ ⊕*www.nouveaucaribbean.com* ▭*AE, D, MC, V* ☺*Closed Sun. June–Oct. No lunch.*

MAHO

$$ ✕**Bamboo Bernies.** *Eclectic.* This dramatic and hip addition to the top level of the Maho central shopping area features red lacquer walls, lounging tables, Indonesian art, a first-rate bar, and electro-house tunes. You can get terrific sushi and sashimi, both the classic Japanese varieties and the Americanized ones (California roll, for example). All are good, as are the Asian hot appetizers and exotic cocktails like the Tranquillity (citrus vodka and smoky oolong tea). If you're not into Asian fare, try the salmon, ribs, or beef. The young crowd keeps this place hopping way past midnight. ⊠ *Sonesta Maho Beach Resort & Casino, Rhine Rd., Maho* ☎599/545–3622 ⊕*www.bamboobernies.net* ▭*MC, V* ☺*No lunch weekdays.*

$$$ ✕**Bliss.** *Eclectic.* Part restaurant, part lounge and nightclub, Bliss is one of the most popular nightspots in St. Maarten. The open-air dining room, decorated in cool Caribbean colors, has great views of the ocean. The contemporary menu features dishes like grilled sirloin, lobster bruschetta, and slow-baked salmon. Stay after dinner and have a drink at the bar, and listen to the DJ (or occasional live band) and dance under the stars. ⊠ *Caravanserai Resort, 2 Beacon Hill Rd., Maho* ☎599/545–3996 ▭*AE, D, MC, V* ☺*No lunch.*

KEY

- **1** *Restaurants*
- **1** *Hotels*

Philipsburg

Great Salt Pond

Great Bay

Walter Nisbet Rd. (Pondfill Rd.)

Post Office

C.A. Cannegetter St.

Back St.

Front St.

Wathey Square

Captain Hodge Pier

Emmaplein

W. G. Buoncamper Rd.

Saint Maarten Museum

Bobby's Marina

Great Bay Marina

Juancho Yrausquin Blvd.

Restaurants	Hotels
Antoine, **1**	Holland House Beach Hotel, **2**
Au Petit Cafe Francais, **5**	Pasanggrahan Royal Inn, **3**
Chesterfield's, **9**	Sea Palace, **1**
Green House, **8**	Sonesta Great Bay Beach Resort, **4**
Kangaroo Court Café, **3**	
L'Escargot, **2**	
Ocean Lounge, **6**	
Shiv Sagar, **7**	
Taloula Mango's, **4**	

$$$ ✕ **Pizza Pasta Trattoria Italiana.** *Italian.* Tucked away on a quiet street near Casino Royale, this Italian eatery is extremely popular with locals. The menu includes favorites like penne Bolognese and eggplant Parmesan, but the real winners are the thin-crust pizzas. The freshly brewed iced tea is great on a hot day. With its laid-back atmosphere and friendly staff, this is a cozy spot for families with small children or a place where you just run in and grab a quick bite. However, the noise level can be deafening. ⊠ *Maho Shopping Plaza, Maho* ☎ 599/545–4034 ▭ *No credit cards* ⊗ *No lunch Sun.*

PHILIPSBURG

$$$ ✕ **Antoine.** *French.* You'd be hard-pressed to find a more
★ enjoyable evening in Philipsburg. Owner Jean Pierre Pomarico's warmth shines through as he greets guests and ushers them into the comfy seaside restaurant. Low-key, blue-accented decor, white bamboo chairs, watercolors lining the walls, and candles—along with the sound of the nearby surf—create a relaxing atmosphere. The lobster thermidor (a succulent tail oozing with cream and Swiss cheese) is a favorite, but other specialties include lobster bisque, seafood linguine, and a beef fillet with béarnaise sauce. At

Restaurant Antoine in Philipsburg

$35, the prix-fixe menu is a great deal. ✉ *119 Front St., Philipsburg* ☎ *599/542–2964* ⊕ *www.antoinerestaurant. com* ⌂ *Reservations essential* 🖃 *AE, D, MC, V.*

$ ✕ **Au Petit Café Français.** *Café.* This tiny bistro is found in the quaint shopping area just off Front Street. Although there are only a small number of tables (both indoor and out), you should still stop by for a quick, inexpensive snack or for a freshly ground cup of coffee. Watching employees make crêpes is half the fun; eating them is the other half. You can also order hearty salads, pizza, and hot or cold sandwiches on fresh bread. It is open from 8 AM to 4:30 PM. ✉ *120 Old St., Philipsburg* ☎ *599/552–8788* 🖃 *No credit cards* ⊘ *Closed Sun. No dinner.*

$$ ✕ **Chesterfield's.** *Caribbean.* On the Great Bay waterfront, this is an excellent place for a cocktail, a beer, or a relaxed meal on the open-air deck. Both the locals and tourists seem to love it. Seafood is the main focus, but steaks, burgers, and pasta and poultry are not wanting. ✉ *Great Bay Marina, Philipsburg* ☎ *599/542–3484* ⊕ *www.chesterfields-restaurant.com* 🖃 *MC, V.*

$$ ✕ **The Green House.** *Eclectic.* The famous happy hour is just one of the reasons people flock to the Green House. This waterfront restaurant balances a relaxed atmosphere, reasonable prices, and quality food with a just-right, flavorful bite. All the beef served is Black Angus, and some people say the burgers and steaks are the best on the island. If you're seeking something spicy, try the creole shrimp. The daily specials, like the Friday-night Lobster Mania, are widely popular. ⊠ *Bobby's Marina, Philipsburg* ☎ *599/542–2941* ▤⊕ *www.thegreenhouserestaurant.com* ▤ *AE, D, MC, V.*

$$ × **Kangaroo Court Café.** *Café.* Grab a table on the lovely back patio of this little café. Almond trees shade it so well that nets are installed to keep nuts and leaves from hitting diners. Although it's best known for coffees, the café also serves great sandwiches, salads, and pizzas. Wash it all down with a fruit frappé or a selection from one of the island's largest selections of wines by the glass. Incidentally, the odd name comes from the location, next to the courthouse in Philipsburg. ⊠ *6 Front St., Philipsburg* ☎ *599/542–7557* ▤ *AE, D, MC, V* ⊗ *Closed Sun. No dinner.*

$$$ × **L'Escargot.** *French.* The wraparound veranda, the bunches of grapes hanging from the chandeliers, and the Toulouse Lautrec–style murals add to the colorful atmosphere of this restaurant in a 150-year-old gingerbread creole house. As the name suggests, snails are a specialty, and are offered several ways. But the menu also includes many other French standards like onion soup, crispy duck, and veal cordon bleu. There's a Friday night cabaret show, complete with cancan in the tradition of *La Cage aux Folles.* ⊠ *96 Front St., Philipsburg* ☎ *599/542–2483* ⊕ *www.lescargotrestaurant .com* ▤ *AE, MC, V.*

★ Fodor'sChoice × **Ocean Lounge.** *Eclectic.* A brilliant young chef, $$$ attentive service, and an airy modern veranda perched on the Philipsburg boardwalk give Ocean Lounge its distinct South Beach vibe. You'll want to linger over tasty small plates and interesting cocktails, as you watch the scene with tourists of all varieties passing by two-by-two on romantic evening strolls, or determined cruise-ship passengers surveying the surrounding shops by day. The daily tasting menu at $39 ($47 with two glasses of good wine) offers a chance to sample the cuisine, which includes delicious fresh salad preparations, sesame-crusted sushi-grade tuna with pasta, beef tenderloin with seared foie gras, truffle risotto, and many seafood entrées. ⊠ *Holland House Beach Hotel, 43 Front St., Philipsburg* ☎ *599/542–2572* ⊕ *www.hhbh. com* ▤ *AE, D, MC, V.*

$$ × **Shiv Sagar.** *Indian.* The colors of India—notably yellow and green—enliven this second-floor restaurant in Philipsburg. What it lacks in decor it more than makes up for in flavor. The menu emphasizes northern Indian specialties, including marvelous tandooris and curries, but try one of the less familiar dishes such as *madrasi machi* (red snapper with hot spices) or *saag gosht* (lamb sautéed with spinach).

Caribbean lobster, a popular luxury in St. Maarten/St. Martin

✉ *20 Front St., opposite First Caribbean International Bank, Philipsburg* ☎ *599/542–2299* ⊕ *www.shivsagarsxm.com* ▭ *AE, D, DC, MC, V* ⊗ *Closed Sun. dinner.*

$$ ✕ **Taloula Mango's.** *Eclectic.* Ribs are the specialty at this casual beachfront restaurant, but the jerk chicken and thin-crust pizza, not to mention a few vegetarian options like the tasty falafel, are not to be ignored. On weekdays lunch is accompanied by live music; every Friday during happy hour a DJ spins tunes. In case you're wondering, the restaurant got its name from the owner's golden retriever. ✉ *Sint Rose Shopping Mall, off Front St. on beach boardwalk, Philipsburg* ☎ *599/542–1645* ⊕ *www.taloulamangos. com* ▭ *AE, D, MC, V.*

SIMPSON BAY

$$ ✕ **The Boathouse.** *Seafood.* Sitting on Simpson Bay's waterfront, this eatery now has new owners, a fresh look and a revised menu. Still featured are seafood dishes like coconut shrimp and red snapper stuffed with crabmeat, but now they cater more to carnivores. Steaks and burgers are more succulent than ever. The bar is a great place to catch live music throughout the week. Open for lunch and dinner, or if you would rather, just hang out at the bar. ✉ *74 Airport Rd., Simpson Bay* ☎ *599/544–5409* ▭ *D, MC, V.*

$$$ ✕ **Ciao.** *Italian.* The former Los Gauchos has received an ☾ extreme menu makeover, even though the decor is pretty much the same. Instead of Argentine steaks, expect great

pizzas like the *quatro formaggi* (a mix of four cheeses) made in a wood-burning oven. You'll also be greeted by a variety of fish, pasta, and other calorie-laden offerings like gnocchi with Gorgonzola cream sauce that scream Italia. Service is friendly, but can also be somewhat spotty. There's an outdoor patio, and the restaurant serves breakfast, lunch, and dinner. ⊠ *Pelican Resort Marina, Simpson Bay* ☎ *599/544-4084* ⚲ *Reservation essential* ▭ *MC, V.*

$$$ ✕ **Pineapple Pete.** This popular, casual, and fun place has an
☾ interior that looks like a streetscape, where the walls have siding and doors on each side. One of those doors leads to a game room with seven pool tables, four dart boards, an arcade, and a large TV tuned to a sports channel, of course. A friendly, efficient staff will serve you burgers, seafood, and ribs, but try one of the specialties like the tasty crab-stuffed shrimp appetizer. Follow it up with succulent, herb-crusted rack of lamb. There's free Wi-Fi and live entertainment Tuesday through Sunday. *Paradise Mall, Airport Rd., across from the Paradise Plaza Casino, Simpson Bay* ☎ *599/544–6030* ⊕ *www.pineapplepete.com* ⚲ *Reservations essential* ▭ *D, MC, V.*

$$$ ✕ **Saratoga.** *Eclectic.* At Simpson Bay Yacht Club you can
★ choose to be inside or on the waterside terrace. The menu changes daily, but you can never go wrong with one of Chef John Jackson's fish specialties, including red snapper with a mango salsa or yellowfin tuna "filet mignon" with miso-roasted veggies. You might start with oysters flown in from France, or sesame seaweed salad. The wine list includes 150 different bottles, including many by the glass. ⊠ *Simpson Bay Yacht Club, Airport Blvd., Simpson Bay* ☎ *599/544–2421* ⊕ *www.sxmsaratoga.com* ⚲ *Reservations essential* ▭ *AE, D, MC, V* ⊗ *Closed Sun. Closed Aug. and Sept. No lunch.*

$ ✕ **Top Carrot.** *Vegetarian.* Open from 7 AM to 6 PM, this café and juice bar is a popular breakfast and lunch stop. It features vegetarian entrées, sandwiches, salads, homemade pastries, and, more recently, fresh fish. Favorites include a pastry stuffed with pesto, avocado, red pepper, and feta cheese, or a cauliflower, spinach, and tomato quiche. The house-made granola and yogurt are local favorites, but folks also drop in just for espresso and the large selection of teas. Adjacent to the restaurant is a gift shop with Asian-inspired items and spiritual books. ⊠ *Airport Rd., near Simpson Bay Yacht Club, Simpson Bay* ☎ *599/544–3381* ▭ *MC, V* ⊗ *Closed Sun. No dinner.*

$ × **Zee Best.** *Café.* This friendly bistro serves one of the best breakfasts on the island. There's a huge selection of fresh-baked pastries—try the almond croissants—plus sweet and savory crepes, omelets, quiches, and freshly baked croissants and other treats from the oven. Specialties include the St. Martin omelet, filled with ham, cheese, mushrooms, onions, green peppers, and tomatoes. Best of all, breakfast is served until 2 PM—perfect for late risers. Lunch includes sandwiches, salads, and the chef's famous spaghetti Bolognese. Grab a table in the dining room or on the terrace; it's a good place to relax with a newspaper and a cup of cappuccino. Zee Best turns into Piccolo restaurant for dinner. There is another location at Port de Plaisance. ⊠ *Plaza del Lago, Simpson Bay* ☎ *599/544–2477* ▭ *No credit cards* ⊘ *No dinner Sun.*

FRENCH SIDE

BAIE NETTLÉ

★ Fodor'sChoice × **La Cigale.** *French.* On the edge of Baie Net-
$$$– tlé, La Cigale has wonderful views of the lagoon from its
$$$$ dining room and its open-air patio, but the charm of the restaurant comes from the devoted attention of adorable owner Olivier, helped by his mother and brother, and various cousins, too. Stephane Istel's delicious food is edible sculpture: ravioli of lobster with wild mushrooms and foie gras is poached in an intense lobster bisque, an ethereal starter of cream-of-asparagus-and-broccoli soup sings, and house-smoked swordfish and salmon is garnished with goat cheese and seaweed salad drizzled with dill-lime vinaigrette. The pecan pie will make you forget the American version forever. ⊠ *101 Laguna Beach, Baie Nettlé* ☎ *599/87–90–23* ▭ *MC, V* ⊘ *Closed Sun. Sept.–Oct. No lunch.*

$$–$$$ × **Les Boucaniers.** *Caribbean.* Dine here, and you can enjoy
🕙 good creole and French food and still wriggle your toes in the sand. The creole "assortment" offers a mini-culinary education of *accras* (codfish balls), avocado mousse, *boudin noir* (blood sausage), and stuffed crab. Dessert features the most delicious Valrhona chocolate *pot de crème*—its not your grandma's chocolate pudding! There's also a kid's menu for €9. ⊠ *Lot 501, Baie Nettlé* ☎ *0590/29–21–75* ⊕ *www.lesboucaniers-sxm.com* ▭ *MC, V.*

$$–$$$ × **Le Ti' Sucrier.** *Eclectic.* Turn off an inauspicious stretch of
🕙 road toward Simpson Bay, and you'll find yourself at this friendly beachfront restaurant that is a favorite of locals and longtime visitors. The menu is constantly changing because

the chef-owner doesn't want his clientele to get bored, but you should find French standards like vichyssoise as well as salads, a sprinkling of Asian favorites like dumplings and spring rolls, and perhaps a surprise or two. Sometimes there are Cajun-spiced scallops, an Antillean squid casserole, and even prime rib—so everyone can be happy. ⊠ *Route des Terres Basses, Baie Nettlé* ☎ *590/52–43–71* ⊕ *www.tisucrierrestaurant.com* ⊟ *AE, MC, V* ⊙ *Closed Sun. No lunch.*

$$$–   ✕ **Ma Ti' Beach.** *French.* Here's a great choice for a casual
$$$$ beach bar with better-than-average food, right across from the Mercure Resort on the road to Marigot. Open for lunch and dinner, it offers great views across the turquoise water to Anguilla. You can always get fresh lobster from the tank, and the excellent traditional French onion soup with a cheesy crust. Prices are happily modest. ⊠ *Anse Margot, across the road from the Mercure Resort, Baie Nettlé* ☎ *590/87–01–30* ⊟ *MC, V* ⊙ *Closed Tues.*

BAIE ORIENTALE

★ Fodor'sChoice ✕ **L'Astrolabe.** *French.* Chef Stephan Decluseau
$$$–   gets raves for his modern interpretations of classic French
$$$$ cuisine served around the pool at this cozy, relaxed restaurant in the Esmeralda Resort. Truffled pumpkin soup with a creamy cheese mousse; foie gras terrine with apricot, mango, and honey jam; an amazing Moroccan lamb tagine with dates and sun-dried tomatoes; and deliciously fresh fish dishes are just some of the offerings. There are lots of choices for vegetarians, a three-course prix-fixe for €44, and a lobster party with live music every Friday night. ⊠ *Esmeralda Resort, Box 5141, Baie Orientale* ☎ *0590/87–11–20* ⊟ *AE, MC, V* ⊙ *No lunch; no dinner Wed.*

$–$$ ✕ **Palm Beach.** *American.* The newest addition to the Baie Orientale beach clubs is as stylish as its Florida namesake. Balinese art and furniture, big comfy chaises on the beach, and an active bar set the stage. Pretty girls are the decor. There are three big tree-house-like lounges for lunch or the afternoon. The menu of salads, grills, and burgers is served in a pavilion shaded by sail-like awnings. Take the exit to BooBoo Jam after the gas station. ⊠ *Baie Orientale* ☎ *690/35–99–06* ⊟ *MC, V* ⊙ *No dinner.*

$$–$$$ ✕ **Waïkiki Beach.** *Eclectic.* It's an all-day party here, not unlike something you might expect if St-Tropez were transported to the Caribbean. It's everything you ever hoped for in a beach club, including sexy bodies. There's a beach bar, massages, great music—no wonder this place is called

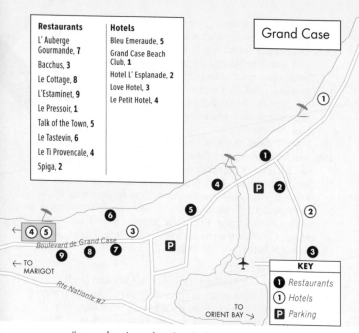

Restaurants

L' Auberge Gourmande, **7**

Bacchus, **3**

Le Cottage, **8**

L'Estaminet, **9**

Le Pressoir, **1**

Talk of the Town, **5**

Le Tastevin, **6**

Le Ti Provencale, **4**

Spiga, **2**

Hotels

Bleu Emeraude, **5**

Grand Case Beach Club, **1**

Hotel L' Esplanade, **2**

Love Hotel, **3**

Le Petit Hotel, **4**

Grand Case

Boulevard de Grand Case

← TO MARIGOT

Rte Nationle #7

TO ORIENT BAY →

KEY

1 *Restaurants*

① *Hotels*

P *Parking*

"more than just a beach." Stylish, light, fresh fare that's perfect for a beach meal includes sushi, salads, light grills, and ice-cream desserts, all complemented by potent potables. Sit at a picnic table, or on a lounge/bed and enjoy the good food and great people-watching. If there's a big cruise-ship group, however, you may just want to head down to the beach. During the Christmas holiday season, top DJs are brought in for partying into the night. ✉ *5 Baie Orientale, Baie Orientale* ☎ *590/87–43–19* ⊕ *www.waikikibeachsxm. com* ⊟ *AE, MC, V.*

FRENCH CUL DE SAC

\$\$\$–
\$\$\$\$ ✕ **Sol é Luna.** *Caribbean.* Charming and romantic, this restaurant puts its best tables on the balcony, from which you can best appreciate the great views. Begin your meal with an appetizer like the roasted vegetables with goat cheese, lobster ravioli, or tuna carpaccio, then move on to the lamb shank with date-ginger puree or the filet mignon with mashed potatoes. Don't be surprised if you see a proposal or two during your meal, as this is one of the most romantic restaurants on the island. ✉ *61 Rte. de Mont Vernon, French Cul de Sac* ☎ *590/29–08–56* ⊟ *MC, V* ☺ *Closed mid-June–early July and Sept.–early Oct.*

GRAND CASE

★ Fodor's Choice ✕ **Bacchus.** *French.* If you want to lunch with
$$$ the savviest locals, you have to scrape yourself from the
beach and head into the industrial park outside Grand Case,
where Benjamin Laurent, the best wine importer in the
Caribbean, has built this lively, deliciously air-conditioned,
reconstruction of a wine cellar. He serves up first-rate start-
ers, salads, and main courses made from top ingredients
brought in from France, lovingly prepared by top chefs. The
wines are sublime, and you will get an amazing education
along with a great lunch. You won't mind eating indoors
here; think of it as the perfect sunblock! Enter at the HOPE
ESTATE sign in the roundabout across from the road that
leads to the Grand Case Airport. ⊠ *Hope Estate 18–19,
Grand Case Rd., Grand Case* ☎ *0590/87–15–70* ⊕ *www.
bacchussxm.com* ⊟ *AE, MC, V* ☉ *No dinner, closed Sun.*

$$$– ✕ **L'Auberge Gourmande.** *French.* A fixture of Boulevard
$$$$ Grand Case, L'Auberge Gourmande is in one of the oldest
creole houses in St. Maarten/St. Martin. The formal dining
room is framed by elegant arches. Chef Didier Rochat's
light Provençal cuisine is a delight, with menu choices like
roasted rack of lamb with an herb crust over olive mashed
potatoes, Dover sole in lemon butter, and pork tenderloin
stuffed with apricots and walnuts. There are vegetarian
options, a kids' menu for €13, and a good selection of
wines. ⊠ *89 bd. de Grand Case, Grand Case* ☎ *590/87–
73–37* ⊟ *MC, V* ☉ *No lunch.*

$$$– ✕ **L'Estaminet.** *French.* The name of this restaurant is an
$$$$ old-fashioned word for "tavern" in French, but the food is
anything but archaic. The creative, upscale cuisine served
in this modern, clean space is fun and surprising, utilizing
plenty of molecular gastronomy. This means that intense
liquid garnishes might be inserted into your goat cheese
appetizer or perhaps given to you in a tiny toothpaste
tube, or even a plastic syringe. The bright flavors, artistic
plating, and novelty make for a lively meal that will be
remembered fondly. Under no circumstances should you
pass up the chocolate tasting for dessert. ⊠ *139 bd. de
Grand Case, Grand Case* ☎ *590/29–00–25* ⊟ *AE, MC, V*
☉ *Closed Mon. Jun.–Nov.*

$$$– ✕ **Le Cottage.** *French.* Inventive, beautiful, classic French
$$$$ cuisine is prepared with a light touch and presented with
flair, and perhaps a bit of humor here. There are tasting
menus, prix-fixe menus, huge portions of hearty French
food served by a genial staff, a lively community gathered
on the street-front porch. Don't miss the caramel dessert

ing, which features a perfect soufflé, or the house-
de salted caramel meringues. ⊠ *97 bd. de Grand Case,
nd Case* ☎ *590/29–03–30* ⊕ *www.restaurantlecottage.
com* ▤ *AE, MC, V.*

★ **Fodor's** Choice ✕ **Le Pressoir.** *French.* In a carefully restored West
$$$– Indian house painted in brilliant reds and blues, Le Pressoir
$$$$ has charm to spare. The name comes from the historic salt
press that sits opposite the restaurant, but the thrill comes
from the culinary creations of Chef Franc Mear and the
hospitality of his beautiful wife Melanie. If you are indeci-
sive or just plain smart, try any (or all) of the degustations
(tastings) of four soups, four foie gras preparations, or four
fruit desserts, each showcasing sophisticated preparations
with adorable presentations. A foie-gras pâte is served in a
dollhouse-size terrine, with a teensy glass of sauternes. ⊠ *30
bd. de Grand Case, Grand Case* ☎ *590/87–76–62* ▤ *AE,
MC, V* ⊙ *Closed Sun. No lunch.*

WORD OF MOUTH. **You should not visit St. Martin without enjoy-
ing at least one dinner at Le Pressoir (we chose to eat there
twice on our last visit). Each course was outstanding, and the
wine list is superb. Though the menu is a bit pricey, the food,
service, and charm of the place make it worth every penny.
—AddieLangdon**

★ **Fodor's** Choice ✕ **Le Tastevin.** *French.* In the heart of Grand Case,
$$$– Le Tastevin is on everyone's list of favorites. The attractive
$$$$ wood-beamed room is the "real" St. Martin style, and the
tasty food is enhanced by Joseph, the amiable owner, who
serves up lunch and dinner every day on a breezy porch
over a glittering blue sea. The menu changes frequently,
and includes fusion treatments of local ingredients such as
mahimahi in a pineapple tomato sauce, and rack of lamb
with glazed garlic and rosemary. There are two tasting
menus, one at €45 that includes a half-bottle of wine, and
another at €75 that offers special wine pairings. ⊠ *86 bd. de
Grand Case, Grand Case* ☎ *590/87–55–45* ⌕ *Reservations
essential* ▤ *AE, MC, V* ⊙ *Closed mid-Aug.–Sept.*

$$$– ✕ **Le Ti Provençale.** *French.* Its always a good idea to follow
$$$$ the French locals for the best food in St. Martin; Chef Hervé
Sageot has won the gold medal as the chef of the year in
the local Taste of St. Martin festival for three years run-
ning. The pretty room over the water offers good service
and a full blackboard of daily specials. It's all about the
fish here, and the day's catch is brought to your table for
you to "meet" and for you to discuss its preparation. This

offers a great opportunity to learn about local seafood. The fish soup is made from rouget (red mullet) and served with the traditional garlicky rouille. But the restaurant does serve more than just fish; there are good pastas and lamb and steaks if your preference does not include seafood. The restaurant is open for both lunch and dinner, and there is a little beach club too. ⊠ *48 bd. de Grand Case, Grand Case* ☎ *590/87–05–65* ▤ *MC, V.*

$$$ ✕ **Spiga.** *Italian.* In a beautifully restored creole house, Spiga's tasty cuisine fuses Italian and Caribbean ingredients and cooking techniques Look for dishes like lamb with tagliatelle, or crab cakes on peas. Save room for the lemon-ricotta cake and try the selection of grappas. ⊠ *4 Rte. de L'Esperance, Grand Case* ☎ *590/524–783* ▤ *D, MC, V* ⊙ *Closed mid-Sept.–late Oct. Closed Tues. June–mid-Sept. No lunch Sun.*

★ Fodor'sChoice ✕ **Talk of the Town.** *Caribbean.* Although St.
$–$$ Martin is known for its upscale dining, each town has its roadside barbecue stands, called lolos, including the island's culinary capital of Grand Case. They are open from lunchtime until evening, but earlier in the day you'll find fresher offerings. Locals flock to the square of a half-dozen stands in the middle of Grand Case, on the water side. Not to say that these stands offer haute or fine cuisine, but they are fun, relatively cheap, and offer an iconic St. Martin meal. Talk of the Town is one of the most popular. With plastic utensils and paper plates, it couldn't be more informal. The menu includes everything from succulent grilled ribs to stewed conch, fresh snapper, and grilled lobster at the most reasonable price on the island. Don't miss the johnnycakes and side dishes like plantains, curried rice, beans, and coleslaw that come with your choice. The service is friendly, if a bit slow, but sit back with a beer and enjoy the experience. On weekends there is often live music. **Sky's the Limit** is another iconic lolo, just two picnic tables over. At this writing the lolos are still offering a one-to-one exchange between euros and dollars. ⊠ *Bd. de Grand Case, Grand Case* ☎ *No phone* ▤ *No credit cards.*

MARIGOT

$$$– ✕ **Bistrot Nu.** *French.* It's hard to top the simple, unadorned
$$$$ fare and reasonable prices you can find at this intimate restaurant tucked in a Marigot alley. Traditional French and creole food—coq au vin, fish soup, snails—is served in a friendly, intimate dining room. The prix-fixe menu is a very good value. The place is popular, and the tables are

routinely packed until it closes at midnight. It can be difficult to park here, so take your chances at finding a spot on the street—or try a taxi. ⊠ *Allée de l'Ancienne Geôle, Marigot* ☎ *590/87–97–09* ▭ *MC, V* ⚑ *Reservations essential* ☉ *Closed Sun.*

$$$ ✕**Claude Mini-Club.** *Caribbean.* An island institution, Claude Mini-Club has delighted patrons with its blend of creole and French food since 1969. The whole place is built treehouse style around the trunks of coconut palms, and the lofty perch means you have great views of Marigot Harbor. The chairs and tablecloths are a mélange of sunny yellows and oranges. The €40 dinner buffet on Wednesday and Saturday nights is legendary. It includes more than 30 dishes, often including conch soup, roast leg of lamb, Black Angus roast beef, and roast pig. Fresh snapper is one of the excellent specialties on the à la carte menu. There's live music nightly. ⊠ *49 bd. de France, Marigot* ☎ *590/87–50–69* ▭ *AE, MC, V* ☉ *Closed Sun.*

$$-$$$ ✕**Enoch's Place.** *Caribbean.* The blue-and-white-striped awning on a corner of the Marigot Market makes this place hard to miss. But Enoch's cooking is what draws the crowds. Specialties include garlic shrimp, fresh lobster, and rice and beans (like your St. Martin mother used to make). Try the saltfish and fried johnnycake—a great breakfast option. The food more than makes up for the lack of decor, and chances are you'll be counting the days until you can return. ⊠ *Marigot Market, Front de Mer, Marigot* ☎ *590/29–29–88* ▭ *No credit cards* ☉ *Closed Sun. No dinner.*

$$ ✕**La Belle Epoque.** *Eclectic.* A favorite among locals, this brasserie is a good choice at the Marigot marina. Whether you stop for a drink or a meal, you'll soon discover that it's a great spot for boat- and people-watching. The menu has a bit of everything: big salads, pizza, and seafood are always good bets. There's also a good wine list. And its open nonstop seven days a week for breakfast through late dinner. ⊠ *Marina de la Port Royale, Marigot* ☎ *590/87–87–70* ▭ *AE, MC, V.*

$$$- ✕**La Vie en Rose.** *French.* This restaurant on the quiet side of
$$$$ Marigot's harborfront is all about romance. It's like Paris with palm trees. Starters include five-pepper marinated salmon with *fromage blanc* (a soft, fresh white cheese) or a light vegetable-pesto lasagna. For traditionalists, there are frogs' legs. Main courses of fresh fish have tasty vegetable garnishes, and heartier meat entrées like roast veal and rack of lamb will please carnivores. Desserts are delightful,

especially the trio of crème brûlées. The service is polite and professional. ⊠ *Front de Mer, Marigot* ☎ *590/87–54–42* ▭ *AE, MC, V.*

$$$$ ✕ **Le Chanteclair.** *French.* Dinner in Marigot's Marina Royale, with its string of pleasant restaurants wrapping around the harbor filled with gleaming boats, is a St. Martin must. This family-run restaurant is a favorite, serving French dishes with an inventive Caribbean twist in a sunshine-yellow room. In high season, you'll have to reserve ahead. The fixed-price *assiettes dégustations* (tasting plates) at €50 and €55 set the meal around theme ingredients such as foie gras or lobster. However, you can also order à la carte. The desserts are just as creative, especially the *l'innommable au chocolat,* the "unnamable" dessert made with chocolate and vanilla ice cream. The menu proudly proposes their philosophy: "The good food is the foundation of true happiness." Not the best English, perhaps, but a worthy observation. ⊠ *Marina de la Port Royale, Marigot* ☎ *590/87–94–60* ▭ *MC, V* ⊘ *Closed Sun. mid-Sept.–mid-Oct.*

$$$ ✕ **Tropicana.** *French.* This bustling bistro at the Marina Royale is busy all day long, thanks to a varied menu, (relatively) reasonable prices, and friendly staff. Salads are a

Breakfast overlooking Maho Bay at the Sonesta Maho Beach Resort

must for lunch, especially the salad Niçoise with medallions of crusted goat cheese. Dinner includes some exceptional steak and seafood dishes. The wine list is quite extensive. Desserts are tasty, and you'll never be disappointed with old standbys like the crème brûlée. You can dine outside or inside along the yacht-filled waterfront, which is busy with shoppers during the day. ⊠ *Marina de la Port Royale, Marigot* ☎ 590/87–79–07 ▤ D, MC, V.

PIC DU PARADIS

$$$ ✕ **Hidden Forest Café.** *Eclectic.* Schedule your trip to Loterie Farm to take advantage of the lovely tree-house pavilions where lunch or dinner has a safari vibe and where the yummy food is inventive and fresh, with touches of Asia. Curried spinach chicken with banana fritters is a popular pick, but there are great choices for vegetarians, too, including cumin lentil balls; those with stouter appetites dig into the massive Black Angus tenderloin. Loterie Farm's other eatery, Treelounge, is open for lunch and dinner Monday–Saturday, and stays open late with a band on Saturday nights. ⊠ *Route du Pic Paradis, Pic Paradis* ☎ 590/87–86–16 ⊕ *www.loteriefarm.net* ▤ MC, V ☉ Closed Mon.

SANDY GROUND

★ Fodor'sChoice ✕ **Mario's Bistro.** *Eclectic.* Don't miss dinner at
$$$$ this romantic eatery, a perennial favorite for its ravishing cuisine, romantic ambience, and most of all the marvelously friendly owners. Didier Gonnon and Martyne Tardif are

St. Maarten vs. St. Martin

CLOSE UP

If this is your first trip to St. Maarten/St. Martin, you're probably wondering which side will better suit your needs. That's hard to say, because in some ways the difference between the two can seem as subtle as the hazy boundary line dividing them. But there are some major differences.

St. Maarten, the Dutch side, has the casinos, more nightlife, and bigger hotels. St. Martin, the French side, has no casinos, less nightlife, and hotels that are smaller and more intimate, many with kitchenettes and most including breakfast. Although there are many good restaurants on the Dutch side, if fine dining makes your holiday, the French side rules.

The biggest difference might be currency—the Netherlands Antilles guilder on the Dutch side, the euro on the French side. And the relative strength of the euro can translate to some expensive surprises. Of course, many establishments on both sides (even the French) accept U.S. dollars.

out front, while chef Mario Tardif is in the kitchen creating dishes such as sautéed sea scallops with crab mashed potatoes and truffle oil, baked mahimahi with a macadamia-nut crust, orange-endive confit, and fennel salsa, and rack of lamb with caramelized onions and goat cheese. ⊠ *At Sandy Ground Bridge, Sandy Ground* ☎ *590/87–06–36* ⚑ *Reservations essential* ☐ *MC, V* ☉ *Closed Sun. and Aug.–Sept. No lunch.*

WHERE TO STAY

St. Maarten/St. Martin accommodations range from modern mega-resorts like the Radisson and the Westin Dawn Beach to condos and small inns. On the Dutch side many hotels cater to groups, and although that's also true to some extent on the French side, you can find a larger collection of intimate accommodations there. ■TIP➔ Off-season rates (April through the beginning of December) can be as little as half the high-season rates. And current economic conditions are making every stay much more affordable.

TIME-SHARE RENTALS

Time-share properties are scattered around the island, mostly on the Dutch side. There's no reason to buy a share, as these condos are rented out whenever the owners are not in residence. If you stay in one, be prepared for a sales

BEST BETS FOR LODGING

Fodor's Choice ★

Caribbean Princess, Domaine de Lonvilliers, Holland House Beach Hotel, The Horny Toad, Palm Court, Radisson St. Martin, La Samanna, **Westin Dawn Beach Resort & Spa**

BEST FOR ROMANCE
La Samanna, Le Domaine de Lonvilliers, Palm Court, Princess Heights

BEST BEACHFRONT
The Horny Toad, La Samanna, Le Domaine de Lonvilliers

BEST POOL
Radisson St. Martin, Westin Dawn Beach Resort & Spa

BEST SERVICE
La Samanna, Le Domaine de Lonvilliers, Pasanggrahan Royal Inn

BEST FOR KIDS
Alamanda Resort, Divi Little Bay Beach Resort, Radisson St. Martin, Sonesta Great Bay Beach Resort & Casino

pitch. Most rent by the night, but there are often substantial savings if you secure a weekly rate. Not all offer daily maid service, so make sure to ask before you book.

PRIVATE VILLAS

Villas are a great lodging option, especially for families who don't need to keep the kids occupied, or groups of friends who just like hanging out together. Since these are for the most part freestanding houses, their greatest advantage is privacy. These properties are scattered across the island, often in gated communities or on secluded roads. Some have bare-bones furnishings, while others are over-the-top luxurious, with gyms, theaters, game rooms, and several different pools. There are private chefs, gardeners, maids, and other staffers to care for both the villa and its occupants.

Villas are secured through rental companies. They offer properties with weekly prices that range from reasonable to more than many people make in a year. Check around, as prices for the same property varies from agent to agent. Rental companies usually provide airport transfers and concierge service, and for an extra fee will even stock your refrigerator.

VILLA RENTAL AGENTS

French Caribbean International (⊠ 5662 Calle Real, Suite 333, Santa Barbara, CA ☎ 805/967–9850 or 800/322–2223 ⊕ www.frenchcaribbean.com) offers rental properties on the

French side of the island. **Island Hideaways** (⊠ *3843 Highland Oaks Dr., Fairfax, VA* ☎ *800/832–2302 or 703/378–7840* ⊕ *www.islandhideaways.com*), the island's oldest rental company, rents villas on both sides. **Island Properties** (⊠ *62 Welfare Rd., Simpson Bay, St. Maarten* ☎ *599/544–4580 or 866/978–5852* ⊕ *www.islandpropertiesonline.com*) has properties scattered around the island. **Jennifer's Vacation Villas** (⊠ *Plaza Del Lago, Simpson Bay Yacht Club, Simpson Bay, St. Maarten* ☎ *631/546–7345 or 011/599–54–43107* ⊕ *www.jennifersvacationvillas.com*) rents villas on both sides of the island. **Pierrescaraïbes** (⊠ *Plaza Caraibes, Bldg A. Rue Kennedy, Marigot, St. Martin* ☎ *866/978–5795 or 590/51–02–85* ⊕ *www.pierrescaraibes.com*), owned by American Leslie Reed, has been renting and selling upscale St. Martin villas to satisfied clients for over a decade. The company's well-designed Web site makes it easy to get a sense of the first-rate properties available in all sizes and prices. The company is associated with Christie's Great Estates. **Romac Southeby's International Realty** (⊠ *54 Simpson Bay Rd., Simpson Bay, St. Maarten* ☎ *599/544–2924 or 877/537–9282* ⊕ *www.romacsothebysrealty.com*) rents luxury villas, many in gated communities. **Villas of Distinction** (⊠ *951 Transport Way, Petaluma, CA* ☎ *800/289–0900* ⊕ *www.villasofdistinction.com*) is one of the oldest villa-rental companies the French side of the island. **WIMCO** (⊠ *Box 1461, Newport, RI 02840* ☎ *401/849–8012 or 866/449–1553* ⊕ *www.wimco.com*) has more hotel, villa, apartment, and condo listings in the Caribbean than just about anyone else.

WHAT IT COSTS IN DOLLARS AND EUROS				
¢	$	$$	$$$	$$$$
HOTELS				
under $80	$80–$150	$150–$250	$250–$350	Over $350
under €60	€60–€110	€110–€180	€180–€260	Over €260

Hotel prices are per night for a double room in high season, excluding taxes, service charges, and meal plans. Hotel prices in Dutch St. Maarten are in dollars; hotel prices in French St. Martin are sometimes in euros, sometimes in dollars.

Hot Deals in High Season

The most expensive time to visit St. Maarten/St. Martin is the high season, which runs from mid-December to April. But this shouldn't deter bargain hunters. Finding good deals takes perseverance, patience, and flexibility. When you're booking a room, call the hotel directly and ask about special offers. Even the most upscale resorts offer discount rates for certain rooms and certain days of the week even in high season. Also, there is often a big difference between accommodations even within the same property, especially if there is renovation going on. Be sure to ask if you have special requests or concerns about smoking, accessibility, and amenities. Packages with special themes like water sports or spas can also save you money. Check out deals where kids stay free, you get a free night when you book a certain number of nights, or packages include meals. Some of the hotels are getting more relaxed about minimum stays.

There's a lot of competition at the island's shops and boutiques. You can always try bargaining, especially in the jewelry stores. You can sometimes get as much as 25% off. Ask, "Is this your best price?" They will let you know if they're in the mood to deal. Very low prices on "designer" items, however, should be greeted with skepticism, as fakes abound. Casinos are always giving something away—chips, drinks, limo service. At restaurants, the prix-fixe lunch or dinner is usually the better deal. On slower nights like Monday and Tuesday, many restaurants offer specials. Look for special offers at the local tourism board and in the local newspaper, the *Daily Herald*.

DUTCH SIDE

COLE BAY

$$–$$$ ☒ **Princess Port de Plaisance Resort.** *Vacation Rental.* Although ♻ on the water (rather than on the beach), this resort still offers enough activities to satisfy travelers. During the day you can laze around at the pool, pamper yourself at the spa, work out with a trainer, or head out from the on-site marina for some water sports. If you're living too much of the high life, visit the anti-aging clinic. In the evening, the giant Princess Casino has live entertainment. There are several popular restaurants, including Zee Best, Peg Leg Pub, and the Courtside Café, which offers a health-conscious menu. (Don't worry, not everything on the menu is good for you.) Spacious suites offer garden or pool views.

Most have a fully equipped kitchen. It's a short drive to beaches. **Pros:** lovely landscaping; quiet, huge casino; children under 18 stay free. **Cons:** not on the beach; needs refurbishing. ⊠ *Union Rd., Cole Bay* ☎ *599/544–4311 or 866/786–2278* ⊕ *www.princessportdeplaisance.com* ⇨ *88 units* ⚿ *In-room: safe, kitchen. In-hotel: 5 restaurants, bar, tennis courts, pools, gym, spa, Internet terminal* ≡ *AE, D, MC, V* ⍓*EP.*

CUPECOY

$$$ ⚏ **Wyndham Sapphire Beach Hotel & Resort.** *Vacation Rental.* A picturesque beach, paths through lush gardens, and a short walk to restaurants, shops, and nightlife—what more could you want in a time-share? Well, maybe a room with a balcony overlooking Simpson Bay Lagoon or the Caribbean Sea. Those on the ocean side have private hot tubs on their balconies, making the view even more memorable. The accommodations, which have recently been freshened up with paint and new furniture, are island-style with fully equipped kitchens and Italian marble bathrooms. **Pros:** American-style breakfast; good rates for longer stays. **Cons:** meager gym. ⊠ *9 Rhine Rd., Cupecoy* ☎ *599/545–2179 or 877/999–3223* ⊕ *www.sbcwi.com* ⇨ *150 units* ⚿ *In-room: kitchen, Wi-Fi. In-hotel: restaurant, pool, gym, spa, beachfront, laundry service* ≡ *AE, D, MC, V* ⍓*BP.*

LITTLE BAY

$$$–
$$$$ ⚏ **Belair Beach.** *Vacation Rental.* This time-share complex has an unbeatable location on Little Bay Beach, one of St. Maarten's nicest and least crowded stretches of sand. The accommodations, all of them suites, include living and dining areas, fully equipped kitchens, and terraces. The property has been freshened up with new beds, tiles, and a new elevator. For a fee, Jody's Place, an on-site convenience store, will fill your refrigerator before you arrive. Grab a light meal at the beachfront Gingerbread Café. The staff can arrange car rentals and island activities. **Pros:** close to Philipsburg; away from the crowds. **Cons:** no full-service restaurant; rooms are a bit dated. ⊠ *Little Bay Beach Rd., Little Bay* ☎ *599/542–3366* ⊕ *www.belairbeach.com* ⇨ *72 suites* ⚿ *In-room: safe. In-hotel: pool, beachfront, water sports, Internet terminal* ≡ *MC, V* ⍓*EP.*

$$–$$$ ⚏ **Divi Little Bay Beach Resort.** *Resort.* Bordering the lovely
ⓒ but sparsely populated Little Bay, this newly renovated property is well located and is awash with water sports. Apartment units in its time-share boast granite kitchens and modern bathrooms. Activities will keep you busy,

DID YOU KNOW?

French hotelier Christophe Leroy, owner of La Table du Marché in Saint-Tropez and Marrakech, has taken over Le Domaine de Lonvilliers.

including trips on the bay in the resort's own glass-bottom boat. It's also a quick trip to the heart of Philipsburg. **Pros:** good location; lovely beach. **Cons:** ongoing renovations; pool areas not great. ⊠ *Little Bay Rd., Box 961, Little Bay* ☎ *599/542–2333 or 800/367–3484* ⊕ *www.diviresorts. com* ⤴ *218 rooms* ⚬ *In-room: kitchen (some), refrigerator (some). In-hotel: 2 restaurants, bars, tennis court, pools, gym, spa, beachfront, diving, water sports, children's programs (ages 3–12), laundry facilities, laundry service* ⊟ *AE, D, DC, MC, V* ⦿*EP.*

MAHO

$$$ ⊞ **Royal Islander Club La Terrasse.** *Vacation Rental.* This ⚘ smaller and nicer sister resort to the Royal Island Club La Plage is right across the street and shares many of the same amenities, including the larger resort's beach. Suites have fine vistas, either of the garden, the pool, or the ocean. There are one-, two-, and three-bedroom units; a lock-out studio (with a kitchenette only) can be created from the two-bedroom units for couples who need a smaller space. Furnished with rattan furniture, each of the tiled units has a fully equipped kitchen and marble-topped bathroom. There's weekly maid service, but for an extra fee the maid will come daily. **Pros:** in a hip area, near restaurants and bars. **Cons:** not on the beach; because this is a time-share rooms can be hard to book during peak periods. ⊠ *1 Rhine Rd., Maho* ☎ *599/545–2388* ⊕ *www.royalislander.com* ⤴*67 units* ⚬ *In-room: kitchen, Wi-Fi. In-hotel: 2 restaurants, pool* ⊟ *AE, D, MC, V* ⊘ *Closed 1st 2 wks in Sept.* ⦿*EP.*

$$–$$$ ⊞ **Sonesta Maho Beach Resort & Casino.** *Resort.* The island's ⚘ largest hotel, which is on Maho Beach, isn't luxurious or fancy, but this full-service resort offers everything right on the premises at reasonable rates. There is a long beach, a big pool area, casino, gym, and spa. The complex has a theater, five clubs, three restaurants, and 40 shops. Seven other restaurants and an outlet mall surround the resort complex. Renovations are planned, and at this writing some sections of the hotel are closed for repairs. **Pros:** huge facility; lots of shopping; nonstop nightlife. **Cons:** resort is aging; not the place for a personal, quiet getaway. ⊠ *1 Rhine Rd., Box 834, Maho* ☎ *599/545–2115, 800/223–0757, or 800/766–3782* ⊕ *www.sonesta.com/mahobeach* ⤴*537 rooms* ⚬ *In-room: safe, Internet, Wi-Fi. In-hotel: 3 restaurants, bars, tennis courts, pools, gym, spa, beachfront* ⊟ *AE, D, DC, MC, V* ⦿*EP.*

The casino at the Sonesta Maho Beach Resort

MULLET BAY

$$$–
$$$$

🏨 **Towers at Mullet Bay.** *Vacation Rental.* Some consider powdery Mullet Bay Beach one of the island's best, and that is where you will find this time-share resort. This property has the island's only golf course, but the links are poorly maintained. Accommodations are pleasant, with pull-out sofas, king-size beds, and either patios or balconies. Each unit has a full kitchen with a refrigerator big enough for a family's needs and even a dishwasher to handle the cleanup. **Pros:** close to restaurants and shops; on a gorgeous beach; every unit has a Nintendo Wii and movies on-demand. **Cons:** disappointing golf course; no restaurant on site. ⊠ *28 Rhine Rd., Mullet Bay* ☎ *599/545–3069 or 800/235–5889* 🛏 *81 units* 🛎 *In-room: kitchen, Internet, DVD. In-hotel: golf course, pool, gym, laundry service* 🖃 *AE, MC, V* 🍴 *EP.*

OYSTER POND

$$–$$$$

🏨 **Oyster Bay Beach Resort.** *Resort.* Jutting out into Oyster Bay, this happening, newly renovated condo resort sits on Dawn Beach. Rooms are spacious and neat, with fresh paint and granite bath vanities, as well as Caribbean decor. Each has a kitchenette (with dishwasher) and a balcony with a fine view of St. Barth or the marina in Oyster Bay. The open-air lobby is a popular gathering spot, and the resort offers a long list of activities and a large pool. Some of the units are time-shares, and one section is quite a bit older than the others (newer units are larger). Time-share users (but not regular guests) are assessed $5–$12 per day for air-conditioning. **Pros:** lots of activities; nightly entertainment; comfortable accommodations. **Cons:** isolated location; need a car to get around. ✉ *10 Emerald Merit Rd., Oyster Pond ⌂ Box 239, Philipsburg ☎ 599/543–6040 or 866/978–0212 ⊕ www.obbr.com ⇨ 157 units ₺ In-room: safe, kitchen. In-hotel: 2 restaurants, bar, pool, spa, gym, beachfront, bicycles, laundry facilities, Internet terminal ☰ AE, D, MC, V ⊙EP.*

$$$– **🖼 Princess Heights.** *Vacation Rental.* Sitting on a hill 900
$$$$ feet above Oyster Bay, newly renovated, spacious suites offer privacy, luxury, and white-balustrade balconies with a smashing view of St. Barth. Each apartment has one or two bedrooms with pillow-top mattresses, stainless-steel kitchen appliances whose side-by-side refrigerator comes stocked with complimentary beverages, granite bathrooms with whirlpool tubs, and rain showers, plus flat-screen TVs and daily maid service. Send a grocery list in advance, and your kitchen will be stocked prior to your arrival. There's a fee for the service, but it saves searching for a grocery store. The property is 4 mi (6 km) from Philipsburg. A second building was recently added. **Pros:** away from the crowds; friendly staff, lovely accommodations; gorgeous vistas. **Cons:** not on the beach; numerous steps to climb; not easy to find; need a car to get around; no restaurant. ✉ *156 Oyster Pond Rd., Oyster Pond ☎ 599/543–6906 or 800/441–7227 ⊕ www.princessheights.com ⇨ 51 suites ₺ In-room: safe, kitchen, refrigerator, Wi-Fi. In-hotel: pool, gym, laundry service ☰ AE, MC, V ⊙EP.*

$$$$ **🖼 Villa Le Cliff.** *Vacation Rental.* The community where this villa is located has such a friendly feel that you wouldn't think twice about going next door to borrow a cup of sugar from your neighbor if you can tear yourself away from the amazing vistas. The spacious rooms have handsome beamed ceilings and attractive furnishings. Chefs will appreciate the fully equipped kitchen with its Viking range. Take a seat at dawn and watch the sun rise over St. Barth. If you need extra space, there's a fourth bedroom with a separate entrance for an additional price. **Pros:** master bedroom on its own level; nice fixtures in bathrooms. **Cons:** a 10-minute walk to the beach. ✉ *Dawn Beach Estates, Oyster Bay ⊕ www.romacsothebysrealty.com ⇨ 3 bedrooms, 3 baths ₺ DVD, twice-weekly maid service, pool, laundry facilities ☰ MC, V ⊙EP.*

2

$$$$ ⊞ **Villa Selah.** *Vacation Rental.* This bright yellow house sits high on a hill amid a verdant landscape. Simply furnished, it has a comfortable living area where people tend to gather. Every room has a great view. The master bedroom has cathedral ceilings, a private terrace, and a bathroom with its own hot tub. **Pros:** reasonably priced; lovely location; good for families; property and pool have been freshened up recently. **Cons:** not on the beach; a bit isolated; stairs to climb. ⊠ *54 Limpet Rd., Oyster Pond* ⊕ *www.islandproperties online.com* ➾ *3-bedrooms, 2½-baths* ⚲ *Dishwasher, DVD, Wi-Fi, daily maid service, hot tub, laundry facilities, pool* ⊟ *MC, V* ⑂ *EP.*

★ Fodor'sChoice ⊞ **Westin Dawn Beach Resort & Spa, St. Maarten.**
$$$– *Resort.* Straddling the border between the Dutch and French
$$$$ sides, the modern Westin sits on one of the island's best
ⵀ beaches. An enormous pool, two excellent restaurants, four bars, a state-of-the art spa, fitness center, casino, nightclub, and family-friendly activities give you plenty of choices. The spacious rooms feature the chain's signature Heavenly beds and ample baths, flat-screen TVs, and balconies. The two-bedroom suites and apartments are especially appealing, and if you are thinking about a condo or villa, those at the Westin certainly are worth considering. They're huge and equipped to perfection with wet bars, full kitchens, and electronics galore. Don't miss the incredible Sunday brunch on the patio overlooking the beach. Like all Westin properties, the resort is smoke-free. A ballroom and conference facilities accommodate up to 1,000 guests. Dawn Beach is one of the most scenic spots on the island and *the* place to be at sunrise. **Pros:** on Dawn Beach; plenty of activities; no smoking allowed. **Cons:** very big; a bit off the beaten track. ⊠ *144 Oyster Pond Rd., Oyster Pond* ☎ *599/543–6700* or *800/228–3000* ⊕ *www.westin.com* ➾ *308 rooms, 6 suites, 99 1-, 2-, and 3-bedroom condo units* ⚲ *In-room: safe, kitchen (some), refrigerator, Internet. In-hotel: 4 restaurants, bars, gym, spa, children's programs (ages 3–12)* ⊟ *AE, MC, V* ⑂ *EP.*

PELICAN KEY

$$ ⊞ **Atrium Beach Resort.** *Vacation Rental.* Lush tropical foliage
ⵀ in the glassed-in lobby—hence the name—makes a great first impression. All the spacious suites and studios open to the lobby, and have lagoon or ocean views. The kitchenettes are equipped with microwaves, refrigerators, and ice makers. With plenty of activities for kids, this property is a perfect place for families. **Pros:** family-friendly environ-

The Wedding Planner

Preparing for your big day is always stressful, even if you aren't planning an event that will take place on an island in the Caribbean. Wedding planners are there to make the process as painless as possible. Give them as little as two months lead time and they will push through the necessary paperwork, help choose the venue, and coordinate the entire event. Securing a minister, photographer, florist, caterer, and driver are all tasks taken off your shoulders. Unconventional events like clothing-optional or underwater weddings are no sweat for these pros. Fees vary according to services. The basic package, which includes securing all the necessary documents, is $940.

Another option is using service provided by your hotel. Larger resorts have on-site wedding coordinators who take care of everything. Small hotels also have wedding and honeymoon packages.

St. Maarten Marry Me.com (☎ 599/542–2214 in St. Maarten or 305/768–0233 in the U.S. ⊕ www.sintmaarten marry-me.com) offers a full line of services for your wedding. The island-based company works with many of the hotels.

Weddings in St. Maarten (☎ 599/557–5478 or 599/581–5843 ⊕ www.stmaarten-beach weddings.com) offers A-to-Z wedding consulting services. Owner Jean Rich's motto is, "If you can dream it, I can do it."

---

ment; short walk to restaurants. **Cons:** rooms lack private balconies; neighborhood is crowded; taxes and service charges add a whopping 25% to basic rates. ⊠ 6 Billy Folly Rd., Pelican Key ☎ 599/544–2126 ⊕ atrium.festiva.travel ➴ 85 rooms ⌂ In-room: kitchen, refrigerator, Internet. In-hotel: tennis court, pools, gym, laundry facilities, Wi-Fi hotspot ⊟ AE, MC, V ⊚ EP.

$$$ ☼ **Diamond Resort International Flamingo Beach.** Vacation ⓒ Rental. There are so many activities at this resort that you might not return to your room before bedtime. That would be a shame, as the accommodations have lovely balconies overlooking Simpson Bay. Wicker furniture and bright colors keep things inside feeling cheery. Bedrooms have king-size beds, and there are sofa beds in the living rooms. Kitchens are fully equipped. **Pros:** close to a variety of restaurants and nightlife options. **Cons:** area gets crowded; small beach. ⊠ 6 Billy Folly Rd., Pelican Key ☎ 599/544–3900 or 800/438–2929 ⊕ www.diamondresorts-getaway.com ➴ 206 units ⌂ In-room: safe, kitchen. In-hotel:

Westin Dawn Beach Resort & Spa

restaurant, tennis courts, pool, beachfront, water sports, laundry service ⊟ *AE, D, MC, V* ⦿ *EP.*

$$–$$$$ 🏨 **Pelican Resort Club.** *Vacation Rental.* Tucked away on Pelican Key, this resort has a lot going for it, bordering both the bay and the ocean and giving you a front-row seat for island sunsets from your terrace. The spacious suites are tastefully decorated with Caribbean-style furniture, fully equipped kitchens, and many with sleeper sofas, making them just right for families. A new, modern 83-unit building was completed in 2009, and features flat-screen TVs, DVDs, and granite countertops. Kids can enjoy the pool or playground while grown-ups head to the on-site spa. **Pros:** family-friendly resort; near nightlife options. **Cons:** maid service only weekly; crowded area. ⊠ *Billy Folly Rd., Pelican Key* ☎ *877/736–4586 or 599/544–2503* ⊕ *www. pelicanresort.com* ⇆ *425 units* ⸓ *In-room: safe, kitchen. In-hotel: 2 restaurants, bars, tennis courts, pools, spa, beachfront, Internet terminal* ⊟ *AE, MC, V* ⦿ *EP.*

$$$$ 🏨 **Villa Bella Vita.** *Vacation Rental.* From this villa entryway you gaze down into a stark white living room—a view every bit as dramatic as the one outdoors. This place has everything: a workout room with an adjoining outdoor spa, a game room, plus a theater room with a projection TV and a pull-down screen. Each bedroom is different, with its own unique fragrance, but all have a walk-in closet and flat-screen TV. Large bathroom showers have multiple showerheads and custom toiletries. Extra amenities include a Jet

Ski available for guest use and free worldwide phone calls. **Pros:** free long-distance; every amenity you can imagine. **Cons:** a short ride to the beach; sometimes shown to prospective renters while it's occupied. ⊠ *6 Opal Rd., Pelican Key ⊕ www.jennifersvacationvillas.com ☞ 6 bedrooms 7½ baths ⚭ Safe, dishwasher, DVD, Wi-Fi, daily maid service, fully staffed, on-site security, water toys, laundry facilities ⊟ AE, MC, V* ⦿*EP.*

PHILIPSBURG

★ Fodor'sChoice 🏨 **Holland House Beach Hotel.** *Hotel.* An ideal
$$–$$$ location for shoppers and sun worshippers, this historic hotel faces the Front Street pedestrian mall; to the rear are the boardwalk and a lovely stretch of Great Bay Beach. The breezy lobby provides easy access from street to beach, and has free Internet access at a computer terminal. Rooms, all of which have balconies, have been completely redecorated in a bright and clean Euro-modern style. Rooms on each floor have different pastel color accents, like pale lavender or mint. The linens are by Frette. The four spacious junior suites have separate seating areas and two flat-screen TVs and are worth the extra cost. There's also a first-rate restaurant. **Pros:** excellent location; free Wi-Fi; young, engaging management. **Cons:** in a busy location; no pool ⊠ *43 Front St., Box 393, Philipsburg* 🕾 *599/542–2572* ⊕ *www.hhbh. com ☞ 48 rooms, 6 suites ⚭ In-room: safe, refrigerator, Wi-Fi. In-hotel: restaurant, bar, Internet terminal, beachfront* ⊟ *AE, D, DC, MC, V* ⦿*EP.*

$–$$ 🏨 **Pasanggrahan Royal Inn.** *Inn.* One of the few remain-
★ ing authentic West Indian properties on St. Maarten is steeped in history. The island's oldest hotel once served as the governor's mansion. Walls of the entranceway are lined with pictures of Dutch royalty. Specialty rooms (such as the Queen's Room, referring to Queen Beatrice) have hand-carved furniture, four-poster beds with mosquito netting, and private balconies, although they are more about atmosphere than creature comforts. Standard rooms have more of an island feel, with plantation-style furniture. The hotel's restaurant, set in the tropical garden, serves reasonably priced meals; the view looking out over Great Bay isn't bad, either. In case you're wondering, *pasanggrahan* means "guesthouse" in Indonesian. **Pros:** well situated; friendly staff; historic. **Cons:** on the main drag; crowded beach; bathrooms are basic. ⊠ *15 Front St., Box 151, Philipsburg* 🕾 *599/542–3588* ⊕ *www.pasanhotel.com ☞ 18 rooms ⚭ In-*

room: safe, refrigerator. In-hotel: restaurant, bar, beach-front, Internet terminal ⊟ AE, D, MC, V ⍥ EP.

$$ 🖭 **Sea Palace.** Vacation Rental. This hotel, which is right on the beach in Philipsburg, is painted an eye-popping shade of pink that is hard to miss. A renovation has added new rattan furnishings, TVs, and bathroom sinks. The funky lobby has a glass-brick reception desk. Balconied rooms boast views of the cruise ships sailing into Great Bay. Each unit has a fully equipped kitchenette. **Pros:** in the heart of Philipsburg; walking distance to shopping. **Cons:** area crowded when cruise ships dock; not much for kids to do. ⊠ 147 Front St., Philipsburg 🕾 599/542–2411 or 599/542–2700 ⊕ www.seapalace.net 🛏 32 units ⌂ In-room: kitchen. In-hotel: restaurant, beachfront, Wi-Fi hotspot ⊟ MC, V ⍥ EP.

$$–$$$$ 🖭 **Sonesta Great Bay Beach Resort & Casino.** Resort. Location, location, location. Away from the docks that are usually crawling with cruise ships, but only a 10-minute walk from downtown Philipsburg, this resort is especially well positioned. Vibrant hues of orange and yellow accent the comfortable, Caribbean-style guest rooms. All have terraces with fine views. The impressive circular marble lobby faces Great Bay and overlooks the cruise-ship pier on one side and mountains on the other. One big plus is the white-sand beach, which is rarely crowded. **Pros:** good location; nice beach and pool; enough activities to keep you busy. **Cons:** hallways are white and bare, giving them a hospital-like feel; Wi-Fi is expensive. ⊠ 19 Little Bay Rd., Philipsburg ⌂ Box 91, Philipsburg 🕾 599/542–2446 or 800/223–0757 ⊕ www.sonesta.com/greatbay 🛏 257 rooms ⌂ In-room: safe, Wi-Fi. In-hotel: 3 restaurants, bars, tennis court, pools, gym, spa, beachfront, water sports, children's programs (ages 4–12) ⊟ AE, D, DC, MC, V ⍥ EP.

SIMPSON BAY

$$$$ 🖭 **Diamond Resort Royal Palm Beach.** Vacation Rental. Step out onto your balcony for a sweeping view of the ocean and the large swimming pools that shimmy up to it. Caribbean-style furnishings and soothing pastels grace all the two-bedroom suites. The living room also has a sleeper sofa, so larger families have plenty of room. (The three bathrooms are nice, too). One nice touch is room service—an unusual amenity for time-shares. There are also resort-style services, like babysitting and a concierge. **Pros:** near restaurants and bars. **Cons:** only 2-bedroom units available; on a busy street. ⊠ Airport Rd., Simpson Bay 🕾 599/544–3912 or

800/438–2929 ⊕ www.diamondresortsgetaway.com ⇨ 140 2-bedroom suites ♁ In-room: kitchen. In-hotel: restaurant, room service, bar, gym, water sports, Internet terminal ⊟ AE, D, MC, V ⦾ EP.

★ Fodor's Choice **The Horny Toad.** *Hotel.* Because of its stupendous view of Simpson Bay, the immaculate and comfortable rooms, and the creative decor, this lovely guesthouse is widely considered the best on this side of the island. Its virtues are many, but the one thing that keeps patrons coming back year after year is the hospitality of owner Betty Vaughn (ask her how the inn got its name). Treating her numerous return guests like long-lost relatives, she is so welcoming that you simply can't resist her charms. It's no wonder, you really feel like you are visiting the beach house of your favorite aunt. Book early, because the Toad fills up fast. The ground level is wheelchair-accessible. **Pros:** tidy rooms; friendly vibe; beautiful beach is usually deserted. **Cons:** rooms are very basic; need a car to get around. ✉ *2 Vlaun Dr., Simpson Bay ☎ 599/545–4323 or 800/417–9361 ⊕ www.thtgh.com ⇨ 8 rooms ♁ In-room: kitchen, no TV, Wi-Fi. In-hotel: beachfront, laundry service, Internet terminal, no kids under 7 ⊟ AE, D, MC, V ⦾ EP.*

$$

$$–$$$ **La Vista.** *Time-Share.* Hibiscus and bougainvillea line brick walkways that connect the 32 wood-frame bungalows and beachfront suites of this intimate and friendly, family-owned time-share resort perched at the foot of Pelican Key. The accommodations, which are under renovation at this writing, are somewhat sparsely furnished and have small bathrooms, but the balconies showcase awesome views. The beach is rocky but good for snorkeling. **Pros:** close to restaurants and bars. **Cons:** no-frills furnishings; not the best beach. ✉ *53 Billy Folly Rd., Pelican Key, Box 2086, Simpson Bay ☎ 599/544–3005 or 888/790–5264 ⊕ www.lavistaresort.com ⇨ 32 suites, penthouses, and cottages ♁ In-room: safe, kitchen (some). In-hotel: restaurant, pools, beachfront, laundry facilities ⊟ AE, D, MC, V ⦾ EP.*

$–$$ ★ **Mary's Boon Beach Plantation.** *Hotel.* A shaded courtyard welcomes guests at this quirky, informal guesthouse on a 3-mi-long stretch of Simpson Bay. It has the feel of the Florida Keys. Guests often gather next to the beachfront restaurant's honor bar, which always has free popcorn. Pilot Mary Pomeroy chose this site because of its proximity to the airport. (Ask someone to tell you about her life and her mysterious disappearance.) Renovated studio, one-, and two-bedroom units now have flat-screen TVs, wooden shutters with screens, and new linens as well as cathedral ceilings, enormous four-poster beds, and verandas. **Pros:** small and intimate; interesting history. **Cons:** need a car; charge for Internet; because of airport proximity, it can be quite noisy; mosquitoes abound year-round. ✉ *117 Simpson Bay Rd., Simpson Bay* ☎ *599/545–7000* ⊕ *www. marysboon.com* ↪ *37 rooms* ♿ *In-room: kitchen (some), Wi-Fi. In-hotel: restaurant, bars, pool, beachfront, Internet terminal* ▭ *AE, D, MC, V* ☞ *6-night min. late Dec.–mid-Mar.* ⦿*EP.*

$ ◫ **Royal Turtle Inn.** *Inn.* This tiny property, which is now under new ownership, appeals to those who like small inns with simple surroundings and a lagoon view, and who don't mind a three-minute walk to the beach. Inexpensive rates make the beach walk all the easier to bear. Rooms are nicely furnished and have romantic touches like four-poster beds. The sundeck is one of the most popular spots on the nicely landscaped grounds. Breakfast at Turtle Pier Restaurant is included. **Pros:** personalized service; intimate atmosphere; rates include tax. **Cons:** faces a very busy street. ✉ *114 Airport Rd., Simpson Bay* ☎ *599/545–2563* ⊕ *www.theroyalturtle.com* ↪ *8 rooms* ♿ *In room: refrigerator, Wi-Fi. In hotel: pool* ▭ *MC, V* ⦿*BP.*

FRENCH SIDE

ANSE MARCEL

$$$$ ◫ **Hotel Le Marquis.** *Hotel.* If you crave spectacular vistas and intimate surroundings and don't mind heights or steep walks, this is a fun property, with a funky St. Barth vibe. Contemporary Caribbean decor in the spacious rooms means a splash of bright colors, marble bathrooms, and a private terrace with a hammock. If you wish, arrange for spa treatments or breakfast in your room, or take advantage of the multiday packages of spa pampering. The young management is very guest-oriented, and the hotel offers complimentary airport transfers. Although not on the beach, the hotel does offer a free shuttle to Anse Marcel, and the property has its own beach chairs and offers signing privileges at restaurants there. Check for other package promotions that include a car and meals. **Pros:** romantic honeymoon destination; doting staff; amazing views. **Cons:** not on the beach; no restaurant; on a steep hill. ✉ *Pigeon Pea Hill, Anse Marcel* ☎ *590/29–42–30* ⊕ *www.hotel-marquis.com* ↪ *17 rooms* ♿ *In-room: safe, refrigerator, DVD (some). In-hotel: bar, gym, spa* ▭ *AE, MC, V* ⦿*BP.*

Condo Rentals

Condo rentals are another lodging option. They appeal to travelers who aren't interested in the one-size-fits-all activities offered by the resorts. Condos are much cheaper than villas, but you get many of the same amenities, including kitchens, and save money by cooking your own meals. To rent a condo, contact the rental company or the individual owner.

CyberRentals (☎ 512/684–1098 ⊕ www.cyberrentals.com) is a listing service. To rent a condo, you contact the owner directly.

🏠 **The Cliff at Cupecoy Beach** (⊠ Rhine Rd., Cupecoy ☎ 866/978–5839 or 599/546–6633 ⊕ www.cliffsxm.com) These luxurious, high-rise condos are rented out when the owners are not in residence. Depending on the owner's personal style, they can be downright fabulous. For extra privacy, separate elevators serve only two apartments on every floor. All units have large living and dining rooms

plus fully equipped kitchens with stainless-steel appliances and granite countertops. All have with sweeping vistas, but upper-level residences showcase Anguilla, Simpson Bay, and Basses Terres. The fitness center boasts a gym with sauna, whirlpool, and both indoor and outdoor pools. The mega-chic Dior Spa overlooks the huge indoor swimming pool **Pros:** great views; good for families; close to Maho casinos and restaurants; tight security. **Cons:** it's apartment living, so if you are looking for resort-y or beachy, this is not your place; there is a concierge, but no other hotel services; no restaurant.

Jennifer's Vacation Villas (☎ 631/546–7345 or 011/599–54-43107 ⊕ www.jennifers vacationvillas.com) rents condos near Simpson Bay Beach.

Sint Maarten Condos Rentals (☎ 501/984–2483 ⊕ www. stmaartencondos.com) rents condos on Pelican Key.

★ Fodor'sChoice 🏠 **Le Domaine de Lonvilliers by Christophe Leroy.**
$$$$ *Resort.* International sophisticates are excited to see what the chic restaurateur-chef of St-Tropez's Table du Marché and super-luxe vacation properties in Marrakech and Avoriaz will make of this classic property on 148 acres of lush gardens bordering the exceptionally beautiful and secluded beach in Anse Marcel. But at this writing, even the first wave of guests is already raving about the food in the restaurant and the professional staff. Renovations by hot French design talent Michaela Fabbri will continue through

2010, to spruce up the rooms and the public spaces, but in the meantime, excellent promotional rates will surely establish this comfortable, low-key resort as an important player in the St. Martin scene. The renovated rooms have remarkably efficient details like ample closets, lots of glass shelves with plugs for electronics, separate showers, his and hers closets and dressing areas, high-tech kitchenettes, flat-screen TVs, and in-room safes that can accommodate laptops. Many have big round Jacuzzi tubs for two. Big balconies with comfortable chairs look over the water and swaying palms lining the walks. If you like the French Riviera or St. Barth, you will love the pool area, which seems lifted directly from a plush hotel in Nice. Perched above the sweeping arc of sand are chic lounge-beds around the convivial bar, where you can lunch or even have a massage in a tented cabana. **Pros:** excellent restaurant; chic atmosphere; lovely gardens; beachfront setting. **Cons:** some rooms have round bathtubs right in the middle of the room; you will need a car to get around; beach is shared with the busy Radisson. ⊠ *Anse Marcel* ☎ *590/52–35–35* ⊕ *www.hotel-le-domaine.com* ↪ *124 rooms, 5 suites* ⌂ *In-room: safe, kitchen (some), Wi-Fi. In-hotel: 2 restaurants, room service, bar, pool, gym, spa, beachfront, laundry service, Wi-Fi hotspot, parking (free)* ⊟ *AE, DC, MC, V* ⊗ *Closed Sept.* ⍓ *BP.*

★ Fodor'sChoice ⊠ **Radisson St. Martin Resort, Marina & Spa.** *Resort.*

$$$– An $80-million facelift has brought the Radisson up to par
$$$$ with any other of the best full-service resorts in the Caribbean. The family-friendly resort has a lovely beach area, huge infinity pool, marina, shops, and a brand-new spa and fitness facility (opened in 2010). The guest-enrichment program adds cooking classes, French lessons, rum tastings, and massage workshops. There are also activities like poolside yoga, Caribbean dance lessons, and a full water-sport agenda. The rooms, while not huge, are decorated in an up-to-date Euro-mod style, with Sleep Number beds, flat-screen TVs, and Internet. One-bedroom suites overlooking the marina have sleeper sofas and enough space for a small family. There are two restaurants: one is casual with a kind-of buffet menu and a rotisserie station, the other more formal. The attractive, open-air lobby has a pleasant bar with artisan rums and tapas. **Pros:** brand-new resort (opened in 2009); activities galore; plenty of space; great beach. **Cons:** need a car to get around; lots of families at school vacation times; the restaurant fare is pretty pedestrian. ⍓ *BP 581 Marcel Cove, Anse Marcel* ☎ *590/87–67–09*

DID YOU KNOW?

La Samanna, which was built by James Frankel and opened in 1974, overlooks Baie Longue on the French side of St. Martin.

*or 888/201–1718 ⊕ www.radisson.com ⌁189 rooms, 63
suites ⚭ In-room: refrigerator, Wi-Fi, safe, DVD. In-hotel:
2 restaurants, bar, pool, spa, gym, beachfront, water sports
⊟AE, MC, V ⋈BP.*

BAIE LONGUE

★ Fodor'sChoice ⊡ **La Samanna.** *Resort.* A long stretch of pretty,
$$$$ white-sand beach borders this venerable resort. The service
is warm and professional, and ongoing refurbishments and
improvements, not to mention seasoned, savvy management, continue to revive this classic property. Seven new
suites are smartly designed with modern upgrades and
private plunge pools on the roof; five new three- and four-
bedroom villas opened in 2010 with drop-dead views,
impeccable decor, and a full private staff that will please
even the pickiest mogul. Unrenovated rooms are somewhat
lacking in the same chic ambience, and standard rooms
are small. Activities include one-on-one Pilates instruction and yoga in the workout facility. The serene Elysées
Spa is surrounded by a lush private garden and waterfall,
and the treatment rooms include a private outdoor area
with a shower. The hotel's 15,000-bottle wine cellar is in
a class by itself, and private dinners in the cellar can be
easily arranged and tailored to guest interests. For cocktails, there's a tented Moroccan bar that leads out to a
smashing cliff-side pool deck. **Pros:** great beach; convenient
location; romantic, attentive service; excellent spa. **Cons:**
rather pricey for standard rooms; small pools; ongoing
renovations in some areas. ⊠ *Baie Longue ⊕ Box 4077,
Marigot 97064 ☎590/87–64–00 or 800/854–2252 ⊕www.
lasamanna.orient-express.com ⌁27 rooms, 54 suites ⚭ In-
room: safe, kitchen (some), refrigerator (some), Wi-Fi.
In-hotel: 2 restaurants, bar, tennis courts, pool, gym, spa,
beachfront, water sports ⊟AE, MC, V ☉ Closed Sept. and
Oct. ⋈BP.*

BAIE ORIENTALE

$$$– ⊡ **Alamanda Resort.** *Resort.* One of the few resorts directly
$$$$ on the white-sand beach of Orient Bay, this hotel has a
☾ funky feel and spacious, colonial-style suites with terraces
that overlook the pool, beach, or ocean. Two-level rooms
also have private decks. Alamanda Café is surrounded by
a fragrant tropical garden; the Kakao Beach restaurant
looks out toward the ocean. A hotel card gives you access
to activities and restaurants at any resort in the area. The
staff at the 24-hour activity desk will be happy to arrange
island activities. **Pros:** pleasant property; friendly staff;

right on Orient Beach. **Cons:** some rooms are noisy; could use some updating. ⊠ *Baie Orientale* ⊡ *BP 5166, Grand Case 97071* ☎ *590/52–87–40 or 800/622–7836* ⊕ *www. alamanda-resort.com* ⇆ *42 rooms* ⚑ *In-room: safe, kitchen. In-hotel: 2 restaurants, room service, tennis courts, pool, gym, water sports, laundry service, Internet terminal* ⊟ *AE, MC, V* ⎢⊙⎢ *BP.*

★ FodorsChoice ⊡ **Caribbean Princess.** *Vacation Rental.* These
$$$$ 12 large, nicely decorated, well-equipped, and updated
☺ two- and three-bedroom condos have big kitchens and living rooms, lovely balconies over Orient Beach (a few steps away), new furniture, and share a pretty pool. They are under the same management as Palm Court. Since the condos offer some hotel services, this is a great choice for families or a group of friends. The village of Orient Bay has a small market, restaurants, and services; guests at the resort get signing privileges at all the Orient Bay restaurants and sport operators. **Pros:** the comforts of home; nice interior design; direct beach access. **Cons:** not a full-service resort. ⊠ *C5 Parc de la Baie Orientale, Baie Orientale* ☎ *0590/52–94–94* ⊕ *www.cap-caraibes.com* ⇆ *12 condos* ⚑ *In-room: safe, kitchen, DVD, Wi-Fi. In-hotel: pool, beachfront, diving, water sports, laundry facilities, laundry service, Internet terminal, Wi-Fi hotspot, parking (free), some pets allowed* ⊟ *AE, MC, V* ⊙ *Closed Sept.* ⎢⊙⎢ *CP.*

$$$– ⊡ **Club Orient Resort.** *Resort.* For something rather different,
$$$$ consider letting it all hang out at this clothing-optional hotel on Baie Orientale. There are villas, suites, and studios that can accommodate from three to seven people each. Members of naturist organizations can score a 10% discount. Unlike many of the guests, the smaller suites are modest, with knotty-pine walls, but all units have fully-equipped kitchens, outdoor showers, and front and back patios. But realistically, privacy is a rare commodity here; it's a lot like a camp. For a bit of adventure, try a nude catamaran cruise (but wear sunscreen, of course), one of many activities offered. **Pros:** nice location; on-site convenience store. **Cons:** no TVs; a bit pricey, rooms are the bare minimum. ⊠ *1 Baie Orientale, Baie Orientale* ☎ *590/87–33–85 or 877/456–6833* ⊕ *www.cluborient.com* ⇆ *137 rooms* ⚑ *In room: safe, Wi-Fi. In hotel: 2 restaurants, tennis courts, water sports, gym* ⊟ *AE, D, MC, V* ⎢⊙⎢ *EP.*

$$$$ ⊡ **Esmeralda Resort.** *Resort.* Almost all of these traditional
☺ Caribbean-style, kitchen-equipped villas, which can be configured to meet the needs of different groups, have their own private pool, and the fun of Orient Beach, where the

hotel has its own private beach club, is a two-minute walk away. The more expensive rooms really are worth the extra bucks here. The activities desk can arrange everything from snorkeling and tennis to car rentals and babysitting, and you have the convenience of signing privileges at all the restaurants and activity outfitters on Orient Beach. The resort has two restaurants—the excellent L'Astrolabe for fine dining and the beachfront Coco Beach Club for anything from sushi, salads, and burgers to all-day long lounging at the prime spot at the quiet end of the beach. **Pros:** beachfront location; private pools; plenty of activities; frequent online promotions. **Cons:** rooms are very dark, some really need updating; water-pressure complaints; need a car to get around. ⌂ *Box 5141, Baie Orientale 97071* ☎ *590/87–36–36 or 800/622–7836* ⊕ *www.esmeralda-resort.com* ⤢ *65 rooms* ♿ *In-room: safe, kitchen (some), refrigerator. In-hotel: 2 restaurants, room service, tennis courts, pools, beachfront, water sports, laundry service, Internet terminal* ⊟ *AE, MC, V* ⊗ *Closed Sept.–Oct.* ⍩ *EP.*

$$$$ ☷ **Green Cay Village.** *Vacation Rental.* Surrounded by five acres of lush greenery high above Baie Orientale, these villas are perfect for families or groups of friends who are looking for privacy and the comforts of home. Each of the West Indian–style villas has a good-size private pool with nice outdoor furniture and a barbecue grill. There is daily maid service, a rarity in condo accommodations. The interiors are spacious and neat—the largest has three bedrooms, two baths, a living room, a full kitchen, and a dining patio—and a great deal for a family or group. If you rent just the cheaper studios, you get a kitchenette and a large bedroom with a sitting area. Whichever you choose, the staff can arrange a cook to take care of all your meals. The beach and restaurants are a short walk or drive away. Refrigerators come stocked with essentials like milk and eggs, and airport pick-ups can be arranged. There are also reserved parking spaces near the villa. **Pros:** beautiful setting; near Baie Orientale; perfect for families with teens or older kids. **Cons:** need a car to get around; beach is a five-minute walk. ⌂ *Parc de la Baie Orientale, Box 3006, Baie Orientale* ☎ *590/87–38–63 or 866/592–4213* ⊕ *www. greencayvillage.com* ⤢ *16 villas* ♿ *In-room: kitchen, refrigerator. In-hotel: tennis court, pools, laundry service* ⊟ *AE, MC, V* ⍩ *CP.*

$$$– ☷ **Hotel La Plantation.** *Hotel.* Perched high above Orient Bay,
$$$$ this colonial-style hotel is a charmer, and guests give high marks to the recent renovations. French doors open to a

2

wraparound veranda with an expansive view of Orient Bay (the best views are from the top level). Each spacious villa is composed of a huge suite with kitchen and a big living room and two studios that can be rented together or separately. All are accented with yellow, green, and stenciled wall decorations. Mosquito nets hang over king-size beds, and good-size bathrooms have large showers and two sinks. Alongside the pool is the cozy Café Plantation, where complimentary breakfast is served. Be sure to check into advantageous free-night promotions especially in the slower months. **Pros:** relaxing atmosphere; eye-popping views. **Cons:** small pool; beach is a 10-minute walk away. ⊠ *C5 Parc de La Baie Orientale, Baie Orientale* ☎ *590/29–58–00* ⊕ *www.la-plantation.com* ⤳ *17 suites, 34 studios* ⚬ *In-room: safe, kitchen (some), refrigerator. In-hotel: restaurant, tennis courts, pool, gym* ⊗ *Closed Sept.–mid-Oct.* ⊟ *AE, MC, V* ⊚ *BP.*

$$$–
$$$$ 　☒ **L'Hoste.** *Resort.* You can't miss the multistory candy-colored villas right on beautiful Orient Beach. Young guests flock here for gentle prices, huge rooms, and the friendly, relaxed atmosphere. The hotel's La Playa Beach Club is also relaxed and inviting, and the boutiques, spa, and nonstop party on the beachfront are big draws. There's a cute little pool in the garden and a gazebo for reading. All rooms have small kitchens. **Pros:** spacious rooms; funky, friendly atmosphere. **Cons:** not fancy; not all the rooms have been updated at this writing, so be sure to ask. ⊡ *Box 5146, Baie Orientale 97150* ☎ *590/87–42–08* ⊕ *www.hostehotel.com* ⤳ *56 junior suites* ⚬ *In-room: safe, kitchen, DVD, Wi-Fi. In-hotel: 2 restaurants, room service, bars, pool, beachfront, diving, water sports, Wi-Fi hotspot, parking (free), some pets allowed* ⊟ *AE, D, DC, MC, V* ⊚ *EP.*

★ Fodor's Choice 　☒ **Palm Court.** *Hotel.* Completely renovated in
$$$$ 2007 by a Parisian travel pro, the romantic beachfront units of this *hotel de charme* are steps from the fun of Orient Beach yet private, quiet, and stylishly up to date. Immaculate spacious rooms are dramatically decorated in spice colors and accessories that suggest Morocco; all have big balconies with loungers. There is a pretty pool in the manicured garden where breakfast is served, and each unit has a fridge and microwave so you can keep and warm up snacks. Guests get signing privileges at all the beach bars; spots at chic Waïkiki Beach Club are reserved for guests of this hotel. The upper-floor units have water views, but the lower level offers immediate access to the pool and garden. **Pros:** big rooms; fresh and new; nice garden. **Cons:** across

Palm Court Hotel, St. Martin

from, but not on the beach; some complaints about the a/c. ⊠ *Parc de la Baie Orientale, Baie Orientale* ☎ *590/87–41– 94* ⊕ *www.sxm-palm-court.com* ⤳ *24 rooms* ♿ *In-room: safe, refrigerator, Wi-Fi. In-hotel: 1 restaurant, pool, Wi-Fi hotspot, parking (free), some pets allowed* ⊟ *AE, MC, V* ⊗ *Closed Sept.* ⦿ *CP.*

GRAND CASE

$$$– $$$$ ⦿ **Bleu Emeraude.** *Vacation Rental.* Brand new in 2009, the 11 apartments in this tidy complex sit right on a sliver of Grand Case Beach. Studios, as well as one-and two-bedroom apartments (the biggest one accommodating up to 6 people), all have great views and are beautifully furnished in white and sky-blue with red accents; all have big sliding glass doors. Apartments are accessible to those in wheelchairs by elevator, and there is both outdoor and indoor parking, You may be able to get a crib or highchair on request, but these are limited in availability. **Pros:** brand-new; walk to restaurants; attractive decor. **Cons:** it's not resort-y at all. ⊠ *240 bd. de Grand Case, Grand Case* ☎ *0590/87–27–71* ⊕ *www.bleuemeraude.com* ⤳ *4 studios, 6 1-bedroom apartments, 1 2-bedroom apartment* ♿ *In-room: safe, kitchen, DVD, Wi-Fi (some). In-hotel: beachfront Wi-Fi, parking (free), some pets allowed* ⊟ *MC, V* ⦿ *CP.*

$$$– $$$$ ⦿ **Grand Case Beach Club.** *Resort.* This popular beachfront property on a cove at the east end of Grand Case has a friendly staff and spectacular sunset views. Spacious studios and one- and two-bedroom units are individually

owned, and while not glamorous, are clean and comfortable; each has a nice balcony. The resort has a lighted synthetic grass tennis court (bring tennis balls from home, but they supply racquets), a gym, a small pool, a restaurant, and nonmotorized water sports all included in the price. All rooms were updated in 2009, and have fully-equipped kitchens with updated appliances and granite counters and either ocean or (cheaper) garden views; Wi-Fi service is free throughout the property. Room service is available from the Sunset Café. **Pros:** reasonable price; comfortable rooms; walking distance to restaurants. **Cons:** small beach; dated buildings. ✉ *21 rue de Petit Plage, at north end of bd. de Grand Case, Box 339, Grand Case* ☎ *590/87–51–87 or 800/344–3016* ⊕ *www.grandcasebeachclub.com* ↴ *72 apartments* ⚫ *In-room: safe, kitchen, refrigerator. In-hotel: restaurant, bar, tennis court, beachfront, pool, gym, water sports, laundry facilities, laundry service, Wi-Fi hotspot* ⊟ *AE, MC, V* ⊙ *CP*.

$$$– $$$$ ⚬ ⌧ **Hôtel L'Esplanade.** *Hotel.* Enthusiasts return again and again to the classy, loft-style suites in this immaculate enclave. Units are decorated in dark wood plantation-tropic style with big four-poster beds; kitchens are sleek and modern and are stocked with basics before you arrive. This attention to detail and great service is a hallmark of Kristin Petrelluzzi, who also owns Le Petit Hotel nearby on Grand Case Beach. Private terraces with sunset and bay views are a lovely touch. The pool is in the pretty garden. Guests walk a path down the hillside to Grand Case. **Pros:** attentive management; very clean; updated room decor; family-friendly feel. **Cons:** lots of stairs to climb; not on the beach. ✉ *Box 5007, Grand Case, 97150* ☎ *590/87–06–55 or 866/596–8365* ⊕ *www.lesplanade.com* ↴ *24 units* ⚫ *In-room: safe, kitchen. In-hotel: pools, laundry service* ⊟ *AE, MC, V* ⊙ *EP*.

$$$– $$$$ ⌧ **Le Petit Hotel.** *Hotel.* Surrounded by some of the best restaurants in the Caribbean, this beachfront boutique hotel, sister hotel to Hotel L'Esplanade, oozes charm and has the same caring, attentive management. A Mediterranean staircase leads to its nine spacious rooms and a one-bedroom suite. Each room has some high-tech touches, such as CD and DVD players and a flat-screen TV. There's no pool, but the beach is great, and you can always take a dip in the pool at the Esplanade. Baskets are provided at the self-serve breakfast buffet, so you can take your croissants, coffee, and freshly squeezed juice back to your private terrace. **Pros:** walking distance to everything in

Grand Case; friendly staff; clean, updated rooms. **Cons:** many stairs to climb; no pool. ⊠ *248 bd. de Grand Case, Grand Case* ☎ *590/29–09–65* ⊕ *www.lepetithotel.com* ⇨ *9 rooms, 1 suite* ⚭ *In-room: safe, kitchen. In-hotel: beachfront* ⊟ *AE, MC, V* ⊚| *CP.*

$–$$ ⊞ **Love Hotel.** *Hotel.* This cozy, seven-room guesthouse right on Grand Case Beach has been renovated by the young owners themselves, but at this writing only five rooms are finished. Simple but fresh (in an international, Ikea style), the rooms will appeal to young travelers, who will especially like the gentle prices (which are even cheaper by the week). There is a friendly café-bar-restaurant on the ground floor, and giant beanbag loungers on the beach a few steps down. "Love" means no TV in the rooms. "Be romantic!" say hoteliers Muriel and William Demy. **Pros:** young, fun vibe; in-town location. **Cons:** pretty basic rooms; ongoing construction; staff not always helpful. ⊠ *140 bd. de Grand Case, Grand Case* ☎ *0590/29–87–14* ⊕ *www.love-sxm.com* ⇨ *7 rooms* ⚭ *In-room: safe, no TV. In-hotel: restaurant, bar, beachfront, Wi-Fi hotspot* ⊟ *MC, V* ⊚| *EP.*

HAPPY BAY

$$$$ ⊞ **Belle de Nuit.** *Vacation Rental.* This architectural gem on the hill above pretty, quiet Happy Bay (though not directly on the beach) was designed by popular architect Mauricio Lanari. The grounds are beautiful, and a spacious pool deck with an infinity pool overlooks the blue sea to Anguilla. Rooms are tasteful and huge, with stylish furnishings. There are five big bedrooms, and a private path to the beach, making it great for a group who might want to come and go at their own pace. **Pros:** soaring, high ceilings; luxurious details. **Cons:** three of the bedrooms have direct access to the pool terrace, which might not be good for groups with small children; a/c is only in bedrooms; not close to anything (requires a car). ⊠ *Happy Bay* ☎ *590/52–02–85* ⊕ *www.pierrescaraibes.com* ⇨ *5 bedrooms, 5½ baths* ⚭ *No a/c (some), safe, dishwasher, DVD, Internet, weekly maid service, laundry facilities, some pets allowed, no smoking* ⊟ *AE, MC, V* ⊚| *EP*

OYSTER POND

$$–$$$ ⊞ **Captain Oliver's Resort.** *Resort.* This cluster of pink bungalows is perched high on a hill above a lagoon. The bungalows are nothing fancy, but they do come with lots of lush landscaping and a fine view of the Caribbean and St. Barth. Rooms are clean and simple, and have private verandas. The restaurant has live music every Saturday.

The reasonable prices mean that people return again and again. **Pros:** restaurant is reasonably priced; ferry trips leave from the hotel. **Cons:** not on the beach. ⊠ *Oyster Pond* ☎ *590/87–40–26 or 888/790–5264* ⊕ *www.captainolivers. com* ⇆ *50 suites* ⚹ *In-room: safe, refrigerator. In-hotel: restaurant, bars, pool, Internet terminal* ⊟ *AE, D, MC, V* ⊘ *Closed Sept. and Oct.* ⫿⊙⫿*BP.*

TERRES BASSES

$$$$ ⌨ **Amber.** *Vacation Rental.* Because this villa sits high above ☾ Baie Rouge, you can be anywhere on its wraparound terrace and enjoy fine views of the Caribbean. The contemporary living room has glass doors that you can fling open for a different perspective on the ocean. Two of the four bedrooms have king-size beds; the third has two singles, and the fourth bedroom has one single. Adjoining bathrooms are quite attractive, with dark tile walls and floors. The fully equipped kitchen has a central island that can accommodate more than one cook. The rental company stocks the refrigerator with the basics—milk, bread, eggs, butter, orange juice, coffee—so you don't have to go shopping the first day you arrive. **Pros:** great views; good for families with children. **Cons:** fourth bedroom is small. ⊠ *Terres Basses* ⊕ *blueescapes.com* ⇆ *4 bedrooms, 4 baths* ⚹ *Safe, dishwasher, Wi-Fi, daily maid service, on-site security, laundry facilities* ⊟ *AE, MC, V* ⫿⊙⫿*EP.*

$$$$ ⌨ **Beau Rivage.** *Vacation Rental.* After a dip in the pool, you ☾ can take a break from the sun under this villa's gorgeous gazebo. Located two steps from Baie Rouge, you can be in the ocean in no time. The living room, with vaulted ceilings and sleek contemporary furniture, has glass doors that open onto views of Anguilla. The kitchen is equipped with everything a chef could ask for. Bedrooms are roomy, with king-size beds. Note, this is a no-smoking property. **Pros:** beachfront property; perfect for large families. **Cons:** beachfront property doesn't come cheap. ⊠ *Terres Basses* ⊕ *www.islandhideaways.com* ⇆ *1 3-bedroom, 3½-bath villa* ⚹ *Dishwasher, Wi-Fi, daily maid service, pool, beachfront* ⊟ *AE, D, MC, V* ⫿⊙⫿*EP.*

$$$$ ⌨ **La Savanne.** *Vacation Rental.* This Spanish colonial–style ☾ home is perched on a hillside facing beautiful Baie Longue. Its layout makes it a good fit for large families or several couples traveling together. The master bedroom suite is by itself upstairs, giving it added privacy. Three of the bedrooms have king-size beds, while the fourth has a queen. A covered terrace with dining and sitting areas overlooks the

pool and gazebo. The living room, furnished with contemporary pieces, has plenty of high-tech gadgets. The cheerful white kitchen has granite countertops and is equipped with everything you need to make a big meal. **Pros:** lovely views; plenty of privacy; good for a family. **Cons:** master suite has a low ceiling. ⊠ *Terres Basses* ⊕ *www.stmartinluxuryvillas. com* ↝ *4 bedrooms, 4 baths* ⚭ *Dishwasher, DVD, on-site security, pool, laundry facilities, no-smoking* ⊟ No credit cards Ⓞl *EP.*

$$$ ☷ **Villa La Nina.** *Vacation Rental.* From the flower-bordered
☽ terrace you can see the tranquil Baie Longue in the distance. A red-tiled gazebo allows you to sit alongside the pool without worrying about getting too much sun. This small, but comfortable, French-style villa is decorated in restrained shades of yellow and blue. The open-air kitchen and its breakfast bar overlook the pretty pool (shared with another villa). **Pros:** well suited for a small family; shared gym facilities and tennis court. **Cons:** not on the beach; one bedroom has twin beds. ⊠ *Terres Basses* ⊕ *www.wimco. com* ↝ *2 bedrooms, 2 baths* ⚭ *Safe, dishwasher, DVD, daily maid service, fully staffed, pool, laundry facilities, no smoking* ⊟ *AE, MC, V* Ⓞl *EP.*

$$$$ ☷ **Villa Mirabelle.** *Vacation Rental.* On a hillside overlooking Simpson Bay sits this charming villa. Rooms have vaulted ceilings and views of the gardens or the lagoon. The gourmet kitchen is stocked with everything you need. The living area makes you want to grab a book and curl up on one of its couches. Each of the three bedrooms has a king-size bed; all open onto the covered terrace leading down to the pool and the ocean. **Pros:** easy walk to Baie Rouge; short drive to Marigot; has a generator in case of power failures **Cons:** staying with children under 11 requires a $1,000 security deposit. ⊠ *Simpson Bay Lagoon, Terres Basses* ⊕ *www.wimco.com* ↝ *3 bedrooms, 3 baths* ⚭ *Dishwasher, safe, DVD, Wi-Fi, daily maid service, pool, laundry facilities, no-smoking* ⊟ *AE, MC, V* Ⓞl *EP.*

BEACHES

Warm surf and a gentle breeze can be found at the island's 37 beaches, and every one of them is open to the public. What could be better? Each is unique: some bustling and some bare, some refined and some rocky, some good for snorkeling and some for sunning. Whatever you fancy in the beach landscape department, it's here, including a clothing-optional one at the south end of Baie Orientale.

Baie Orientale, widely considered St. Martin's best beach

Petty theft from cars in beach parking lots is an unfortunate fact of life in St. Maarten and St. Martin. Leave nothing in your parked car, not even in the glove compartment or the trunk.

DUTCH SIDE

Cupecoy Beach. This picturesque area of sandstone cliffs, white sand, and shoreline caves is a necklace of small beaches that come and go according to the whims of the sea. Even though the western part is more developed, the surf can be rough. It's popular with gay locals and visitors. It's near the Dutch-French border. Break-ins have been reported in cars, so don't leave anything at all in your vehicle. ⊠ *Cupecoy, between Baie Longue and Mullet Bay.*

☺ **Dawn Beach.** True to its name, Dawn Beach is the place to
★ be at sunrise. On the Atlantic side of Oyster Pond, just south of the French border, this is a first-class beach for sunning and snorkeling. It's not usually crowded, and there are several good restaurants nearby. To find it, follow the signs to Mr. Busby's restaurant. ⊠ *South of Oyster Pond, Dawn Beach.*

☺ **Great Bay.** This is probably the easiest beach to find because it curves around Philipsburg. A bustling, white-sand beach, Great Bay is just behind Front Street. Here you'll find boutiques, eateries, and a pleasant boardwalk. Because of

Cupecoy Beach, St. Maarten

the cruise ships and the salt pond, it's not the best place for swimming. If you must get wet, do it west of Captain Hodge Pier or seek out a quieter area like around Antoine's Restaurant. ✉ *Philipsburg.*

Guana Bay. If you're looking for seclusion, you'll find it here. There are no umbrellas, no lounge chairs, and a beach shack with no regular service. What this bay does have is a long expanse of soft sand. The surf is strong, making this beach a popular surfer hangout. It's definitely not recommended for kids because of the rough surf. It's five minutes northeast of Philipsburg. Turn on Guana Bay Road, which is behind Great Bay Salt Pond. ✉ *Upper Prince's Quarter.*

☾ **Little Bay.** Despite its popularity with snorkelers and divers as well as kayakers and boating enthusiasts, Little Bay isn't usually crowded. Maybe the gravelly sand is the reason. But, it does boast panoramic views of St. Eustatius, Philipsburg, the cruise-ship terminal, Saba, and St. Kitts. The beach is west of Fort Amsterdam and accessible via the Divi Little Bay Resort. ✉ *Little Bay Rd., Little Bay.*

Mullet Bay Beach. Many believe that this mile-long, powdery white-sand beach near the medical school is the island's best. Swimmers like it because the water is usually calm. When the swell is up, the surfers hit the beach. It's also the place to listen for the "whispering pebbles" as the waves wash up. ✉ *Mullet Bay, south of Cupecoy, Mullet Bay.*

Simpson Bay Beach. This secluded, half-moon stretch of white-sand beach on the island's Caribbean side is a hidden gem. It's mostly surrounded by private residences. There are no big resorts, no jet skiers, no food concessions, and no crowds. It's just you, the sand, and the water. Southeast of the airport, follow the signs to Mary's Boon and the Horny Toad guesthouses. ✉ *Simpson Bay.*

2

FRENCH SIDE

Almost all the French-side beaches, whether busy Orient Bay or less busy Friar's Bay, have beach clubs and restaurants, much as you would find in the south of France. For about $25 a couple you get two *transats* (chaises) and a *parasol* (umbrella) for the day, not to mention chair-side service delivering drinks and food. The restaurants at the more chic clubs are generally more expensive, and some are more popular with day-trippers from the cruise ships, but you can check everything out before you commit. Only some beaches have bathrooms and showers, so if that is your preference, inquire.

Anse Heureuse (*Happy Bay*). Not many people know about this romantic, hidden gem. Happy Bay has powdery sand, gorgeous luxury villas, and stunning views of Anguilla. The snorkeling is also good. To get here, turn left on the rather rutted dead-end road to Baie de Péres (Friars Bay). The beach itself is a 10- to 15-minute walk from the last beach bar. ✉ *Happy Bay.*

Baie de Grand Case. Along this skinny stripe of a beach bordering the culinary capital of Grand Case, the old-style gingerbread architecture sometimes peeps out between the bustling restaurants. The sea is calm, and there are tons of fun lunch options from bistros to beachside lolos (barbecue stands). Several of the restaurants rent chairs and umbrellas; some include their use for lunch patrons. In between there is a bit of shopping, certainly for beach necessities but also for the same kinds of handcrafts found in the Marigot market. ✉ *Grand Case,.*

Baie des Péres (*Friars Bay*). This quiet cove close to Marigot has beach grills and bars, with chaises and umbrellas, calm waters, and a lovely view of Anguilla. Kali's Beach Bar, open daily for lunch and (weather permitting) dinner, has a Rasta vibe and color scheme—it's the best place to be on the full moon for music, dancing, and a huge bonfire, but you can get lunch, beach chairs, and umbrellas there in any moon-phase. To get to the beach, take National Road 7 from Marigot, go toward Grand Case to the Morne Valois hill, and turn left on the dead-end road at the sign. ⊠ *Friar's Bay.*

Baie Longue (*Long Bay*). Though it extends over the French Lowlands, from the cliff at La Samanna to La Pointe des Canniers, the island's longest beach has no facilities or vendors. It's the perfect place for a romantic walk. But car break-ins are a particular problem here. To get here, take National Road 7 south of Marigot. The entrance marked LA SAMANNA is the first entrance to the beach. For a splurge, lunch at the resort or sunset drinks are a must. ⊠ *Baie Longue.*

★ Fodor's Choice **Baie Orientale** (*Orient Bay*). Many consider this the island's most beautiful beach, but its 2 mi of satiny white sand, underwater marine reserve, variety of water sports, beach clubs, and hotels also make it one of the most crowded. Lots of "naturists" take advantage of the clothing-optional policy, so don't be shocked. Early-morning nude beach walking is de rigueur for the guests at Club Orient, at the southeastern end of the beach. Plan to spend the day at one of the clubs; each one has umbrellas of a different color, and all boast terrific restaurants and lively bars. You can have an open-air massage, try any sea toy you fancy, and stay until dark. To get to Baie Orientale from Marigot, take National Road 7 past Grand Case, past the Aéroport de L'Espérance, and watch for the left turn. ⊠ *Baie Orientale.*

Baie Rouge (*Red Bay*). You can bask on the gorgeous beach here—home to a couple of beach bars, complete with chaises and umbrellas—along with the millionaires renting the big-ticket villas in the "neighborhood." Baie Rouge and its salt ponds make up a nature preserve, the location of the oldest habitations in the Caribbean. This area is widely thought to have the best snorkeling beaches on the island. You can swim the crystal waters along the point and explore a swim-through cave. The beach is fairly popular with gay men in the mornings and early afternoons. There are two restaurants here, including Chez Raymond, which is open every day (cocktail hour starts when the conch shell blows, so keep your ears open). There is a sign and a right turn after you leave Baie Nettlé. ⊠ *Baie Rouge.*

☺ **Le Galion.** A coral reef borders this quiet beach, part of the island's nature preserve, which is paradise if you are

A Day in St. Eustatius

The Quill, St. Eustatius' dormant volcano

Unless you're a diver or a history buff, chances are you have never heard of St. Eustatius, or Statia, as it is often called. So many ships once crowded its harbor that it was tagged the Emporium of the Western World. That abruptly changed in 1776. With an 11-gun salute to the American *Andrew Doria*, Statia became the first country to recognize U.S. independence. Great Britain retaliated by economically devastating the island.

Fort Oranje, where the famous shots came from, is a history buff favorite. In Oranjestad, it has protected the island since 1636. Its courtyard houses the original Dutch Reformed Church (1776). Holen Dalim, one of the oldest synagogues in the Caribbean (1738), is on Synagogepad (Synagogue Path).

The island's interior is gorgeous. For hikers, the Quill is the challenge. The long and windy trail to the top of the 1,968-foot crater is lined with wild orchids, frilly ferns, elephant ears, and various other kinds of flora. Beaches, on the other hand, hold little attraction. There's no real sandy spot on the Caribbean shore, and the beaches on the Atlantic side are too rough for swimming.

Statia is a pleasant change from the bustle of St. Maarten. No matter how much time you spend on the island, locals will wave or beep at you in recognition. You never feel like a stranger. For more information, contact the **Statia Tourist Office** (☎ *599/318–2433* ⊕ *www. statiatourism.com*).

traveling with children. The water is calm, clear, and quite shallow, so it's a perfect place for families with young kids. It's a full-service beach, with chair rentals, restaurants, and water-sports operators. Kite-boarders and windsurfers like the trade winds at the far end of the beach. On Sundays there are always groups picnicking and partying. To get to Le Galion, follow the signs to the unmissable Butterfly Farm and continue toward the water. ⊠ *Quartier d'Orleans.*

☼ **Ilêt Pinel.** A protected nature reserve, this kid-friendly island is a five-minute ferry ride from French Cul de Sac ($7 per person round-trip). The ferry runs every half-hour from mid-morning until dusk. The water is clear and shallow, and the shore is sheltered. If you like snorkeling, don your gear and paddle along both coasts of this pencil-shaped speck in the ocean. You can rent equipment on the island or in the parking lot before you board the ferry for about $10. Plan for lunch any day of the week at the water's edge at a palm-shaded beach hut at **Karibuni** (except in September, when it's closed) for the freshest fish, great salads, tapas, and drinks—try the frozen mojito for a treat. ⊠ *Ilêt Pinel.*

SPORTS AND THE OUTDOORS

BIKING

Mountain biking is a great way to explore the island. Beginner and intermediate cyclists can ride the coastal trails from Cay Bay to Fort Amsterdam or Mullet Beach. More serious bikers can cruise the Bellevue Trail from Port de Plaisance to Marigot. Bring your bathing suit—along the way you can stop at Baie Rouge or Baie des Prunes for a dip. The bike trails to Fort Louis offer fabulous views. The most challenging ride is up Pic du Paradis. If you would feel better tackling this route with a guide, ask at one of the bike shops. Several locally known guides can help you make this trip.

DUTCH SIDE

☼ **TriSport** (⊠ *Airport Rd. 14B, Simpson Bay* ☎ *599/545–4384* ⊕ *www.trisportsxm.com*) rents bikes that come with helmets, water bottle, locks, and repair kits. Rates are $17 per half day, $24 overnight, and $110 per week.

Sailing, a popular activity in St. Maarten/St. Martin

FRENCH SIDE

Loterie Farm (✉ *Rte. de Pic du Paradis, Pic du Paradis* ☎ *590/87–86–16 or 590/57–28–55*) arranges mountain-biking tours around Pic du Paradis.

Rent A Scoot (✉ *Baie Nettlé* ☎ *590/87–20–59*) rents bikes for €10 per day or €60 per week.

BOATING AND SAILING

The island is surrounded by water, so why not get out and enjoy it? The water and winds are perfect for skimming the surf. It'll cost you around $1,200 to $1,500 per day to rent a 28- to 40-foot powerboat, considerably less for smaller boats or small sailboats. Drinks and sometimes lunch are usually included on crewed day charters.

DUTCH SIDE

Lagoon Sailboat Rental (✉ *Airport Rd., near Uncle Harry's, Simpson Bay* ☎ *599/557–0714* ⊕ *www.lagoonsailboatren-tal.com*) has 20-foot day sailers for rent within Simpson Bay Lagoon for $150 per day, with a half day for $110. Either explore on your own or rent a skipper to navigate the calm, sheltered waters around Simpson Bay Yacht Club and miles of coastline on both the French and Dutch sides of the islands.

Random Wind (✉ *Ric's Place, Simpson Bay* ☎ *599/587–5742* ⊕ *www.randomwind.com*) offers half- and full-day sailing and snorkeling trips on a traditional 54-foot clipper. Charter prices depend on the size of the group and whether lunch is served. The regularly scheduled Paradise Daysail costs $95 per person and includes food and drink. Departures are on the Dutch side, from Ric's Place at Simpson Bay, at 9 AM Tuesday through Friday.

Sailing experience is not necessary for the **St. Maarten 12-Metre Challenge** (✉ *Bobby's Marina, Philipsburg* ☎ *599/542–0045* ⊕ *www.12metre.com*), one of the island's most popular activities. Participants compete on 68-foot racing yachts, including Dennis Connor's *Stars and Stripes* (the actual boat that won the America's Cup in 1987) and the *Canada II*. Anyone can help the crew grind winches, trim sails, and punch the stopwatch, or you can just sit back and watch everyone else work. The thrill of it is priceless, but book well in advance; this is the most popular shore excursion offered by cruise ships in the Caribbean.

FRENCH SIDE

The **Moorings** (✉ *Captain Oliver's Marina, Oyster Pond* ☎ *590/87–32–54* ⊕ *www.moorings.com*) has a fleet of Beneteau yachts as well as bareboat and crewed catamarans for those who opt for a sailing vacation.

FISHING

You can angle for yellowtail snapper, grouper, marlin, tuna, and wahoo on deep-sea excursions. Costs range from $150 per person for a half day to $250 for a full day. Prices usually include bait and tackle, instruction for novices, and refreshments. Ask about licensing and insurance.

DUTCH SIDE

Lee's Deepsea Fishing (✉ *Welfare Rd. 82, Simpson Bay* ☎ *599/544–4233* ⊕ *www.leesfish.com*) organizes excursions, and when you return, Lee's Roadside Grill will cook your tuna, wahoo, or whatever else you catch and keep.

Rudy's Deep Sea Fishing (✉ *14 Airport Rd., Simpson Bay* ☎ *599/545–2177 or 599/522–7120* ⊕ *www.rudysdeepsea fishing.com*) has been around for years, and is one of the more experienced sport-angling outfits.

FRENCH SIDE

Big Sailfish Too (✉ *Anse Marcel* ☎ *690/27–40–90*) is your best bet on the French side of the island.

Horseback riding in the surf, St. Maarten

GOLF

DUTCH SIDE

St. Maarten is not a golf destination. Although **Mullet Bay Golf Course** (✉ *Airport Rd., north of airport, Mullet Bay* ☎ *599/545–3069*), on the Dutch side, is an 18-hole course, it's the island's *only* one. At this writing, only nine holes are open, as the beach side was damaged in 2008 by Hurricane Omar. But the course is serviceable, if you are really desperate for a golf fix. Otherwise, take the ferry from Marigot over to Anguilla for the top-notch (albeit expensive) Temenos course.

HORSEBACK RIDING

Island stables offer riding packages for everyone from novices to experts. A 90-minute ride along the beach costs $50 to $70 for group rides and $70 to $90 for private treks. Reservations are necessary. You can arrange rides directly or through most hotels.

DUTCH SIDE

On the Dutch side contact **Lucky Stables** (✉ *Traybay Dr. 2, Cay Bay* ☎ *599/544–5255 or 599/555–7246* ⊕ *www. luckystables.com*), which offers mountain- and beach-trail rides, including a romantic champagne night ride. Rides start at $45.

FRENCH SIDE

Bayside Riding Club (⊠ *Galion Beach Rd., Baie Orientale* ☎ *590/87–36–64 or 599/557–6822* ⊕ *www.baysideriding club.com*), on the French side, is a long-established outfit that can accommodate all levels of riders.

KAYAKING

Kayaking is becoming very popular, and is almost always offered at the many water-sports operations on both the Dutch and the French sides. Rental starts at about $15 per hour for a single and $19 for a double.

DUTCH SIDE

On the Dutch side, **Blue Bubbles** (⊠ *Dawn Beach Resort, Oyster Pond* ☎ *599/542–2502* ⊕ *www.bluebubblessxm.com*) offers lagoon paddles and snorkeling tours by kayak.

TriSports (⊠ *Airport Rd. 14B, Simpson Bay* ☎ *599/545–4384* ⊕ *www.trisportsxm.com*) organizes similar kayaking and snorkeling excursions.

FRENCH SIDE

On the French side, kayaks are available at **Kauak Tour** (⊠ *French Cul de Sac* ☎ *599/557–0112 or 690/47–76–72*).

Near Le Galion Beach, **Wind Adventures** (⊠ *Orient Bay* ☎ *590/29–41–57* ⊕ *www.wind-adventures.com*) offers kayaking.

PARASAILING

DUTCH SIDE

Blue Bubbles (⊠ *Dawn Beach Resort, Oyster Pond* ☎ *599/542–2502* ⊕ *www.bluebubblessxm.com*) offers parasailing, jet skiing, and other water-sports adventures.

Westport Water Sports (⊠ *Simpson Bay* ☎ *599/544–2557*), at Kim Sha Beach, has Jet Skis for rent and offers parasailing excursions. Fees are $60 for a single fly and $100 for a double fly.

FRENCH SIDE

Kontiki Watersports (⊠ *Northern beach entrance, Baie Orientale* ☎ *590/87–46–89*) offers parasailing for $40 per half hour on Baie Orientale, giving you aerial views of Green Key, Tintamarre, Ilêt Pinel, and St. Barth. You can also rent Jet Skis for $45 for a half hour.

SCUBA DIVING

Diving in St. Maarten/St. Martin is mediocre at best, but those who want to dive will find a few positives. The water temperature here is rarely below 70°F (21°C). Visibility is often 60 to 100 feet. The island has more than 30 dive sites, from wrecks to rocky labyrinths. Right outside of Philipsburg, 55 feet under the water, is the HMS *Proselyte*, once explored by Jacques Cousteau. Although it sank in 1801, the boat's cannons and coral-encrusted anchors are still visible.

Off the north coast, in the protected and mostly current-free Grand Case Bay, is **Creole Rock.** The water here ranges in depth from 10 feet to 25 feet. Other sites off the north coast include **Îlêt Pinel,** with its good shallow diving; **Green Key,** with its vibrant barrier reef; and **Tintamarre,** with its sheltered coves and geologic faults. On average, one-tank dives start at $55; two-tank dives are about $100. Certification courses start at about $400.

The Dutch side offers several full-service SSI- (Scuba Schools International) and/or PADI-certified outfitters. There are no hyperbaric chambers on the island.

DUTCH SIDE

Blue Bubbles (⊠ *Dawn Beach Resort, Oyster Pond* ☎ 599/542–2502 ⊕ *www.bluebubblessxm.com*) offers Snuba, a shallow-water diving technique that is a great way to try undersea exploring.

Dive Safaris (⊠ *La Palapa Marina, Simpson Bay* ☎ 599/545–3213 ⊕ *www.divestmaarten.com*) has a shark-awareness dive where participants can watch professional feeders give reef sharks a little nosh.

Ocean Explorers Dive Shop (⊠ *113 Welfare Rd., Simpson Bay* ☎ 599/544–5252 ⊕ *www.stmaartendiving.com*) is St. Maarten's oldest dive shop, and offers different types of certification courses.

FRENCH SIDE

Blue Ocean (⊠ *Sandy Ground Rd., Baie Nettlé* ☎ 590/87–89–73 ⊕ *www.blueocean.ws*) is a full-service PADI dive education center, starting right at the Web site itself, which features a wealth of information for the novice diver, albeit only in French at this writing.

Neptune (⊠ *Plage d'Orient Bay, Baie Orientale* ☎ 690/50–98–51 ⊕ *www.neptune-dive.com*) is a PADI-certified outfit and very popular for its friendly owners Fabien and Sylvie, whose extensive experience thrills happy clients of reef, wreck, and cove dives. There is also an extensive program for beginners.

Octopus (✉ *15 bd. de Grand Case, Grand Case* ☎ *590/87–20–62* ⊕ *www.octopusdiving.com*) offers diving certification courses and all-inclusive dive packages, using the latest equipment and a 30-foot power catamaran called *Octopussy.* The company also offers private and group snorkel trips starting at $40, including all necessary equipment.

At Grand Case Beach Club, **O2 Limits** (✉ *Bd. de Grand Case, Grand Case* ☎ *690/50–04–00*) offers a full menu of diving options and the only Nitrox technology on St. Martin.

SEA EXCURSIONS

DUTCH SIDE

You can take day cruises to Prickly Pear Cay, off Anguilla, aboard the *Lambada,* or sunset and dinner cruises on the 65-foot sail catamaran *Tango* with **Aqua Mania Adventures** (✉ *Pelican Marina, Simpson Bay* ☎ *599/544–2640 or 599/544–2631* ⊕ *www.stmaarten-activities.com*).

The 50-foot catamaran ***Bluebeard II*** (✉ *Simpson Bay* ☎ *599/587–5935* ⊕ *www.bluebeardcharters.com*) sails around Anguilla's south and northwest coasts to Prickly Pear Cay, where there are excellent coral reefs for snorkeling and powdery white sands for sunning.

For low-impact sunset and dinner cruises, try the catamaran ***Celine*** (✉ *Skip Jack's Restaurant, Simpson Bay* ☎ *599/526–1170 or 599/552–1335* ⊕ *www.sailstmaarten.com*).

☾ The sleek 76-foot catamaran ***Golden Eagle*** (☎ *599/542–3323* ⊕ *www.sailingsxm.com*) takes day-sailors to outlying islets and reefs for snorkeling and partying.

FRENCH SIDE

A cross between a submarine and a glass-bottom boat, the 34-passenger ***Seaworld Explorer*** (✉ *Bd. de Grand Case, Grand Case* ☎ *599/542–4078* ⊕ *www.atlantisadventures. com*) offers a 1½-hour excursion that crawls along the water's surface from Grand Case to Creole Rock. While seated below the water line, passengers view marine life and coral through large windows. Divers jump off the boat and feed the fish and eels. The excursion costs $39.

CLOSE UP

A Day in Saba

The Bottom, Saba.

Erupting out of the Caribbean, that 5-square-mi rock is called Saba (pronounced *say*-ba). The 14-minute flight from St. Martin has you landing on the world's smallest commercial runway—bordered on three sides by 100-foot cliffs. Arrive by boat and you will not see a beach. What little sand there is on this island comes and goes at the whim of the sea.

Hire a cab to navigate "The Road" and its 14 hairpin turns. The thoroughfare, under construction for 15 years, leads to the island towns of Windwardside, Hells Gate, and the Bottom (a funny name for a place that is about halfway up the mountain). Gingerbread-like cottages hang off the hillsides, making this island feel like a step back in time.

The Road may be a thrill ride, but most people visit Saba to

do some hiking, diving, and relaxing. Its most famous trek is up the 1,064 steps to the summit of 2,855-foot Mt. Scenery. Goats occupy the snakelike Sulphur Mine Trail, which winds around to an abandoned mine with a colony of bats. Extraordinary underwater wonders attract divers. Saba National Marine Park, which circles the island, has a labyrinth formed by an old lava flow and various tunnels and caves filled with colorful fish.

The isle is renowned for its 151-proof rum, Saba Spice. The rum, along with lace and hand-blown glass, is the most popular souvenir. For more information, contact the **Saba Tourist Office** (☎ 599/416–2231 or 599/416-2322 ⊕ *www.sabatourism.com*).

⁄ORKELING

Some of the best snorkeling on the Dutch side can be found around the rocks below Fort Amsterdam off Little Bay Beach, in the west end of Maho Bay, off Pelican Key, and around the reefs off Oyster Pond Beach. On the French side, the area around Orient Bay—including Caye Verte, Ilêt Pinel, and Tintamarre—is especially lovely, and is officially classified and protected as a regional underwater nature reserve. Sea creatures also congregate around Creole Rock at the point of Grand Case Bay. The average cost of an afternoon snorkeling trip is about $45 to $55 per person.

DUTCH SIDE

☾ **Aqua Mania Adventures** (✉ *Pelican Marina, Simpson Bay* ☎ *599/544–2640 or 599/544–2631* ⊕ *www.stmaarten-activities.com*) offers a variety of snorkeling trips. The newest activity, called Rock 'n Roll Safaris, lets participants not only snorkel, but navigate their own motorized rafts.

☾ **Blue Bubbles** (✉ *Dawn Beach Resort, Oyster Pond* ☎ *599/542–2502* ⊕ *www.bluebubblessxm.com*) has both boat and shore snorkel excursions.

Eagle Tours (✉ *Bobby's Marina, Philipsburg* ☎ *599/542–3323* ⊕ *www.sailingsxm.com*) is geared more to cruise groups, but anyone can sign on for the 4-hour power rafting, or sailing trips that include snorkeling, a beach break, and lunch. The sailing trips are done aboard a 76-foot catamaran. Some cruises stop in Grand Case or Marigot for a bit of shopping.

FRENCH SIDE

Arrange equipment rentals and snorkeling trips through **Kontiki Watersports** (✉ *Northern beach entrance, Baie Orientale* ☎ *590/87–46–89*).

SPAS

Spas have added a pampering dimension to several properties on both the French and Dutch sides of the island. Treatments and products vary depending on the establishment, but generally include several different massage modalities, body scrubs, facials, and mani-pedis; all the spas offer men's treatments, too. Be sure to phone to book in advance, however, as walk-ins are hardly ever accommodated. There are massage cabanas on some beaches, especially on the French side, and most of the beach clubs in Baie Orientale will have a blackboard where you can sign up or will give you the phone number for a massage therapist. Sometimes these beachside massages can be arranged at the spur of the moment. Hotels that don't have spas can usually arrange in-room treatments.

DUTCH SIDE

★ Fodor'sChoice **Christian Dior Spa** (⊠ *The Cliff at Cupecoy Beach, Rhine Rd., Cupecoy* ☎ *599/546–6620* ⊕ *cliffsxm.com/spa*), with its oceanfront setting, is undeniably dramatic, and the treatments are certainly creative. The Intense Youthfulness Treatment combines a 30-minute back massage with a facial cleansing therapy and shiatsu head massage. A two-hour Harmonizing Body Massage combines several techniques such as reflexology and shiatsu. Guests have all-day use of the pool, steam room, and sauna. A full line of Dior products is available for purchase. The spa is open weekdays 9 to 6 and Saturday 9 to 4.

Good Life Spa (⊠ *Sonesta Maho Beach Resort & Casino, 1 Rhine Rd., Maho* ☎ *599/545–2540 or 599/545–2356* ⊕ *www.thegoodlifespa.com*) offers aloe-vera treatments (to combat sunburn) and a wide range of scrubs and wraps. There's also a fitness center. It's open weekdays from 8 to 8, Saturday from 8 to 6.

Hibiscus Spa (⊠ *Westin Dawn Beach Resort & Spa, 144 Oyster Pond Rd., Oyster Pond* ☎ *599/543–6700* ⊕ *www. starwoodcaribbean.com*) is an attractive facility offering the usual menu of facials, body treatment, and massages. The Hibiscus Expert Facial is formulated to benefit your skin type. It's open daily from 9 to 7.

★ Fodor'sChoice **The Spa** (⊠ *La Terrasse Maho Village, Rhine Rd., Maho* ☎ *599/545–2808* ⊕ *www.thespasintmaarten.com*) has a huge hydrotherapy pool with seating that resembles lounge chairs as well as a waterfall jet for back treatments and several other jets for the rest of the body. A dozen different kinds of massages are available, including one treatment that is done on the floor. The specialty, a customized couple's massage, is administered in the Yin Yang Room. Besides the massage tables, this room has a huge oval aromatherapy tub. Couples can spend another 90 minutes in the room after the treatment is finished. Champagne and flowers are optional. The spa is open Monday to Saturday from 9:30 to 8.

Ilet Pinel, St. Martin

FRENCH SIDE

★ Fodor'sChoice **La Samanna Spa** (⊠ *La Samanna, Baie Longue* ☎ *590/87–65–69* ⊕ *www.lasamanna.orient-express.com*) has one of the best spas on the island, and you don't have to be a guest at the famous hotel to enjoy a treatment or a day package at this heavenly retreat; just ring for an appointment and start to relax. In the lovely tropical garden setting, immaculate treatment rooms feature walled gardens with private outdoor showers. There are dozens of therapies for your body, face, hair, and spirit on the spa menu, and any can be customized to your desires or sensitivities. There are over a dozen different massage modalities offered, including Indian Ayurvedic, Thai, Japanese, and Chinese, and, of course, facials, scrubs, and soothing treatments for sunburn. The spa is open daily from 9 to 8.

Le Spa (⊠ *Radisson St. Martin Resort, Marina & Spa, BP 581 Marcel Cove, Anse Marsel* ☎ *590/87–67–01* ⊕ *lespaby radisson.com*) opened in 2009, offering a full menu of more than 40 services, including advanced skin-care therapies, integrative massages, exfoliation and body treatments, facials, and nail care performed by skilled Parisian-trained Carita therapists. Tropical ingredients are appropriate to the beach setting, so try the Lulur, Lotus, and Frangipani, a luxurious scrub that begins with a massage using rice, coconut powder, and flowers from Bali.

WATERSKIING

Expect to pay $50 per half hour for waterskiing, $40 to $45 per half hour for jet skiing.

FRENCH SIDE

On the French side, **Kontiki Watersports** (⊠ *Northern beach entrance, Baie Orientale* ☎ *590/87–46–89*) offers rentals of windsurfing boards, Jet Skis, and WaveRunners, and also offers waterskiing, as well as instruction for all of these sports.

WINDSURFING

The best windsurfing is on Galion Bay on the French side. From November to May, trade winds can average 15 knots.

FRENCH SIDE

Club Nathalie Simon (⊠ *Northern beach entrance, Baie Orientale* ☎ *590/29–41–57* ⊕ *www.wind-adventures.com*) offers rentals and lessons in both windsurfing and kite-surfing. One-hour lessons are about €40.

Windy Reef (⊠ *Galion Beach, past Butterfly Farm* ☎ *590/87–08–37* ⊕ *www.windyreef.fr*) has offered windsurfing lessons and rentals since 1991.

NIGHTLIFE

★ St. Maarten has lots of evening and late-night action. To find out what's doing on the island, pick up *St. Maarten Nights, St. Maarten Quick Pick Guide,* or *St. Maarten Events,* all of which are distributed free in the tourist office and hotels. The glossy *Discover St. Martin/St. Maarten* magazine, also free, has articles on island history and on the newest shops, discos, and restaurants. Or buy a copy of Thursday's *Daily Herald* newspaper, which lists all the week's entertainment.

BARS

DUTCH SIDE

Axum Café (⊠ *7L Front St., Philipsburg* ☎ *599/52–0547*), a 1960s-style coffee shop, offers local cultural activities as well as live jazz and reggae. It's open daily, 11:30 AM until the wee hours.

Bamboo Bernies (⊠ *Sonesta Maho Beach Resort & Casino, 1 Rhine Rd., Maho* ☎ *599/545–3622*) is a sophisticated club-restaurant with soft techno music.

The open-air **Bliss** (⊠ *Caravanserai Resort, Simpson Bay* ☎ *599/545–3996*) nightclub, restaurant, and lounge in one, rocks till late.

Buccaneer Bar (⊠ *Behind Atrium Beach Resort, Simpson Bay* ☎ *599/544–5876*) is the place to enjoy a BBC (Bailey's banana colada), a slice of pizza, and a nightly bonfire.

Cheri's Café (⊠ *Airport Rd., Simpson Bay* ☎ *599/545–3361*), across from Maho Beach Resort & Casino, features Sweet Chocolate, a lively band that will get your toes tapping and your tush twisting. Snacks and hearty meals are available all day long on a cheerful veranda decorated with thousands of inflatable beach toys.

Lady C (⊠ *Simpson Bay* ☎ *599/544–4710*), a 70-year-old sailboat, is transformed into a floating party bar. It sits in Simpson Bay Lagoon, making it very convenient for the yachties.

The **Ocean Lounge** (⊠ *Holland House Hotel, 43 Front St., Philipsburg* ☎ *599/542–2572*) is the quintessential people-watching venue. Sip a Guavaberry colada and point your chair toward the boardwalk.

At **Pineapple Pete** (⊠ *Airport Rd., Simpson Bay* ☎ *599/544–6030*) you can groove to live music or visit the game room for a couple of rounds of pool.

The **Red Piano** (⊠ *Hollywood Casino, Simpson Bay* ☎ *599/544–6008*) has live music and tasty cocktails.

Starting each night at 8, the pianist at **Soprano's** (⊠ *Sonesta Maho Beach Resort & Casino, 1 Rhine Rd., Maho* ☎ *599/545–2485*) takes requests for oldies, romantic favorites, or smooth jazz.

Sunset Beach Bar (⊠ *Maho Beach, Maho* ☎ *599/545–3998*) offers a relaxed, anything-goes atmosphere. Enjoy live music Wednesday through Sunday as you watch planes from the airport next door fly directly over your head.

Gambling, the most popular indoor activity in St. Maarten

FRENCH SIDE

On the French side, **Kali's Beach Bar** (⊠ *Baie des Pères* ☎ *690/49–06–81*) is a happening spot with live music until midnight. On the night of the full moon and on every Friday night the beach bonfire and late-night party here is the place to be.

CASINOS

The island's casinos—all 13 of them—are found only on the Dutch side. All have craps, blackjack, roulette, and slot machines. You must be 18 years or older to gamble. Dress is casual (but excludes bathing suits or skimpy beachwear). Most casinos are found in hotels, but there are also some independents.

With some of the best restaurants on the island, **Atlantis World Casino** (⊠ *106 Rhine Rd., Cupecoy* ☎ *599/545–4601*) is a popular destination even for those who don't gamble. It has more than 500 slot machines and gaming tables offering roulette, baccarat, three-card poker, Texas Hold'em poker, and Omaha high poker, not to mention some of the best restaurants on the Dutch side of the island.

Beach Plaza Casino (⊠ *Front St., Philipsburg* ☎ *599/543–2031*), in the heart of the shopping area, has more than 180 slots and multigame machines with the latest in touch-screen technology. Because of its location, it is popular with cruise-ship passengers.

One of the island's largest gambling joints, **Casino Royale** (⊠ *Maho Beach Resort & Casino, Maho Bay* ☎ 599/545–2602) is in bustling Maho, near plenty of restaurants, bars, and clubs.

Coliseum Casino (⊠ *Front St., Philipsburg* ☎ 599/543–2101) is popular with fans of slots, blackjack, poker, or roulette.

Diamond Casino (⊠ *1 Front St., Philipsburg* ☎ 599/543–2583) has 250 slot machines, plus the usual tables offering games like blackjack, roulette, and three-card poker. The casino is in the heart of Philipsburg.

The **Dolphin Casino** (⊠ *Simpson Bay* ☎ 599/544–3411), near the airport, has a giant slot machine at the entrance.

Golden Casino (⊠ *Great Bay Beach Hotel, Little Bay Rd., Great Bay* ☎ 599/542–2446) is on the small side. But fans say the 84 slots machines and tables with Caribbean poker, blackjack, and roulette are more than enough.

Hollywood Casino (⊠ *Pelican Resort, Pelican Key, Simpson Bay* ☎ 599/544–4463) has an upbeat theme and a nice late-night buffet.

Jump-Up Casino (⊠ *1 Emmaplein, Philipsburg* ☎ 599/542–0862) is near the cruise-ship pier, so it attracts lots of day-trippers.

Paradise Plaza Casino (⊠ *Airport Rd., Simpson Bay* ☎ 599/543–4721) has 250 slots and multigame machines. Betting on sporting events is a big thing here, which explains the 20 televisions tuned to whatever game happens to be on at the time.

One of the island's largest gaming halls, **Princess Casino** (⊠ *Port de Plaisance, Union Rd., Cole Bay* ☎ 599/544–4311), has a wide array of restaurants and entertainment options.

Rouge et Noir Casino (⊠ *Front St., Philipsburg* ☎ 599/542–2952) is small but busy, catering mostly to cruise-ship passengers.

Tropicana Casino (⊠ *Welfare Rd., Cole Bay* ☎ 599/544–5654) offers slot machines and games like poker, blackjack, and roulette, as well as live entertainment and a nightly buffet.

Westin Casino (⊠ *Westin Dawn Beach Resort & Spa, 144 Oyster Pond Rd., Oyster Pond* ☎ 599/543–6700) is somewhat more sedate. If you ever get tired of the endless array of slot machines and gaming tables, beautiful Dawn Beach is just outside the door.

DANCE CLUBS

DUTCH SIDE

Greenhouse (⊠ *Bobby's Marina Philipsburg* ☎ *599/542–2941* ⊠ *Billy's Folly Rd., just past the Atrium Beach Resort, Simpson Bay* ☎ *599/544–4173* ⊕ *www.thegreenhouse restaurant.com*) plays soca, merengue, zouk, and salsa, and has a two-for-one happy hour that lasts all night Tuesday. A second branch has opened in Simpson Bay.

Tantra (⊠ *Sonesta Maho Beach Resort & Casino, Maho Bay* ☎ *599/545–2861*) is the eastern Caribbean's largest nightclub (the former Q Club), an Asian-inspired disco at the Casino Royale with a mix of music sure to please everyone.

FRENCH SIDE

Boo Boo Jam (⊠ *Baie Orientale* ☎ *590/87–03–13*) is a jumping joint with a mix of calypso, meringue, salsa, and other beats.

Calmos Café (⊠ *40 bd. de Grand Case, Grand Case* ☎ *0590/29–01–85*) draws a young local crowd. Just walk through the boutique and around the back to the sea and pull up a beach chair or park yourself at a picnic table. It's open all day, but the fun really begins at the cocktail hour, when everyone enjoys tapas. The little covered deck at the end is a perfect for romance. On Sundays there is often live reggae on the beach.

La Chapelle (⊠ *Baie Orientale* ☎ *590/52–38–90*) is a sports bar that transforms itself into a disco at night, right in the little village of Baie Orientale.

La Noche (⊠ *147 bd. de Grand Case, Grand Case* ☎ *0590/29–72–89*) may tempt you during your after-dinner stroll in Grand Case; consider continuing your evening at this sexy lounge decorated in red, where the house music starts at 11 (or later) and continues until the last reveler quits. The dress code is "chic and sexy."

Marigot's waterfront market

SHOPPING

It's true that the island sparkles with its myriad outdoor activities—diving, snorkeling, sailing, swimming, and sunning—but shopaholics are drawn to the sparkle in the jewelry stores. The huge array of such stores is almost unrivaled in the Caribbean. In addition, duty-free shops can offer substantial savings—about 15% to 30% below U.S. and Canadian prices—on cameras, watches, liquor, cigars, and designer clothing. It's no wonder that many cruise ships make Philipsburg a port of call. Stick with the big vendors that advertise in the tourist press, and you will be more likely to avoid today's ubiquitous fakes and replicas. On both sides of the island, be alert for idlers. They can snatch unwatched purses. Just be sure to know the U.S. prices of whatever you plan on buying in St. Maarten so you know if you're getting a deal or just getting dealt a bad hand.

Prices are in dollars on the Dutch side, in euros on the French side. As for bargains, there are more to be had on the Dutch side; prices on the French side may sometimes be higher than those you'll find back home, and the merchandise may not be from the newest collections, especially with regard to clothing. Finally, remember the important caveat about shopping anywhere: if it sounds too good to be true, it usually is.

SHOPPING AREAS

Philipsburg's **Front Street** reinvented itself. Now it's mall-like, with redbrick walk and streets, palm trees lining the sleek boutiques, jewelry stores, souvenir shops, outdoor restaurants, and the old reliables, like McDonald's and Burger King. Here and there a school or a church appears to remind visitors that there's more to the island than shopping. Back Street is where you'll find the **Philipsburg Market Place,** a daily open-air market where you can haggle for bargains on handicrafts, souvenirs, and beachwear. **Old Street,** near the end of Front Street, has stores, boutiques, and open-air cafés offering French crepes, rich chocolates, and island mementos.

On the French side, wrought-iron balconies, colorful awnings, and gingerbread trim decorate Marigot's smart shops, tiny boutiques, and bistros in the **Marina Royale** complex and on the main streets, **Rue de la Liberté** and **Rue de la République.** Also in Marigot are the pricey **West Indies Mall** and the **Plaza Caraïbes,** which house designer shops, although some shops are closing in the economic downturn.

Because of the bad exchange rate with the U.S. dollar, stores on the Dutch side (which have prices in dollars) are usually a better deal than those on the French side, but it's always worth comparing prices. There are goods available on the French side that are not available on the Dutch side, and vice versa.

SPECIALTY STORES

ART GALLERIES

Maybe it's the vibrant colors, the gorgeous sunlight, or the scenic beauty that stimulates the creative juices of the many artists on the island. It must be something special, because there are a great many artists and galleries.

DUTCH SIDE

On the Dutch side of the Island, **Art Gallery Le Saint Geran** (⊠ *117 Front St., Philipsburg* ☎ *599/542–1023*) has a collection of more than 250 original works. There's also a selection of sculptures and ceramics.

Tessa Urbanowicz (⊠ *117 Front St., Philipsburg* ☎ *599/542–1023*) uses pewter, gold, and rhodium to create unique jewelry designs. Her work can also be seen at the Art Gallery Le Saint Geran, although she no longer works there. She can be contacted through her home number or through the gallery.

FRENCH SIDE

On the French side, the watercolor paintings of **Antoine Chapon** (⊠ *Terrasses de Cul-de-Sac, Baie Orientale* ☎ *590/87–40–87*) reflect the peaceful atmosphere of St. Martin and the sea surrounding it.

Contemporary Caribbean artists, including Paul Elliot Thuleau, who is a master of capturing the unique sunshine of the islands, are showcased at **Atelier des Tropismes** (⊠ *107 bd. de Grand Case, Grand Case* ☎ *590/29–10–60* ⊕ *tropismesgallery.com*).

Céramiques d'art Marie Moine (⊠ *76 rue de la Flibuste, Oyster Pond* ☎ *590/29–53–76*) sells ceramics that are unique and affordable.

Dona Bryhiel Art Gallery (⊠ *Oyster Pond* ☎ *590/87–43–93*), before the turnoff to Captain Oliver's Marina, showcases the romantic, naive watercolors painted by the owner. She will delight you with stories of her life and of the paintings, which are steeped in romantic French and Caribbean traditions.

The brilliant oil paintings of **Francis Eck** (⊠ *48 rue due Soleil Bevant, Concordia* ☎ *590/87–12–32*) are true to the primary colors and shapes of the Caribbean.

Galerie Camaïeu (⊠ *8 rue de Kennedy, Marigot* ☎ *590/87–25–78*) sells both originals and copies of works by Caribbean artists.

Gingerbread Galerie (⊠ *Marina Royale, Marigot* ☎ *590/87–73–21*) specializes in Haitian art and sells both expensive paintings and more reasonably priced decorative pieces of folk art.

Josiane Casaubon (⊠ *274 Parc de la Baie Orientale, Baie Orientale* ☎ *590/87–33–66*) displays paintings every afternoon or by appointment.

Minguet Art Gallery (⊠ *Rambaud Hill* ☎ *590/87–76–06*), between Marigot and Grand Case, is managed by the daughter of the late artist Alexandre Minguet. The gallery carries original paintings, lithographs, posters, and postcards depicting island flora and landscapes by Minguet, as well as original works by Robert Dago and Loic BarBotin.

Dutch architecture along Philipsburg's pedestrian mall

CLOTHING

For fashionistas who insist on the upscale best, St. Maarten/
St. Martin has designer shops that won't disappoint.

DUTCH SIDE

Most shops on the Dutch side are clustered around Front
Street in Philipsburg.

Liz Claiborne (⊠ *48A Front St., Philipsburg* ☎ *599/543–0380*)
sells designer women's clothes.

Polo Ralph Lauren (⊠ *31 Front St., Philipsburg* ☎ *599/543–
0195* ⊠ *Plaza Caraïbes, Rue du Général de Gaulle, Marigot*
☎ *590/87–73–24*) has men's and women's sportswear.

Tommy Hilfiger (⊠ *28 Front St., Philipsburg* ☎ *599/542–6315*)
sells sportswear in the designer's trademark colors.

FRENCH SIDE

On the French side, the best luxury brand shops are found
either in the modern, air-conditioned West Indies Mall or
the Plaza Caraïbes center across from Marina Royale in
Marigot. There is also a small center in Grand Case, called
La Petite Favorite, with four shops and a café.

Coco Boutique/Coco Shoes (⊠ *15 Rue du Général De Gaulle,
Marigot* ☎ *590/52–97–76*) carries very up-to-the-minute
trends for the young and chic—both clothing and shoes—

including items by Roberto Durville, Fred Sun, Les Baisers, and more.

Hermès (✉ *Rue du Général de Gaulle, Marigot* ☎ *590/87–28–48*) stocks the famous scarves along with other selections of the famous designer's apparel.

Hip Up (✉ *47 Rue de la Liberté-Marigot, Marigot* ☎ *590/29–31–04* ⊕ *www.hipup.com*) has a a terrific selection of swimsuits, cute cover-ups, and beach accessories like rhinestone-studded flip-flops at this outpost of the popular French retailer. Many of the swimsuits are sold as separates—you pick the top and the bottom in the size and style that suits.

Hip Up Outlet (✉ *Zone Commercial d'Hope Estate 2, Grand Case*) has overstocks and last season's swimwear. This is one of the island's best shopping secrets, since you'll find trendy swimwear and accessories at up to 75% off retail prices (these are real bargains, not just "duty-free" bargains).

Lacoste (✉ *West Indies Mall, Marigot* ☎ *590/52–84–84*) has everything with the alligator logo for men, women, and children, and the offerings are generally the better-quality (and more expensive) made-in-France items, not the made-in-Peru items usually available in the U.S.

L'Atelier (✉ *28 Marina Port la Royale, Marigot* ☎ *590/87–13–71*) is a nice boutique with a well-edited selection of clothes and accessories by Chloé, Alexander McQueen, Valentino, and Free Lance.

Max Mara (✉ *6 rue du Kennedy, Marigot* ☎ *590/52–99–75*) has beautifully made tailored women's clothes with an elegant attitude.

120% Lino (✉ *21 Marina Royale, Marigot* ☎ *590/87–25–43*) has nicely made and classy shirts and pants for men and women made of pure linen in pastel tones.

Tuula (✉ *Rue de President Kennedy, Marigot* ☎ *590/87–50–94*) is another good boutique across from Marina Royale, this one stocking an interesting selection of fashion-forward and one-of-a-kind apparel and accessories.

CRYSTAL AND CHINA
In addition to the stores listed here, both Little Europe and Little Switzerland carry china and crystal.

Divine (⊠4 *Sint Rose Arcade, Front St., Philipsburg* ☎599/542–9955) has a sparkling array of Swarovski crystal and a timely selection of Swatches.

The Dutch Delft Blue Gallery (⊠37 *Front St., Philipsburg* ☎599/542–5204) is famous for blue-and-white porcelain pieces.

Lalique (⊠13 *Sint Rose Arcade, Front St., Philipsburg* ☎599/542–0763) has a fine collection of French crystal.

HANDICRAFTS

Visitors to the Dutch side of the island come for free samples at the **Guavaberry Emporium** (⊠8–10 *Front St., Philipsburg* ☎599/542–2965), the small factory where the Sint Maarten Guavaberry Company makes its famous liqueur. You'll find a multitude of versions, including one made with jalapeño peppers. Check out the hand-painted bottles.

The **Shipwreck Shop** (⊠42 *Front St., Philipsburg* ☎599/542–2962 or 599/542–6710 ⊕ *www.shipwreckshops.com*) has shops all over the island that stock a little of everything: colorful hammocks, handmade jewelry, and lots of the local Guavaberry liqueur, but the main store on Front Street in Philipsburg has the largest selection of wares.

JEWELRY AND GIFTS

Jewelry is big business on both the French and Dutch sides of the island, and many stores have outlets in both places. The so-called duty-free prices, however, may not give you much saving (if anything) over what you might pay at home, and sometimes prices are higher than you would pay at a shop back home. Compare prices in a variety of stores before you buy, and if you know you want to search for an expensive piece of jewelry or high-end watch, make sure you price your pieces at home and bargain hard to ensure you get a good deal.

Artistic Jewelers (⊠8 *rue du Général de Gaulle, Marigot* ☎590/52–24–80⊠61 *Front St., Philipsburg* ☎599542–3456) carries the work of David Yurman, among many others, as well as high-end designer watches.

Art of Time Jewelers (⊠26 *Front St., Philipsburg* ☎599/542–5204), a sister store to Artistic Jewlers, specializes in watches, Montblanc pens, and jewelry by David Yurman, Chopard, and Mikimoto, among others.

Carat (⊠ *16 rue de la République, Marigot* ☎ *590/87–73–40* ⊠ *73 Front St., Philipsburg* ☎ *599/542–2180*) sells jewelry by Pomellato, watches by Bell & Ross, and other luxury brands.

Cartier (⊠ *35 Front St., Philipsburg* ☎ *599/543–7700* ⊠ *Rue de Général de Gaulle, Marigot* ☎ *590/52–40–02*) has a lovely collection of fine jewelry.

Little Europe (⊠ *80 Front St., Philipsburg* ☎ *599/542–4371* ⊠ *2 Front St., Philipsburg* ☎ *599/542–3153* ⊠ *1 rue du Général de Gaulle, Marigot* ☎ *590/87–92–64* ⊕ *www.littleeurope-jewellers.com*) sells fine jewelry, crystal, and china.

Little Switzerland (⊠ *52 Front St., Philipsburg* ☎ *599/542–2523* ⊠ *Harbor Point Village, Pointe Blanche* ☎ *599/542–7785* ⊠ *Westin Dawn Beach Resort & Spa, Dawn Beach* ☎ *599/643–6451*) sells watches, fine crystal, china, perfume, and jewelry.

Manek's (⊠ *Rue de la République, Marigot* ☎ *590/87–54–91*) sells, on two floors, luggage, perfume, jewelry, Cuban cigars, duty-free liquors, and tobacco products.

Oro Diamante (⊠ *62-B Front St., Philipsburg* ☎ *599/543–0342 or 800/635–7950*) carries loose diamonds, jewelry, watches, perfume, and cosmetics.

LEATHER GOODS AND ACCESSORIES

Furla (⊠ *13 Front St., Philipsburg* ☎ *599/542–9958*) is the place for very "in" Italian leather purses.

Longchamp (⊠ *Rue de Général de Gaulle, Marigot* ☎ *590/87–92–76*) is the local outpost for the chic French leather goods company, where you'll find an especially good selection of the Pliage line of foldable, durable coated zipper totes with leather handles.

PERFUME

Lipstick (⊠ *Plaza Caraïbes, Rue du Kennedy, Marigot* ☎ *590/87–73–24* ⊠ *31 Front St., Philipsburg* ☎ *599/542–6052*) has an enormous selection of perfume and cosmetics.

St. Barthélemy

WORD OF MOUTH

"[St. Barts] is a gorgeous island with beautiful beaches. We were surprised how small the island (quick drive everywhere) was, making it very easy to check out everything we wanted to in our week there."

—emrutten

By Elise
Meyer

ST. BARTHÉLEMY BLENDS THE RESPECTIVE essences of the Caribbean, France, and *Architectural Digest* in perfect proportions. A sophisticated but unstudied approach to relaxation and respite prevails: you can spend the day on a beach, try on the latest French fashions, and watch the sunset while nibbling tapas over Gustavia Harbor, then choose from nearly 100 excellent restaurants for an elegant evening meal. You can putter around the island, scuba dive, windsurf in a quiet cove, or just admire the lovely views.

A mere 21 square km (8 square mi), St. Barth is a hilly island, with many sheltered inlets providing visitors with many opportunities to try out picturesque, quiet beaches. The town of Gustavia wraps itself around a modern harbor lined with everything from size-matters mega-yachts to rustic fishing boats to sailboats of all descriptions. Red-roofed villas dot the hillsides, while glass-front shops line the streets. Beach surf runs the gamut from kiddie-pool calm to serious-surfer dangerous, beaches from deserted to packed. The cuisine is tops in the Caribbean, and almost everything is tidy, stylish, and up-to-date. French *savoir vivre* prevails throughout the island.

HISTORY AND CULTURE

Christopher Columbus discovered the island—called "Ouanalao" by its native Caribs—in 1493; he named it for his brother Bartholomé. The first group of French colonists arrived in 1648, drawn by the ideal location on the West Indian Trade Route, but they were wiped out by the Caribs, who dominated the area. Another small group from Normandy and Brittany arrived in 1694. This time the settlers prospered—with the help of French buccaneers, who took advantage of the island's strategic location and protected harbor. In 1784 the French traded the island to King Gustav III of Sweden in exchange for port rights in Göteborg. The king dubbed the capital Gustavia, laid out and paved streets, built three forts, and turned the community into a prosperous free port. The island thrived as a shipping and commercial center until the 19th century, when earthquakes, fires, and hurricanes brought financial ruin. Many residents fled for newer lands of opportunity, and Oscar II of Sweden decided to return the island to France. After briefly considering selling it to America, the French took possession of St. Barthélemy again on August 10, 1877.

TOP REASONS TO GO

■ The island is active, sexy, hedonistic, and hip, with the young, gorgeous international affluent set providing human scenery that's as adorable as the sparkling blue sea vistas.

■ If it's possible for St. Barth to get even more chic, changes in the last year bring the level of style and taste up a notch or two. New restaurants continue to tempt gourmets and gourmands.

■ Those who prefer to indulge in less caloric extravagance will find bliss stalking the latest in clothes and accessories in dozens of the Caribbean's best boutiques.

■ Windsurfing and other water sports make going to the beach more than just a lounging experience.

3

Today the island is a free port, and in 2007 became a Collectivity, a French-administered overseas territory outside of continental France. Arid, hilly, and rocky, St. Barth was unsuited to sugar production, and thus never developed an extensive slave base. Some of today's 3,000 current residents are descendants of the tough Norman and Breton settlers of three centuries ago, but you are more likely to encounter attractive French 20- and 30-somethings from Normandy and Provence who are friendly, English-speaking, and here for the sunny lifestyle.

EXPLORING ST. BARTHÉLEMY

With a little practice, negotiating St. Barth's narrow, steep roads soon becomes fun. Recent infrastructure upgrades and the prevalence of small, responsive cars have improved things a lot. Free maps are everywhere, roads are smooth and well-marked, and signs will point the way. The tourist office has annotated maps with walking tours that highlight sights of interest. Parking in Gustavia is still a challenge, especially during busy vacation times.

🐚 **Corossol.** The island's French-provincial origins are most evident in this two-street fishing village with a little rocky beach.

Ingenu Magras's **Inter Oceans Museum** has more than 9,000 seashells and an intriguing collection of sand samples from around the world. You can buy souvenir shells.

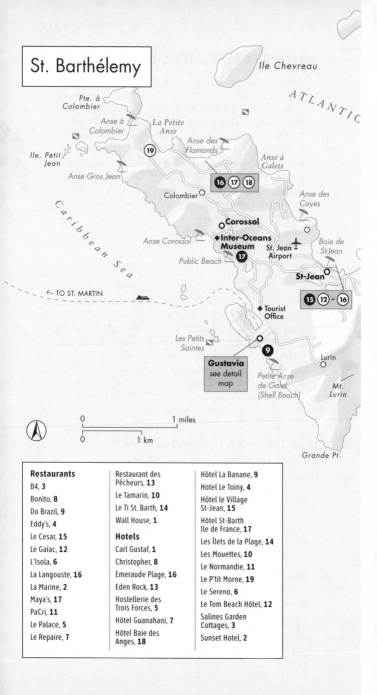

St. Barthélemy

Ile Chevreau

ATLANTIC

Pte. à Colombier

Anse à Colombier

La Petite Anse

Anse des Flamands

Anse à Galets

Ile. Petit Jean

Anse Gros Jean

(19)

Anse des Cayes

16 17 18

Colombier

Caribbean Sea

Corossol

Anse Corossol

◆Inter-Oceans Museum
17

St. Jean Airport

Baie de St-Jean

Public Beach

St-Jean

15 12 – 16

← TO ST. MARTIN

◆ Tourist Office

Les Petits Saintes

Gustavia
see detail map

9

Petite Anse de Galet (Shell Beach)

Lurin

Mt. Lurin

| 0 | 1 miles |
| 0 | 1 km |

Ⓝ

Grande Pt.

Restaurants	Restaurant des Pêcheurs, **13**	Hôtel La Banane, **9**
B4, **3**	Le Tamarin, **10**	Hotel Le Toiny, **4**
Bonito, **8**	Le Ti St. Barth, **14**	Hôtel le Village St-Jean, **15**
Do Brazil, **9**	Wall House, **1**	Hôtel St-Barth Ile de France, **17**
Eddy's, **4**	**Hotels**	Les Îlets de la Plage, **14**
Le Cesar, **15**	Carl Gustaf, **1**	Les Mouettes, **10**
Le Gaïac, **12**	Christopher, **8**	Le Normandie, **11**
L'Isola, **6**	Emeraude Plage, **16**	Le P'tit Morne, **19**
La Langouste, **16**	Eden Rock, **13**	Le Sereno, **6**
La Marine, **2**	Hostellerie des Trois Forces, **5**	Le Tom Beach Hôtel, **12**
Maya's, **17**	Hôtel Guanahani, **7**	Salines Garden Cottages, **3**
PaCri, **11**	Hôtel Baie des Anges, **18**	Sunset Hotel, **2**
Le Palace, **5**		
Le Repaire, **7**		

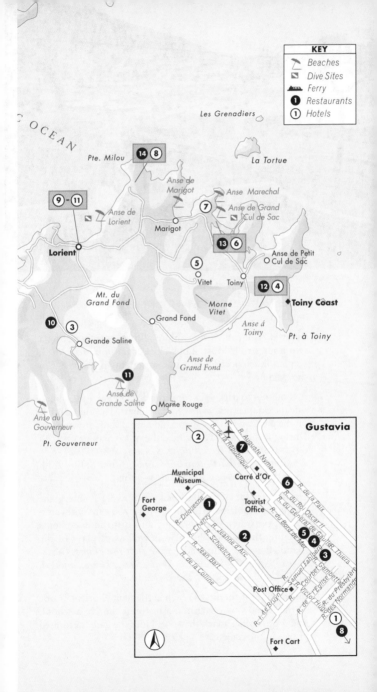

KEY
Beaches
Dive Sites
Ferry
1 Restaurants
1 Hotels

Les Grenadiers

C OCEAN

La Tortue

Pte. Milou 14 8

Anse de
Marigot

Anse Marechal

Anse de Grand
Cul de Sac

9 – 11

Anse de
Lorient

Marigot 7

13 6

Lorient

Anse de Petit
Cul de Sac

Mt. du
Grand Fond

5

Vitet

Toiny

12 4

Toiny Coast

Morne
Vitet

10 3

Grand Fond

Anse à
Toiny

Pt. à Toiny

Grande Saline

Anse de
Grand Fond

11

Anse de
Grande Saline

Morne Rouge

Anse du
Gouverneur

Pt. Gouverneur

Gustavia

2

R. de la République
R. Auguste Nyman

7

Municipal
Museum

Carré d'Or

6

R. de la Paix

Fort
George

1

Tourist
Office

R. du Roi Oscar II
R. du Général de Gaulle
R. du Général Clavier Thiers

R. Duquesne

R. Jeanne d'Arc

2

R. du Bord de Mer

5

4

3

R. Charry

R. Schœlcher

R. Samuel Fahlberg

R. de Jean Bart

Post Office

R.t. de Brin

R. Courbet Gambetta

R. de la Colline

R. Victor Hugo

R. de l'Église

R. du Presbytère

R. Hugues Normandie

1

8

Fort Cart

Gustavia's waterfront promenade

⊠ *Corossol* ☎ *0590/27–62–97* ⌧ *€3* ⊙ *Tues.–Sun. 9–12:30 and 2–5.*

Gustavia. You can easily explore all of Gustavia during a two-hour stroll. Most shops close from noon to 2 or 3, so plan lunch accordingly, but stores stay open past 7 in the evening.

A good spot to park your car is rue de la République, along-side the catamarans, yachts, and sailboats. The **tourist office** on the pier can provide maps and a wealth of information. During busier holiday periods, the office may be open all day. ⊠ *Rue de la République, Gustavia* ☎ *0590/27–87–27* ⊕ *www.saintbarth-tourisme.com* ⊙ *Mon. 8:30–12:30, Tues.–Fri. 8–noon and 2–5, Sat. 9–noon.*

On the far side of the harbor known as La Pointe is the charming **Municipal Museum,** where you can find water-colors, portraits, photographs, and historic documents detailing the island's history, as well as displays of the island's flowers, plants, and marine life. ⊠ *La Pointe, Gustavia* ☎ *599/29–71–55* ⌧ *€2* ⊙ *Mon., Tues., Thurs., and Fri. 8:30–12:30 and 2:30–6, Sat. 9–12:30.*

Lorient. Site of the first French settlement, Lorient is one of the island's two parishes; a restored church, a school, and a post office mark the spot. Note the gaily decorated graves in the cemetery.

St-Jean. There is a monument at the crest of the hill that divides St-Jean from Gustavia. Called *The Arawak*, it symbolizes the soul of St Barth. A warrior, one of the earliest inhabitants of the area (AD 800–2,500), holds a lance in his right hand and stands on a rock shaped like the island; in his left hand he holds a conch shell, which sounds the cry of nature; perched beside him are a pelican (which symbolizes the air and survival by fishing) and an iguana (which represents the earth). The half-mile-long crescent of sand at St-Jean is the island's most popular beach. A popular activity is watching and photographing the hair-raising airplane landings, but be sure to not stand in the area at the beach end of the runway, where someone was seriously injured. You'll also find some of the best shopping on the island here, as well as several restaurants.

NEED A BREAK? If you find yourself in St-Jean and need a picnic or just want some food to take home to your villa for later, stop in at Maya's To Go (✉ *Galeries de Commerce, St-Jean* ☎ *0590/29–83–70* ☉ *Closed Mon.*), which can be found in the Galeries de Commerce shopping center across from the airport. It's a more casual offering from the owners of the Gustavia favorite and is open daily from 7 to 7 (except Monday), has free Wi-Fi on the deck in front, and a full menu of prepared foods, baked goods, sandwiches, and salads for beach picnics or villa dinners.

Toiny Coast. Over the hills beyond Grand Cul de Sac is this much-photographed coastline. Stone fences crisscross the steep slopes of Morne Vitet, one of many small mountains on St. Barth, along a rocky shore that resembles the rugged coast of Normandy. Nicknamed the "washing machine" because of its turbulent surf, it is not recommended even to expert swimmers because of the strong undertow.

WHERE TO EAT

Dining on St. Barth compares favorably to almost anywhere in the world. Varied and exquisite cuisine, a French flair in the decor, sensational wine, and attentive service make for a wonderful epicurean experience in almost any of the more than 80 restaurants. On most menus, freshly caught local seafood mingles on the plate with top-quality provisions that arrive regularly from Paris.

Most restaurants offer a chalkboard full of daily specials that are usually a good bet. But even the pickiest eaters will find something on every menu. Some level of compliance can be paid to dietary restrictions within reason, and especially if explained in French; just be aware that French people generally let the chef work his or her magic. Expect your meal to be costly; however, you can dine superbly and somewhat economically if you limit pricy cocktails, watch wine selections, share appetizers and/or desserts, and pick up snacks and picnic meals from one of the well-stocked markets. Or you could follow the locals to small *crêperies,* cafés, sandwich shops, and pizzerias in the main shopping areas. Lunch is usually less costly than dinner. *Ti Creux* means snack or small bite.

The small *Ti Gourmet Saint-Barth* is a free pocket-size guidebook that's invaluable for addresses and telephone numbers of restaurants and services. Look for the annual *Saint-Barth Tables* for full restaurant menus.

Reservations are strongly recommended, and in high season, essential. However, except during the Christmas–New Year's season it's not usually necessary to book far in advance. A day's—or even a few hours'—notice is usually sufficient. At the end of the meal, as in France, you must request the bill. Until you do, you can feel free to linger at the table and enjoy the complimentary vanilla rum that's likely to appear.

Check restaurant bills carefully. A *service compris* (service charge) is always added by law, but you should leave the server 5% to 10% extra in cash. You'll usually come out ahead if you charge restaurant meals on a credit card in euros instead of paying with American currency, as your credit card might offer a better exchange rate than the restaurant (though since most credit cards nowadays have conversion surcharges of 3% or more, the benefit of using plastic is rapidly disappearing). Many restaurants serve locally caught *langouste* (lobster); priced by weight, it's usually the most expensive item on a menu and, depending on its size and the restaurant, will range in price from $40 to $60. In menu prices below, it has been left out of the range.

		WHAT IT COSTS IN EUROS		
¢	$	$$	$$$	$$$$
RESTAURANTS				
under €6	€6–€9	€9–€15	€15–€22	Over €22

Restaurant prices are per person for a main course at dinner and include a 15% service charge

3

WHAT TO WEAR

A bathing suit and pareu (sarong) are acceptable at beach-side lunch spots. Most women will top it off with a T-shirt or tank top. Jackets are never required and rarely worn by men, but most people do dress fashionably for dinner. Casual chic is the idea; women wear whatever is hip, current, and sexy. You can't go wrong in a tank dress or anything clingy and ruffly with tight jeans and high sandals. The sky is the limit for high fashion at nightclubs and lounges in high season, when you might (correctly) think everyone in sight is a model. Nice shorts (not beachy ones) at the dinner table may label a man *américain,* but many locals have adopted the habit, and nobody cares much. Pack a light sweater or shawl for the occasional breezy night.

ANSE DE TOINY

★ Fodor'sChoice ✕ **Le Gaïac.** *French.* Chef Stéphane Mazières is
$$$$ the only person in the Caribbean to share the Grand Chef designation of the Relais & Châteaux organization with the likes of Daniel Boulud and Thomas Keller. The new management of Hôtel Le Toiny (which includes Francophile Lance Armstrong) has fine-tuned the dramatic, tasteful cliff-side dining porch to showcase his gastronomic art, and this is one dinner that you won't want to miss. Less stuffy than you might remember from seasons past, the food is notable for its innovation and extraordinary presentation, and the warm but consummately professional service, overseen by maître d' Philippe Casadumont, sets a glorious standard. Rare ingredients and unique preparations delight, gossamer sheets of beet encase tuna tartare "cannelloni"; veal is spiked with truffles and salt-roasted with purple artichokes; date fritters garnish rosy slices of lamb from the Pyrenees. A greenhouse has even been installed on this former pineapple field to grow organic produce for the restaurant. The menu changes frequently, evolving and refining ideas. On

Le Gaïac restaurant by candlelight

Tuesday's special Fish Market Night, you choose your own fish to be grilled; there's a €43 buffet brunch on Sunday. This is one restaurant that is a true hedonistic experience, but you're on vacation, after all. ⊠ *Hôtel Le Toiny, Anse de Toiny* ☎ *0590/29–77–47* ▤ *AE, DC, MC, V* ⊙ *Closed Sept.–mid-Oct.*

FLAMANDS

$$$–
$$$$ ✕ **La Langouste.** *Seafood.* This tiny beachside restaurant in the pool courtyard of Hôtel Baie des Anges is run by Anny, the hotel's amiable, ever-present proprietor. It lives up to its name by serving fantastic, fresh-grilled lobster at a price that is somewhat gentler than at most other island venues. Simple, well-prepared fish, pastas, and an assortment of refreshing cold soups, including a corn-and-coconut soup perfumed with lemongrass, are also available. Be sure to try the warm goat cheese in pastry served on a green salad with a fruity salsa. ⊠ *Hôtel Baie des Anges, Flamands* ☎ *0590/27–63–61* ⌂ *Reservations essential* ▤ *MC, V* ⊙ *Closed May–Oct.*

BACK-UP FERRY. Even if you are planning to fly to St. Barth, it's a good idea to keep the numbers and schedules for the two ferry companies handy in case your flight is delayed. An evening ferry could save you from having to scramble for a hotel room in St. Maarten. If you are planning to spend time in St. Martin before traveling on to St. Barth, the ferry is half the cost and somewhat more reliable than the puddle-jumper, and you can leave from Marigot, Oyster Pond, or Philipsburg.

GRAND CUL DE SAC

$$$–
$$$$ ×**Restaurant des Pêcheurs.** *Seafood.* From fresh, morning beachside brioche to a final evening drink in the sexy lounge, you can dine all day in this soaring thatch pavilion that is the epitome of chic. The restaurant at Le Sereno, like the Christian Liaigre–designed resort, is serenity itself. Each menu item is a miniature work of art, beautifully arranged and amiably served. Each day there is a different €44 three-course menu. "Authentic" two-course bouillabaisse *à l'ancienne,* the famous French seafood stew, is served every Friday, and the chef even gives a class in its preparation, but the menu also lists daily oceanic arrivals from Marseille and Quiberon on France's Atlantic coast: roasted, salt-crusted, or grilled to your personal perfection. For splurges, there is a caviar and foie-gras menu. This—and sand between your toes—is heaven. ⊠ *Le Sereno, Grand Cul de Sac* ☏*0590/29–83–00* ⌂ *Reservations essential* ▭ *AE, D, MC, V.*

GRANDE SALINE

$$$–
$$$$
★ ×**Le Tamarin.** *French.* A leisurely lunch here en route to Grande Saline beach is a St. Barth *must.* But new management makes it tops for dinner too. Sit on one of the licorice-colored Javanese couches in the lounge area and nibble excellent sushi, or settle at a table under the wondrous tamarind tree for which the restaurant is named. A unique cocktail each day, ultra-fresh fish provided by the restaurant's designated fisherman, and gentle prices accommodate local residents as well as the holiday crowd. The restaurant is also open year-round. ⊠ *Grande Saline* ☏*0590/27–72–12* ▭ *AE, MC, V* ⊙ *Closed Tues.*

WORD OF MOUTH. "My husband and I both agree, the most romantic place we dined in St. Barth was Le Taramin in Saline beach. We had a late lunch there one day. The place was deserted. It seems to have a Bali-type theme at the inn there, and the food was like an Asian-French fusion type thing. We loved it." —Cold_in_Cleveland

$$$–
$$$$ ×**PaCrì.** *Italian.* An adorable young husband-and-wife team (she is the chef) serve delicious, huge portions of house-

made pasta, wood-oven pizza (at lunch only), and authentic Italian main courses, including chicken Milanese, on a breezy open terrace right near Saline Beach. The menu—handwritten on a chalkboard—changes daily. Don't miss the softball-size hunk of the best artisanal mozzarella you've ever had, flown in from Italy and garnished with prosciutto or tomato and basil. The eggplant Parmesan appetizer is delicious and more than enough for a meal. Like the pastas, the bread and the desserts are made in-house, and *Torta al ciocolato di Cristina* (Cristina's chocolate cake) is only one of the winners. Gorgeous waitstaff of both sexes add to the general air of voluptuousness. ✉ *Rte. de Saline, Anse de Grande Saline* ☎ *0590/29–35–63* ⚓ *Reservations essential* ▭ *AE, MC, V.*

GUSTAVIA

$$$– ✕ **B4.** *French.* Pronounced *before,* this newcomer in 2009
$$$$ occupies the central former location of longtime St. Barth mainstay Le Sapotillier. Offering lighter French cuisine (scallop sashimi, citrus duck, sole meunière, simply prepared turbot) in one half, and a lounge with music, bar, and flat-screen TVs in the other, it's designed to fill up the pocket time after dinner and *before* you head to your other late-night activities. ✉ *13 rue Samuel Fahlberg, Gustavia* ☎ *590/52–45–31* ▭ *AE, MC, V.*

$$$ ✕ **Bonito.** *Latin-American.* The former Mandala space has been completely transformed into a chic beach house, with big white canvas couches in the center, tables around the sides, an open kitchen, and three bar areas. The young Venezuelan owners go to great lengths to see that guests are having as much fun as they are. There is a ceviche bar with eight different varieties, not to mention combos that are prettily arrayed on poured-glass platters for culinary experimentation. Try octopus and shrimp, or wahoo garnished with sweet potatoes and popcorn. Traditionalists might like the fricassee of escargots, or foie gras served with mango, soy, and preserved lemon. Carnivores will love the Angus steaks. ✉ *Rue de la Sous-Préfecture, Gustavia* ☎ *590/27–96–96* ⊕ *www.ilovebonito.com* ⚓ *Reservations essential* ▭ *AE, MC, V* ⊘ *Closed Mon. No lunch.*

$$$– ✕ **Do Brazil.** *Eclectic.* This restaurant is open every day
$$$$ for breakfast, lunch, and dinner, and offers live music for sundown cocktail hour on Thursday, Friday, and Saturday evenings, as well as top DJs spinning the latest club mixes for the evening events that are listed in the local papers.

Right on Gustavia's Shell Beach, you'll find tasty light fare like chilled soups, fruit-garnished salads with tuna, shrimp, and chicken, plus sandwiches, burgers, pastas, and grilled fresh fish for lunch. At dinner there is also a €29 three-course prix-fixe with a dozen choices, including lobster pasta, steaks, ribs, and some of the lunchtime soups and salads, that can help keep the bill in line. The extensive cocktail menu tempts, but at €12 each, your bar bill can quickly exceed the price of dinner. ⊠ *Shell Beach, Gustavia* ☎ *0590/29–06–66* ⊕ *www.dobrazil.com* ⊟ *AE, MC, V.*

$$$– $$$$ ✕ **Eddy's.** *Pan-Asian.* By local standards, dinner in the pretty, open-air, tropical garden here is reasonably priced. The cooking is French-creole-Asian. Fish specialties, especially the sushi tuna sampler, are fresh and delicious, and there are always plenty of notable daily specials. Just remember some mosquito repellent for your ankles. ⊠ *Rue du Centenaire, Gustavia* ☎ *0590/27–54–17* ⌕ *Reservations not accepted* ⊟ *AE, MC, V* ⊘ *Closed Sun. No lunch.*

$$$$ ✕ **La Marine.** *Seafood.* This St. Barth harbor-side classic is run by Carole Gruson, who has created a spiffy decor to match and meld into her hot next-door nightclub, Le Yacht Club (which, despite the ads, is not really "private"). The traditional Thursday- and Friday-night mussels for €25 are always a hit, along with lots of other seafood choices. Tuesday is Caribbean barbecue night, featuring all-you-can-eat grilled spiny lobster along with ribs, side dishes, and desserts. It's a good choice for lunch, too. ⊠ *Rue Jeanne d'Arc, Gustavia* ☎ *0590/27–68–91* ⊟ *AE, MC, V.*

$$$– $$$$ ✕ **Le Palace.** *Caribbean.* Tucked into a tropical garden, this popular in-town restaurant known for its barbecued ribs, beef fillet, and rack of lamb is consistently one of our absolute favorites. Fish-market specialties like red snapper cooked in a banana leaf or grilled tuna are good here, as are grilled duck with mushroom sauce and a skewered surf-and-turf with a green curry sauce. The blackboard lists daily specials that are usually a great choice, like a salad of tomato, mango, and basil. Pierrot, the friendly owner, is sure to take good care of you. ⊠ *Rue Général-de-Gaulle, Gustavia* ☎ *0590/27–53–20* ⌕ *Reservations essential* ⊟ *MC, V* ⊘ *Closed mid-June–July.*

$$– $$$ ✕ **Le Repaire.** *Eclectic.* This friendly brasserie overlooks Gustavia's harbor, and is a popular spot from its opening at noon to its late-night closing. The flexible hours are great if you arrive mid-afternoon and need a substantial snack before dinner. Grab a cappuccino, pull a captain's chair up to the street-side rail, and watch the pretty girls. The

menu ranges from cheeseburgers, which are served only at lunch along with the island's best fries, to simply grilled fish and meat, pastas, and risottos. The composed salads always please. Wonderful ice-cream sundaes round out the menu. ⊠ *Quai de la République, Gustavia* ☎ *0590/27–72–48* ⊟ MC, V.

$$$– × **L'Isola.** *Italian.* St. Barth's chic sister to the Santa Mon-
$$$$ ica, (California) favorite, Via Veneto, is packing in happy guests for Italian classic dishes, dozens of house-made pasta dishes, prime meats, and the huge, well-chosen wine list. Restauranteur Fabrizio Bianconi wants it all to feel like a big Italian party, and with all the celebrating you can hear at dinner, it sure sounds like success. ⊠ *Rue du roi Oscar II, Gustavia* ☎ *590/51-00-05* ⊕ *www.lisolastbarth.com* ⌕ *Reservations essential* ⊟ AE, MC, V ⊘ *Closed Sept.–Oct.*

$$$$ × **Maya's.** *French.* New Englander Randy Gurley and his wife Maya (the French-born chef) provide a warm welcome and a very pleasant dinner on their cheerful dock decorated with big, round tables and crayon-colored canvas chairs, all overlooking Gustavia Harbor. A market-inspired menu of good, simply prepared and garnished dishes like mahimahi in creole sauce, shrimp scampi, and pepper-marinated beef fillet changes daily, assuring the ongoing popularity of a restaurant that seems to be on everyone's list of favorites. ⊠ *Public, Gustavia* ☎ *0590/27–75–73* ⌕ *Reservations essential* ⊟ AE, MC, V.

$$$– × **Wall House.** *Eclectic.* The food is excellent—and the ser-
$$$$ vice is always friendly—at this restaurant on the far side of Gustavia Harbor. The pesto gnocchi are out of this world, and the rare fresh-caught tuna with sea salt and lime ginger mousse is a universal favorite. Local businesspeople crowd the restaurant for the bargain €10 prix-fixe lunch menu. The daily €29 dinner menu is a pretty good deal, too. An old-fashioned dessert trolley showcases some really yummy sweets. ⊠ *La Pointe, Gustavia* ☎ *0590/27–71–83* ⌕ *Reservations essential* ⊟ AE, MC, V ⊘ *Closed Sept. and Oct.*

POINTE MILOU

★ Fodor's Choice × **Le Ti St. Barth Caribbean Tavern.** *Eclectic.* Chef-
$$$$ owner Carole Gruson captures the funky, sexy spirit of the island in her wildly popular hilltop hot spot. We always come here to dance to great music with the attractive crowd lingering at the bar, lounge at one of the pillow-strewn banquettes, or chat on the torch-lighted terrace. By the time your appetizers arrive, you'll be best friends with

the next table. The menu includes Thai beef salad, lobster ceviche, rare grilled tuna with Chinese noodles, and the best beef on the island. Provocatively named desserts, such as Nymph Thighs (airy lemon cake with vanilla custard) and Daddy's Balls (passion-fruit sorbet and ice cream) end the meal on a fun note. Around this time someone is sure to be dancing on top of the tables. There's an extensive wine list. The famously raucous full-moon parties are legendary. ⊠ *Pointe Milou* ☎ *0590/27–97–71* ⚓ *Reservations essential* ⊟ *MC, V.*

ST-JEAN

$$$– $$$$ ✕ **Le Cesar.** *Eclectic.* At this restaurant next to Hôtel le Village St-Jean an unusually wide variety of locally caught ☺ seafood is ably prepared by the former chef of Le Marine. The decor isn't the chicest, but the wicker tables and chairs on the open-air, terra-cotta-tile patio are set apart for nice quiet conversation, and the fresh local fish is well prepared in classic, and new-classic style. Try any of your favorites roasted in a sea-salt crust. There are good grilled meats with a wide choice of vegetable side dishes. There's a €10 children's menu. The flambéed banana dessert is a treat. ⊠ *Les Hauts de Saint-Jean, St-Jean* ☎ *0590/27–70–67* ⚓ *Reservations essential* ⊟ *AE, MC, V.*

WHERE TO STAY

There's no denying that hotel rooms and villas on St. Barth carry high prices. You're paying primarily for the privilege of staying on the island, and even at $800 a night the bedrooms tend to be small. Still, if you're flexible—in terms of timing and in your choice of lodgings—you can enjoy a holiday in St. Barth and still afford to send the kids to college.

The most expensive season falls during the holidays (mid-December to early January), when hotels are booked far in advance, may require a 10- or 14-day stay, and can be double the high-season rates. At this writing, some properties are reconsidering minimum stays, and there are concessions to the current *crise* (economic downturn). A 5% government tourism tax on room prices (excluding breakfast) went into effect in 2008; be sure to ask if it is included in your room rate or added on.

When it comes to booking a hotel on St. Barth, the reservation manager can be your best ally. Rooms within a prop-

Getting a massage on a private deck at Le Sereno

erty can vary greatly. It's well worth the price of a phone call or the time investment of an e-mail correspondence to make a personal connection, which can mean much in arranging a room that meets your needs or preferences. Details of accessibility, views, recent redecorating, meal options, and special package rates are topics open for discussion. Most quoted hotel rates are per room, not per person, and include service charges and airport transfers.

Most hotels on St. Barth are small (the largest has fewer than 60 rooms) and stratospherically expensive, but there are some reasonable options. About half of the accommodations on St. Barth are in private villas. Prices drop dramatically after March, and summer is a great time for a visit. Check hotel Web sites for updates of discounts and special offers that seem to be becoming more common with the current economy.

VILLAS AND CONDOMINIUMS

On St. Barth the term "villa" is used to describe anything from a small cottage to a luxurious, modern estate. Today almost half of St. Barth's accommodations are in villas, and we recommend considering this option, especially if you're traveling with friends or family. Ever more advantageous to Americans, villa rates are usually quoted in dollars, thus bypassing unfavorable euro fluctuations. Most villas have a small private swimming pool and maid service daily except Sunday. They are well furnished with linens,

St. Barth's Spas

Visitors to St. Barth can enjoy more than the comforts of home by taking advantage of any of the myriad spa and beauty treatments that are now available on the island. Three major hotels, the Hotel St-Barth Isle de France, the Hotel Guanahani, and the Carl Gustaf have beautiful, comprehensive, on-site spas. Others, including the Hôtel le Village St-Jean and Hôtel Le Toiny, have added spa cottages, where treatments and services can be arranged on-site. Depending on availability, all visitors to the island can book services at all of these. In addition, scores of independent therapists will come to your hotel room or villa and provide any therapeutic discipline you can think of, including yoga, Thai massage, shiatsu, reflexology, and even manicures, pedicures, and hairdressing. You can find current therapists listed in the local guide, *Ti Gourmet*, or get up-to-date recommendations at the tourist office in Gustavia.

kitchen utensils, and such electronic playthings as CD and DVD players, satellite TV, and broadband Internet. Weekly in-season rates range from $1,400 to "oh-my-gosh." Most villa-rental companies are based in the United States and have extensive Web sites that allow you to see pictures of the place you're renting; their local offices oversee maintenance and housekeeping and provide concierge services to clients. Just be aware that there are few beachfront villas, so if you have your heart set on "toes in the sand" and a cute waiter delivering your kir royale, stick with the hotels or villas operated by hotel properties.

VILLA RENTAL COMPANIES

Marla (☎ *0590/27–62–02* ⊕ *www.marlavillas.com*) is a local St. Barth villa-rental company that represents more than 100 villas, many that are not listed with other companies.

St. Barth Properties, Inc. (☎ *508/528–7727 or 800/421–3396* ⊕ *www.stbarth.com*), owned by American Peg Walsh—a regular on St. Barth since 1986—represents more than 120 properties here and can guide you to the perfect place to stay. Weekly peak-season rates range from $1,400 to $40,000 depending on the property's size, location, and amenities. The excellent Web site offers virtual tours of most of the villas and even details of availability. An office in Gustavia can take care of any problems you may have and offers some concierge-type services.

Wimco (☎ *800/932-3222* ⊕ *www.wimco.com*), which is based in Rhode Island, oversees bookings for more than 230 properties on St. Barth. Rents range from $2,000 to $10,000 for two- and three-bedroom villas; larger villas rent for $7,000 per week and up. Properties can be previewed and reserved on Wimco's Web site (which occasionally lists last-minute specials), or you can obtain a catalog by mail. The company will arrange for babysitters, massages, chefs, and other in-villa services for clients, as well as private air charters.

HOTEL COSTS

Most hotels add a 10%–15% service charge. A 5% room tax may be added to your bill but could also be included in the rate.

WHAT IT COSTS IN DOLLARS AND EUROS				
¢	$	$$	$$$	$$$$
HOTELS				
under $80	$80–$150	$150–$250	$250–$350	Over $350
under €60	€60–€110	€110–€180	€180–€260	Over €260

Hotel prices are per night for a double room in high season, excluding taxes, service charges, and meal plans. Hotels are usually priced in euros, villas in dollars.

ANSE DE TOINY

★ **Fodor's**Choice ☕ **Hôtel Le Toiny.** *Vacation Rental.* When per-
$$$$ fection is more important than price, choose Le Toiny's romantic villas with mahogany furniture and divine white linens with crisp, colorful striped accents, all new in 2008. New management has rejuvenated the venerable enclave, with an eye on sustainability. They've added a water treatment plant, organic cleaning products, and moves toward using solar energy. Each of the spacious suites has a heated private pool. Privacy and serenity are the mission here, but charming and caring service makes all the guests feel like celebrities. Rooms have every convenience of home, including lush bathrooms and fully equipped kitchenettes. High-tech amenities include several flat-screen LCD TVs, stereos, iPod docks, fax machines, espresso makers, and

Bang & Olufsen phones. Each suite has an outdoor shower, a patio hammock, and heated private pool. Breakfast is brought to your terrace each morning, and there is free laundry service. Spa services can be provided in your villa, or you can wander over to the new spa cottage. If ever you want to leave your villa, Sunday brunch and haute cuisine can be had at the alfresco Le Gaïac restaurant, one of the very best on the island, which overlooks the Italian-tile pool. New owners added a walking trail to a small private beach, but you really can't swim in the rough water there. There is a small but state-of-the art fitness center. Two of the villas are wheelchair accessible. Low-season discounts can make a honeymoon here affordable, and the Romance packages include great extras such as the use of a convertible Mini Cooper and a half-day with a professional photographer to document your special trip. **Pros:** extremely private; luxurious rooms; flawless service; environmental awareness. **Cons:** not on the beach; isolated (at least half an hour's drive from town). ✉ *Anse de Toiny* ☎ *0590/27–88–88* ⊕ *www.letoiny.com* ⇆ *14 1-bedroom villas, 1 3-bedroom villa* ⚿ *In-room: safe, kitchen, refrigerator, DVD, Wi-Fi. In-hotel: restaurant, bar, pools, laundry service* ▭ *AE, DC, MC, V* ⊗ *Closed Sept.–late Oct.* ⊚ CP.

COLOMBIER

$$$–
$$$$ ⛄ **Le P'tit Morne.** *Hotel.* Each of the modestly furnished but freshly decorated and painted mountainside studios has a private balcony with panoramic views of the coastline. The small kitchenettes are adequate for creating picnic lunches and other light meals. The snack bar serves breakfast. It's relatively isolated here, and the beach is a 10-minute drive away, but the young and friendly management is eager to help you enjoy your stay. There are weeklong packages that include a car or a dive package. **Pros:** reasonable rates; great area for hiking. **Cons:** rooms are basic; remote location. ✉ *Box 14, Colombier 97133* ☎ *0590/52–95–50* ⇆ *14 rooms* ⚿ *In-room: kitchen. In-hotel: pool* ▭ *AE, MC, V* ⊚ CP.

FLAMANDS

$$$–
$$$$ ⛄ **Hôtel Baie des Anges.** *Hotel.* Everyone is treated like fam-
☼ ily at this casual retreat. The ten clean, spacious rooms are
★ newly decorated in white and pastel sea colors, reflecting hues of serene Anse des Flamands, which is just steps away from your accomodation; each has a kitchenette on a big private terrace and a sofa that converts to an extra bed.

There's also a small pool. The food at La Langouste, the hotel's restaurant, is tasty and reasonably priced. The proprietor also manages a four-bedroom, three-bath villa a bit farther up the hill. **Pros:** on St. Barth's longest beach; family-friendly; excellent value. **Cons:** the area is a bit remote from the town areas, necessitating a car. ✉ *Anse des Flamands, Flamands* ☎ *0590/27–63–61* 🌐 *www.hotelbaiedesanges.fr* *10 rooms* *In-room: safe, kitchen. In-hotel: restaurant, pool, beachfront* ▭ *AE, MC, V* 🍽 *EP.*

★ Fodor'sChoice **Hotel St-Barth Isle de France.** *Resort.* An obses-
$$$$ sively attentive management team ensures that this intimate, casually refined resort remains among the very best accommodations in St. Barth—if not the entire Caribbean. It's not hard to understand why the property boasts a 72% high-season return rate—it just keeps improving each season. A technology upgrade in 2007 added a reception-area computer for guests and broadband to rooms, which are huge and luxuriously outfitted, all with modern four-posters, French fabrics, and fine art, plus superb marble baths (all with a tub or Jacuzzi tub, both rare on the island). In 2009, renovations added four enormous, beyond-fabulous beachfront suites. The beachside La Case de l'Isle restaurant serves fine nouvelle cuisine on a pretty veranda. The beautifully serene spa is by Molton Brown. The beautiful white-sand beach couldn't be more pristine. The little boutique is full of great beachwear. There are many different room options on the beachfront, in the garden, or on the hillside; you can choose from large single rooms to bungalows that can accommodate a family of up to six. Be sure to read the descriptions and make your preferences known when you book, because every room is different. Good off-season multiday, multiroom, spa, and honeymoon packages are often offered on the Web site and are a good value for this top property. **Pros:** prime beach location; terrific management; great spa; excellent restaurant. **Cons:** garden rooms—though large—can be dark; unfortunately, the day will come when you will have to leave this paradise. ✉ *Baie des Flamands* ☎ *0590/27–61–81* 🌐 *www.isle-de-france.com* *32 rooms, 2 villas* *In-room: refrigerator, DVD, Internet, Wi-Fi. In-hotel: restaurant, room service, bar, tennis court, pools, gym, spa, laundry service, water sports, Wi-Fi hotspot* ▭ *MC, V* 🍽 *CP* ⊙ *Closed Sept.–mid-Oct.*

Hotel St-Barth Isle de France

Hotel Guanahani and Spa

Le Sereno

GRAND CUL DE SAC

★ Fodor'sChoice ⊞ **Hotel Guanahani and Spa.** *Resort.* The larg-
$$$$ est full-service resort on the island has lovely rooms and
� suites (14 of which have private pools) and impeccable
personalized service, not to mention one of the island's
only children's programs (though it's more of a nursery).
The devoted management continues to tweak the resort
toward perfection. Rooms, all of which have large bathrooms with Clarins toiletries, were updated in 2008. At
the same time, a stunningly serene Clarins Spa and Frédéric
Fekkai hair salon were added; there are oodles of fantastic
spa services, including massage modalities from all over the
world. Units vary in price, privacy, view, and distance from
activities, so make your preferences known. The Wellness
Suite, which is at the top of the property, can serve as your
own hedonistic domain after the spa closes at night. The
other five ultra-luxurious suites include your own butler
to unpack your suitcases, attend to reservations, laundry,
and other duties. Flat-screen TVs, iPod docks, and DVDs
are new in all rooms, as is resort-wide Wi-Fi service; the
well-equipped gym is newly expanded, and two renovated,
lighted tennis courts boast an Astroturf surface. A beachside sports pavilion has kayaks and paddleboats. Also here
are two well-regarded restaurants, poolside L'Indigo and
sophisticated Bar'tô. There is even a first-rate boutique.
Check the Web site for upcoming promotions and autumn
packages that include meals. **Pros:** fantastic spa; beachside
sports; family-friendly; great service. **Cons:** lots of cats;
steep walk to beach. ⊠ *Grand Cul de Sac* ☎ *0590/27–66–60*
⊕ *www.leguanahani.com* ↪ *33 rooms, 28 suites, 1 3-bed-
room villa* ⌂ *In-room: DVD, Wi-Fi. In-hotel: 2 restaurants,
room service, bar, tennis courts, pools, spa, Wi-Fi hotspot,
water sports, children's programs (ages 2–12)* ⊟ *AE, MC,
V* ⑩ *CP.*

★ Fodor'sChoice ⊞ **Le Sereno.** *Resort.* A St. Barth classic on a
$$$$ beautiful stretch of beach was reborn as a sexy, ultrachic
retreat in 2005 (designed by Parisian architect Christian
Liagre). Cutting-edge modern decor and techno amenities
create a spare but luxurious, Zen-like serenity. The suites
are huge by St. Barth standards, and have spacious living
areas and private sundecks. Large bathrooms, some with
"steeping tubs," have roomy showers and vessel sinks of
solid black granite. Other perks include cloud-soft linens and robes from Porthault, Parisian Ex Voto toiletries,
high-speed Internet, plasma TVs, and iPod docks (for your

own device or their fully loaded ones to borro[…] poolside lounges for two set the romantic tone[…] all-day party. Check the Web site or call to in[…] upcoming packages that will include meals an[…] **Pros:** romantic rooms; beach location; super-chic comfort; fun atmosphere. **Cons:** no a/c in bathrooms; lots of construction planned for this part of the island over next few years. ✉ *B.P. 19 Grand-Cul-de-Sac, Grand Cul de Sac* ☎ *0590/29–83–00* 🌐 *www.lesereno.com* ⇨ *37 suites and villas* ♨ *In-room: safe, refrigerator, DVD, Wi-Fi. In-hotel: restaurant, room service, bar, pool, gym, water sports, laundry service, Wi-Fi hotspot* ▭ *AE, MC, V* 🍽 *EP.*

GRAND SALINE

$$–$$$ **Salines Garden Cottages.** *Vacation Rental.* Budget-conscious beach lovers need look no further than these small garden cottages, a short stroll from what is arguably St. Barth's best beach. Each of the five studios is named for favorite places of the owners: Pavones, Padang, Waikiki, Cap Ferrat, and Essaouira. There's a small but pleasant pool in the garden, and each studio unit has a private terrace. Three have full kitchenettes. You can choose to join the impromptu house party including the owners and residents, or just stay to yourself. The management also rents a luxury villa in Lurin, near Gustavia. **Pros:** only property walkable to Salines Beach; quiet; reasonable rates. **Cons:** far from town; not very private; no phones in rooms. ✉ *Grand Saline* ☎ *0590/51–04–44* 🌐 *www.salinesgarden.com* ⇨ *5 cottages* ♨ *In-room: no phone, safe, kitchen (some), Wi-Fi. In-hotel: bar, pool, Wi-Fi hotspot* ⊗ *Closed mid-Aug.–mid-Oct.* ▭ *AE, MC, V* 🍽 *CP.*

GUSTAVIA

★ Fodor's Choice **Carl Gustaf.** *Hotel.* This sophisticated hotel
$$$$ right in Gustavia received a welcome overhaul in 2006, and its new incarnation is the last word in luxury. The hotel is a good option if you don't want to do much driving—it's within walking distance of everything in town if you don't mind climbing the hill, but there is ample parking if you want a car. Each apartment-suite is lavishly decorated and equipped with every modern convenience: iPod-clock radios, multiple flat-screen TVs, and complete mini-kitchens (except the smallest "spa suite") with a Häagen Dazs–stocked refrigerator-freezer and an espresso machine. One- and two-bedroom suites with private decks and black-

and-gold-tiled plunge pools spill down a hill overlooking quaint Gustavia Harbor. If you need even more space, there are multi-bedroom villas and suites with up to seven super-luxurious bedrooms, private pools, and Jacuzzis. There is even one completely wheelchair-accessible suite, a rarity on the island. Summer rates and special Internet and honeymoon packages are offered. The Victoria restaurant, with glamorous, Euro-modern decor, and thrilling views, is known for its classic French cuisine and is a spectacular venue for sunset cocktails and dinner over the twinkle of the harbor lights. The Carita spa and 24-hour fitness facility offers a resistance pool, steam rooms, saunas, and pampering galore. **Pros:** luxurious decor; in-town location; loads of in-room gadgets; excellent restaurant; beautiful spa. **Cons:** not on the beach; outdoor space limited to your private plunge pool. ⊠ *Rue des Normands, Box 700, Gustavia* ☎ *0590/29–79–00* ⊕ *www.hotelcarlgustaf.com* ⇱ *14 suites* ☖ *In-room: kitchen, refrigerator, DVD, Wi-Fi. In-hotel: restaurant, bar, pool, gym, Wi-Fi hotspot, parking (free)* ⊟ *AE, MC, V* ☲ *CP.*

$–$$ ☲ **Sunset Hotel.** *Hotel.* Ten simple, utilitarian rooms (one can accommodate three people) right in Gustavia sit across from the harbor and offer an economical and handy, if not luxurious, accommodation option for those who want to stay in town. The five "superior" rooms are in the front with views; the back ones are pretty dark. This is St. Barth's sort-of answer to a business hotel. There is Wi-Fi on the terrace, where breakfast is available for an extra charge. **Pros:** reasonable rates; in town. **Cons:** no elevator; not resortlike in any way. ⊠ *Rue de la Républic, Gustavia* ☎ *590/27–77–21* ⊕ *www.saint-barths.com/sunset-hotel* ⇱ *10 rooms* ☖ *In-room: safe, refrigerator, Wi-Fi (some). In-hotel: Wi-Fi hotspot* ⊟ *AE, MC, V* ☲ *EP*

LORIENT

$$$$ ☲ **Hotel La Banane.** *Hotel.* A young vibe, and a sociable attitude attract chic visitors to the nine smallish pavilion rooms with Euro-style contemporary furnishings, white-draped four-poster beds, and pale aqua walls. Spacious, stylish baths have open showers with waterfall shower-heads, pretty turquoise glass-tile walls, and Aqua de Parma toiletries. Each room has a small front porch with a ban-quette, but guests gather around the central pool with fun sun beds and whimsical white café tables to try specialties from the lounge bar in the shade. A nice touch is a library with books and lots of DVDs. The hotel's location behind a small shopping center may be construed as either a bother or a convenience, but Lorient Beach is a two-minute walk away. Breakfast is served around the palm-shaded pool. K'fe Massaï, the African-themed restaurant, is very popular. **Pros:** short walk to beach; friendly and social atmosphere at pool areas; great baths. **Cons:** rooms are small; location of entrance through parking lot is not attractive. ✉ *Lorient* ☎ *0590/52–03–00* ⊕ *www.labanane.com* ⇨ *9 rooms* ♁ *In-room: DVD, Wi-Fi. In-hotel: restaurant, bar, pools* ▭ *AE, MC, V* ⊗ *Closed Sept. 1–Oct. 15* 🍽 *CP.*

3

$$–$$$ **Les Mouettes.** *Vacation Rental.* This guesthouse offers clean, simply furnished, and economical bungalows that open directly onto the beach. They're also quite close to the road, which can be either convenient for a quick shopping excursion or bothersome on account of the noise. Each air-conditioned bungalow has a bathroom with a shower (rather than full bathtub), a kitchenette, a patio, and one or two double beds, making this place a good bet for families or young visitors on a budget. **Pros:** right on the beach; family-friendly. **Cons:** rooms are basic; right near the road; takes only cash. ✉ *Lorient Beach* ☎ *0590/27–77–91* ⊕ www.st-barths.com/hotel-les-mouettes ⇨ *7 bungalows* ♁ *In-room: kitchen. In-hotel: beachfront* ▭ *No credit cards* 🍽 *EP.*

$$$ ★ **Le Normandie.** *B&B.* Wendy and Dennis Carlton, longtime St. Barth visitors, have renovated this eight-room inn in a Euro-meets-nautical theme, reflecting the eponymous art-deco ocean liner. The rooms are small but stylish, with good bathrooms, and will appeal to young visitors who appreciate the in-town location and the clubby atmosphere of the small pool garden, where breakfast and afternoon wine are served. Another thing is sure—there's nothing to compare at this price on the island. And, it's a two-minute walk to the beach. **Pros:** friendly management; pleasant atmosphere; good value. **Cons:** tiny rooms. ✉ *Lorient* ☎ *0590/27–61–66* ⊕ *www.normandiehotelstbarts.com* ⇨ *8 rooms (7 double, 1 single)* ♁ *In-room: Wi-Fi. In-hotel: bar, pool, Wi-Fi hotspot* ▭ *AE, MC, V* 🍽 *CP.*

POINTE MILOU

$$$$ **Christopher.** *Resort.* This longtime St. Barth favorite of European families underwent a thoughtful and stylish transformation in 2009. The young, experienced management brings professionalism to the personalized service, and the renovated rooms are super-comfortable, and stuffed with

Carl Gustaf

Eden Rock

Hôtel le Village St-Jean

unpretentious but luxurious touches like steeping tubs, flat-screen TVs, iPod docks, and specially commissioned 780-thread-count linens, using environmentally sensitive materials. Each unit has a private front deck with a lounge bed, perfect for late-day relaxing with a book. Set in lush, mature tropical gardens facing amazing sunsets along the rocky shore of tony Point Milou, the huge infinity pool brings the liquid horizon up to your toes; its shallow side is a dream for small kids (it has an alarm at night for safety). Most appreciated are the remarkably moderate prices. An ample buffet breakfast and first-rate gastronomic dinners are served in a lovely modern pavilion. Lunch is a waterfront BBQ, and yummy drinks come from the poolside bar. The spa services can come to your room, or you can have treatments in a rooftop tent. **Pros:** comfortable elegance; family friendly; reasonable price; updated rooms. **Cons:** resort is directly on the water but not on a beach. ⊠ *Pointe Milou* ☎ *590/27–63–63* ⊕ *www.hotelchristopher.com* ⤴ *41 rooms* ᴗ *In-room: safe, refrigerator, DVD, Internet (some), Wi-Fi. In-hotel: 2 restaurants, room service, bars, pool, gym, spa, diving, water sports, laundry service, Internet terminal, Wi-Fi hotspot, parking (free), some pets allowed* ▤ *AE, MC, V* ⊗ *Closed Sept.–mid-Oct.* ⓞ *CP.*

ST-JEAN

★ Fodor'sChoice ⚐ **Eden Rock.** *Resort.* St. Barth's first hotel opened
$$$$ in the 1950s on the craggy bluff that splits Baie de St-Jean.
ᴗ Extensive renovations and an expansion in 2005 raised it into the top category of St. Barth properties. Each of the hotel's 34 unique rooms, suites, and villas is tastefully decorated and luxuriously appointed with plasma satellite TV and high-speed Internet. New, large bathrooms have either deep soaking tubs or walk-in showers; all have loads of fluffy towels and Bulgari amenities. The beachfront villas built on the property are magnificent and sleep up to eight, with full kitchens and beautifully appointed modern living areas. Stunning bay views and great service are uniform. In 2008 the resort added two enormous (two- and three-bedroom) super-deluxe villas, each with two private pools, an art gallery, butler service, private cinema, and use of a Mini Cooper. One, called Villa RockStar, even has a full recording studio. The breakfast buffet, included in the rate, is terrific and reserved for hotel guests only; the on-site restaurants are first-rate and deserving of a visit. **Pros:** chic clientele; beach setting; can walk to shopping and restaurants.

Cons: some suites are noisy because of proximity to street. ⊠ *Baie de St-Jean, St-Jean* ☎ *0590/29–79–99; 877/563–7015 in U.S.* ⊕ *www.edenrockhotel.com* ⌕ *32 rooms, 2 villas* ⚘ *In-room: refrigerator, Internet. In-hotel: 2 restaurants, bars, pool, water sports* ⊟ *AE, MC, V* ⎮⊚⎮ *BP.*

$$$$ ⊡ **Emeraude Plage.** *Hotel.* Right on the beach of Baie de
★ St-Jean, this petite resort consists of small but immaculate
☾ bungalows and villas with modern, fully equipped outdoor kitchenettes on small patios; nice bathrooms add to the comfort. The beach bungalows were renovated in a modern, clean, white-and-brown color scheme that has become the St. Barth "look"; now there are white flat-screen TVs, iPod docks, and, on the patios, new white kitchens. A new beach pavilion serves light fare at breakfast, lunch, and cocktails until 7 PM. The complex is convenient to nearby restaurants and shops. The beachfront two-bedroom villas, one of which has a private Jacuzzi on the deck, are something of a bargain, especially off-season; one of them is wheelchair-accessible. **Pros:** beachfront and in-town location; good value; cool kitchens on each porch. **Cons:** smallish rooms. ⊠ *Baie de St-Jean, St-Jean* ☎ *0590/27–64–78* ⊕ *www.emeraudeplage.com* ⌕ *28 bungalows* ⚘ *In-room: safe, kitchen, Wi-Fi. In-hotel: bar, restaurant, beachfront, laundry service, Wi-Fi hotspot* ⊟ *AE, MC, V* ⊘ *Closed Sept.–mid-Oct.* ⎮⊚⎮ *EP.*

★ **Fodor's**Choice ⊡ **Hôtel le Village St-Jean.** *Hotel.* For two genera-
$$$– tions, the Charneau family has offered friendly service and
$$$$ reasonable rates at its small hotel, making guests feel like
☾ a part of the family. Recent upgrades have raised the bar, but not the prices. Handsome, spacious, and comfortable, the airy stone-and-redwood cottages have high ceilings, sturdy furniture, modern baths, open-air kitchenettes, and lovely terraces with hammocks; one has a Jacuzzi and an indoor-outdoor rain shower. It's even accessible for travelers with disabilities, a rarity on this island of steep hills and rocky steps. You get the advantages of a villa and the services of a hotel here. The regular rooms have refrigerators, and most have king-size beds. In addition, there are three lovely villas of various sizes. Regulars are invited to store beach equipment. The location is great—you can walk to the beach and town from here—and most rooms and cottages have gorgeous views. See if Rooms 12, 15, or 10, perched on the edge of the hillside, are available when you book. The excellent restaurant, Le Cesar ($$–$$$), is open all day long, with occasional live music. A lovely mahogany massage room and well-equipped gym were

added in 2008. Cottages have kitchens; very reasonable summer rates for cottages include a car. **Pros:** great value; convenient location; wonderful management. **Cons:** somewhat old-fashioned; can be noisy, depending on how close your room is to the street below. ☞ *Box 623, Baie de St-Jean, St-Jean 97133* ☎*0590/27–61–39 or 800/651–8366* ⊕*www.villagestjeanhotel.com* ⇄*5 rooms, 20 cottages, 1 3-bedroom villa, 2 2-bedroom villas* ⚖ *In-room: kitchen (some), no TV. In-hotel: restaurant, bar, pool, spa* ⊟*MC, V* ⟟*EP.*

3

$$$$ 🖪 **Les Îlets de la Plage.** *Vacation Rental.* On the far side of the airport, tucked away at the far corner of Baie de St-Jean, these well-priced, comfortably furnished island-style one-, two-, and three-bedroom bungalows (four right on the beach, seven up a small hill) have small kitchens, pleasant open-air sitting areas, and comfortable bathrooms. This is a good choice if you want to be right on the beach with the space and convenience of a villa but the feel of a small resort. Crisp white linens and upholstery, lovely verandas, and daily deliveries of fresh bread from a nearby bakery add to the pleasantness of the surroundings, though only the bedrooms are air-conditioned. **Pros:** beach location; apartment conveniences; front porches. **Cons:** no a/c outside bedrooms; right next to the airport. ☒*Plage de St-Jean, St-Jean* ☎*0590/27–88–57* ⊕*www.lesilets.com* ⇄*11 bungalows* ⚖ *In-room: safe, kitchen, Wi-Fi. In-hotel: pool, gym, beachfront, Internet terminal* ⊟*AE, MC, V* ⊘*Closed Sept.–Nov. 1* ⟟*EP.*

$$$$ 🖪 **Le Tom Beach Hôtel.** *Hotel.* This chic but casual boutique hotel right on busy St-Jean beach is fun for social types, and the nonstop house party often spills out onto the terraces and lasts into the wee hours. The gallery in the entryway features exhibitions that change each fortnight. A path winds through suites set in a garden, over a small pool via a small footbridge, into the hopping, open-air restaurant La Plage. Big, white plantation-style rooms have high ceilings, draped four-poster beds, nice baths, a TV with DVD player, direct-dial phones, and patios. Oceanfront suites are the most expensive; 6 of the 12 were redone in 2009 in the now-ubiquitious St Barth white and taupe. **Pros:** party central at beach, restaurant, and pool; in-town location. **Cons:** trendy social scene is not for everybody, especially light sleepers. ☒*Plage de St-Jean, St-Jean* ☎*0590/27–53–13* ⊕*www.st-barths.com/tom-beach-hotel* ⇄*12 rooms* ⚖ *In-room: safe, refrigerator, DVD, Wi-Fi. In-hotel: restaurant, bar, pool, beachfront, Wi-Fi hotspot* ⊟*AE, MC, V* ⟟*CP.*

VITET

$$$ ☂ **Hostellerie des Trois Forces.** *Inn.* For the young, the spiritual, and the cost-conscious, a respite at one of the seven tiny bungalows at the very top of the highest peak on the island at this so-called "New Age Inn" might be your karmic destiny. Devotees claim that it's magic. What is certain is that the atmosphere is low-key and the location remote, but the views are beyond belief. You might think of this as a camp. There are a tiny pool and a meditation room, but rooms have no phones and no TV, so that you can more easily connect with your traveling companions. (There is Wi-Fi at the pool area in a nod toward keeping you in touch with the outside world.) One of the units has an attached bedroom suitable for a child. Hubert Delamotte, the proprietor, is a renowned chef and member of a prestigious confraternity of chefs; he's also an astrologer, and will no doubt read your chakras to pick your perfect accommodation in the Zodiac-named rooms. In his words: "Here, silence is very loud. Between us and Africa, there is no one." Lunches and dinners are events of the classic French gastronomic variety, and Hubert will, no doubt, capture your heart as he expertly flambés your dessert. **Pros:** far from the hustle and bustle of cosmopolitan St. Barth. **Cons:** remote and a tough drive up the mountain (rent a four-wheel-drive vehicle); rooms and baths are clean but basic. ⊠ *Vitet* ☎ *590/27–61–25* ⊕ *www.3forces. net* ⤙ *7 rooms* ⚐ *In-room: no phone, safe (some), kitchen (some), refrigerator, no TV. In-hotel: restaurant, pool, Wi-Fi hotspot, parking (free), some pets allowed* ⊟ *AE, MC, V* ⍰ *EP.*

BEACHES

There is a beach in St. Barth to suit every taste. Whether you are looking for wild surf, a dreamy white-sand strand, or a spot at a chic beach club close to shopping and restaurants, you will find it within a 20-minute drive.

There are many *anses* (coves) and nearly 20 *plages* (beaches) scattered around the island, each with a distinctive personality; all are open to the public, even if the beach fronts the toniest of resorts. Because of the variety and number of beaches, even in high season you can find a nearly empty beach, despite St. Barth's tiny size. That's not to say that all the island's beaches are equally good or even equally suitable for swimming, but each beach has something unique

DID YOU KNOW?

Every one of St. Barth's twenty-some white-sand beaches is open to the public, whether or not it's the home of a tony resort.

to offer. Unless you are having lunch at a beachfront restaurant that has lounging areas set aside for its patrons, you should bring your own umbrella, beach mat, and water (all of which are easily obtainable all over the island if you haven't brought yours with you on vacation). Topless sunbathing is common, but nudism is supposedly forbidden— although both Grande Saline and Gouverneur are de facto nude beaches. Shade is scarce.

Anse à Colombier. The beach here is the least accessible, thus the most private, on the island; to reach it you must take either a rocky footpath from Petite Anse or brave the 30-minute climb down (and back up) a steep, cactus-bordered—though clearly marked—trail from the top of the mountain behind the beach. Appropriate footgear is a must, and you should know that once you get to the beach, the only shade is a rock cave. But this is a good place to snorkel. Boaters favor this beach and cove for its calm anchorage. ⊠ *Anse à Colombier, Colombier.*

Anse de Grand Cul de Sac. The shallow, reef-protected beach is especially nice for small children, fly-fishermen, kayakers, and windsurfers; and lots of the amusing pelican-like frigate birds that dive-bomb the water fishing for their lunch. You needn't do your own fishing; you can have a wonderful lunch at one of the excellent restaurants. ⊠ *Grand Cul de Sac.*

★ Fodor'sChoice **Anse de Grande Saline.** Secluded, with its sandy ocean bottom, this is just about everyone's favorite beach, and is great for swimmers, too. Without any major development (although there is some talk of developing a resort here), it's an ideal Caribbean strand. However, there can be a bit of wind here, so you can enjoy yourself more if you go on a calm day. In spite of the prohibition, young and old alike go nude. The beach is a 10-minute walk up a rocky dune trail, so be sure to wear sneakers or water shoes. Bring whatever you will need on the beach; although there are several good restaurants for lunch near the parking area, once you get there, the beach is just sand, sea, and sky. The big salt ponds here are no longer in use, and the place looks a little desolate when you approach, but don't despair. ⊠ *Grande Saline.*

Anse de Lorient. This beach is popular with St. Barth's families and surfers, who like its rolling waves and central location. Be aware of the level of the tide, which can come in very fast. Hikers and avid surfers like the walk over the hill to Point Milou in the late afternoon sun when the waves roll in. ⊠ *Lorient.*

Anse des Flamands. This is the most beautiful of the hotel beaches—a roomy strip of silken sand. Come here for lunch and then spend the afternoon sunning, taking a long beach walk and a swim in the turquoise water. From the beach, you can take a brisk hike to the top of the now-extinct volcano believed to have given birth to St. Barth. A new paved sidewalk down the steep hill is popular for those looking for an aerobic workout. ⊠ *Anse des Flamands, Flamands.*

★ **Anse du Gouverneur.** Because it's so secluded, this beach is a popular place for nude sunbathing. It is truly beautiful, with blissful swimming and views of St. Kitts, Saba, and St. Eustatius. Venture here at the end of the day and watch the sun set behind the hills. The road here from Gustavia also offers spectacular vistas. Legend has it that pirates' treasure is buried in the vicinity. There are no restaurants or other services here, so plan accordingly. ⊠ *Anse du Gouverneur, Gouverneur.*

Baie de St-Jean. Like a mini Côte d'Azur—beachside bistros, terrific shopping, bungalow hotels, bronzed bodies, windsurfing, and day-trippers who tend to arrive on BIG yachts—the reef-protected strip is divided by Eden Rock promontory. You can rent chaises and umbrellas at La Plage restaurant or at Eden Rock, where you can lounge for hours over lunch. ⊠ *Baie de St-Jean, St-Jean.*

SPORTS AND THE OUTDOORS

BOATING AND SAILING

St. Barth is a popular yachting and sailing center, thanks to its location midway between Antigua and St. Thomas. Gustavia's harbor, 13 to 16 feet deep, has mooring and docking facilities for 40 yachts. There are also good anchorages available at Public, Corossol, and Colombier. You can charter sailing and motorboats in Gustavia Harbor for as little as a half day. Stop at the Tourist Office in Gustavia for an up-to-the minute list of recommended charter companies.

Marine Service (⊠ *Ferry dock, Gustavia* ☎ *0590/27–70–34* ⊕ *www.st-barths.com/marine.service*) offers full-day outings, either on a 42- or 46-foot catamaran, to the uninhabited Île Fourchue for swimming, snorkeling, cocktails, and

Up to 40 yachts can moor in Gustavia's harbor

lunch. The cost is $100 per person; an unskippered motor rental runs about $260 a day.

Yellow Submarine (✉ *Ferry dock, Gustavia* ☎ *0590/52–40–51* ⊕ *www.yellow-submarine.fr*) takes you "six feet under" (the surface of the sea) for a close-up view of St. Barth's coral reefs through large glass portholes. Once a week you can go at night. It costs €40. Trips depart daily in the morning and in the afternoon, but more often depending on demand, so call first.

DIVING AND SNORKELING

Several dive shops arrange scuba excursions to local sites. Depending on weather conditions, you may dive at **Pain de Sucre, Coco Island,** or toward nearby **Saba.** There's also an underwater shipwreck to explore, plus sharks, rays, sea tortoises, coral, and the usual varieties of colorful fish. The waters on the island's leeward side are the calmest. For the uncertified who still want to see what the island's waters hold, there's an accessible shallow reef right off the beach at Anse de Cayes that you can explore if you have your own mask and fins.

Most of the waters surrounding St. Barth are protected in the island's **Réserve Marine de St-Barth** (✉ *Gustavia* ☎ *0590/27–88–18*), which also provides information at its office in Gustavia. The diving here isn't nearly as rich as in the more dive-centered destinations like Saba and St. Eustatius, but the options aren't bad either, and none of the smaller islands offer the ambience of St. Barth.

Plongée Caraïbe (📠 0590/27–55–94) is recommended for its up-to-the-minute equipment and dive boat.

Splash (✉ *Gustavia* ☎ 0690/56–90–24) does scuba, snorkeling, and fishing, too.

Marine Service operates the only five-star, PADI-certified diving center on the island, called **West Indies Dive** (☎ 0590/27–70–34). Scuba trips, packages, resort dives, night dives, and certifications start at $90, including gear.

FISHING

Most fishing is done in the waters north of Lorient, Flamands, and Corossol. Popular catches are tuna, marlin, wahoo, and barracuda. There's an annual St. Barth Open Fishing Tournament, organized by Ocean Must, in mid-July.

Marine Service (✉ *Gustavia* ☎ 0590/27–70–34 ⊕ *www. st-barths.com/marine.service*) arranges ocean-fishing excursions.

Océan Must Marina (✉ *Gustavia* ☎ 0590/27–62–25) arranges deep-sea fishing expeditions as well as bareboat and staffed boat charters.

GUIDED TOURS

You can arrange island tours by minibus or car at hotel desks or through any of the island's taxi operators in Gustavia or at the airport. The tourist office runs a variety of tours with varying itineraries that run about €46 for a half-day for up to eight people. You can also download up-to-the minute walking- and driving-tour itineraries from the tourist board's Web site (*see* ⇨ *Visitor Information in Travel Smart*).

Mat Nautic (✉ *Quai du Yacht Club, Gustavia* ☎ 0690/49–54–72) can help you arrange to tour the island by water on a Jet Ski or WaveRunner. **St-Barth Tours & Travel** (✉ *Rue Jeanne d'Arc, Gustavia* ☎ 0590/27–52–14) will customize a tour of the island. **Wish Agency** (☎ 0590/29–83–74 ✉ wish.agency@ wanadoo.fr) can arrange customized tours as well as take care of airline ticketing, event planning, maid service, and private party arrangements.

Snorkeling at Anse à Colombier

NIGHTLIFE

Most of the nightlife in St. Barth is centered in Gustavia, though there are a few places to go outside of town. "In" clubs change from season to season, so you might ask around for the hot spot of the moment. There's more nightlife than ever in recent memory, and a late (10 PM or later) reservation at one of the club-restaurants will eventually become a front-row seat at a party. *Saint-Barth Leisures* contains current information about sports, spas, nightlife, and the arts.

Bar de l'Oubli (⊠ *Rue du Roi Oscar II, Gustavia* ☎ *0590/27–70–06*) is where young locals gather for drinks. **Carl Gustaf** (⊠ *Rue des Normands, Gustavia* ☎ *0590/27–82–83*) lures a more sedate crowd, namely those in search of quiet conversation and sunset watching. **Le Nikki Beach** (⊠ *St-Jean* ☎ *0590/27–64–64*) rocks on weekends during lunch, when the scantily clad young and beautiful lounge on the white canvas banquettes. **Le Repaire** (⊠ *Rue de la République, Gustavia* ☎ *0590/27–72–48*) lures a crowd for cocktail hour and its pool table. **Le Sélect** (⊠ *Rue du Centenaire, Gustavia* ☎ *0590/27–86–87*) is St. Barth's original hangout, commemorated by Jimmy Buffett's "Cheeseburger in Paradise." The boisterous garden is where the barefoot boating set gathers for a brew. At this writing, the hot spot is **Le Yacht Club** (⊠ *Rue Jeanne d'Arc, Gustavia* ☎ *0690/49–23–33*); although ads call it a private club, you can probably get in anyway. **The Spot** (⊠ *Lurin* ☎ *0590/52–84–09*) is a disco in the Lurin Hills, where locals go for weekend fun.

SHOPPING

★ Fodor'sChoice St. Barth is a duty-free port, and with its sophisticated crowd of visitors, shopping in the island's 200-plus boutiques is a definite delight, especially for beachwear, accessories, jewelry, and casual wear. It would be no overstatement to say that shopping for fashionable clothing, accessories, and decorative items for the home is better in St. Barth than anywhere else in the Caribbean. New shops open all the time, so there's always something new to discover. Stores often close for lunch from noon to 2, and many on Wednesday afternoon as well, but they are open until about 7 in the evening. A popular afternoon pastime is strolling about the two major shopping areas in Gustavia and St-Jean.

SHOPPING AREAS

In Gustavia, boutiques line the three major shopping streets. Quai de la République, which is right on the harbor, rivals New York's Madison Avenue or Paris's avenue Montaigne for high-end designer retail, including shops for **Louis Vuitton, Bulgari, Cartier, Chopard,** and **Hermès.** These shops often carry items that are not available in the United States. The Carré d'Or plaza is great fun to explore. Shops are also clustered in **La Savane Commercial Center** (across from the airport), **La Villa Créole** (in St-Jean), and **Espace Neptune** (on the road to Lorient). It's worth working your way from one end to the other at these shopping complexes—just to see or, perhaps, be seen. Boutiques in all three areas carry the latest in French and Italian sportswear and some haute couture. Bargains may be tough to come by, but you might be able to snag that *pochette* that is sold out stateside, and in any case, you'll have a lot of fun hunting around.

SPECIALTY STORES

CLOTHING

Shopping for up-to-the-minute fashions is as much a part of a visit to St. Barth as going to the beach. Shops change all the time, both in ownership and in the lines that are carried. Current listings are just a general guide. The best advice is simply to go for a long stroll and check out all the shops on the way. The following is a list of shops that

Shops on Rue de la France, Gustavier

have an interesting variety of current and fun items, but it's by no means an exhaustive one.

Black Swan (⊠ *Le Carré d'Or, Gustavia* ☎ *0590/27–65–16* ⊠ *La Villa Créole, St-Jean*) has an unparalleled selection of bathing suits. The wide range of styles and sizes is appreciated.

Blanc Bleu (⊠ *Gustavia Harbor, Gustavia* ☎ *590/27–99–53*) Classy and comfortable linen and cotton separates for men women and kids mostly in white, blue, and a wonderful soft gray. There are also outposts in St-Jean and at Le Sereno hotel.

Boutique Lacoste (⊠ *Rue Du Bord de Mer, Gustavia* ☎ *0590/27–66–90*) has a huge selection of the once-again-chic alligator-logo wear, as well as a shop next door with a complete selection of the Petit Bateau line of T-shirts popular with teens.

Cafe Coton (⊠ *Rue du Bord du Mer, Gustavia* ☎ *0590/52–48–42*) is a great shop for men, especially for long-sleeve linen shirts in a rainbow of colors and Egyptian cotton dress shirts.

Calypso (⊠ *Le Carré d'Or, Gustavia* ☎ *0590/27–69–74*) carries sexy resort wear that fits the island sensibility.

Fans of the popular **Longchamp** (⊠ *Le Carré d'Or, Gustavia* ☎ *0590/52–00–94*) travel bags, handbags, and leather goods will find a good selection at about 20% off state-side prices.

Ilena (✉ *Villa Creole, St-Jean* ☎ *0590/29–84–05*) has incredible beachwear and lingerie by Chantal Thomas, Sarda, and others, including Swarovski crystal-encrusted bikinis for the young and gorgeous.

The **Hermès** (✉ *Rue de la République, Gustavia* ☎ *0590/27–66–15*) store in St. Barth is an independently owned franchise, and prices are slightly below those in the States.

Kokon (✉ *Rue Fahlberg, Gustavia* ☎ *0590/29–74–48*) offers a nicely edited mix of designs for on-island of off, including the bo'em, Lotty B. Mustique, and Day Birger lines, and cute shoes to go with them by Heidi Klum for Birkenstock.

jee's (✉ *Rue Samuel Fahlberg, Gustavia* ☎ *No phone*) is an excellent source if you are looking for accessories.

Check out **Lili Belle** (✉ *Pelican Plage, St-Jean* ☎ *0590/87–46–14*), for a nice selection of wearable and current styles.

Linde Gallery St Barth (✉ *Les Hauts de Carré d'Or, Gustavia* ☎ *590/29–73–86*) sells vintage sunglasses, accessories, vintage ready-to-wear from the 1970s and '80s, as well as books, CDs, and DVDs.

Linen/EuroPann (✉ *Rue Lafayette, Gustavia* ☎ *0590/27–54–26*) has tailored linen shirts for men in a rainbow of soft colors, and soft slip-on driving mocs in classic styles are a St. Barth must.

Don't miss **Lolita Jaca** (✉ *Le Carré d'Or, Gustavia* ☎ *0590/27–59–98*) for trendy, tailored sportswear.

Made in Saint Barth (✉ *Rue Du Bord de Mer, Gustavia* ☎ *0590/29–78–04*) is the largest of the three shops that stock the chic, locally made T-shirts, totes, and beach wraps that have practically become the logo of St. Barth. The newest styles have hand-done graffiti-style lettering. The shop also has some handcrafts, and other giftable items.

Morgan's (✉ *La Villa Créole, St-Jean* ☎ *0590/27–57–22*) has a line of popular casual wear in the trendy vein.

At **Poupette** (✉ *Rue de la République, Gustavia* ☎ *0590/27–94–49*), all the brilliant color-crinkle silk and chiffon batik and embroidered peasant skirts and tops are designed by the owner. There also are great belts and beaded bracelets.

Saint-Barth Stock Exchange (✉ *La Pointe-Gustavia, Gustavia* ☎ *0590/27–68–12*), on the far side of Gustavia Harbor, is the island's consignment and discount shop.

Stéphane & Bernard (✉ *Rue de la République, Gustavia* ☎ *0590/27–69–13*) stocks a well-edited, large selection of superstar French fashion designers, including Rykiel, Tarlazzi, Kenzo, Féraud, and Mugler, and Eres beachwear.

Look to **St. Tropez KIWI** (✉ *St-Jean* ☎ *0590/27–57–08* ✉ *Gustavia* ☎ *0590/27–68–97*) for resort wear.

SUD SUD.ETC.Plage (✉ *Galerie du Commerce, St-Jean* ☎ *0590/27–98–75*) stocks everything for the beach: inflatables, mats, bags, and beachy shell jewelry.

Vanita Rosa (✉ *Rue Oscar II, Gustavia* ☎ *0590/52–43–25*) showcases beautiful lace and linen sundresses and peasant tops, with accessories galore.

COSMETICS

The Beauty Spot (✉ *La Savane Shopping Center, St-Jean* ☎ *590/51–11–75* ⊕ *www.skinsuncare.com*) offers a great selection of make-up and skin care products, sun-care products, and beauty accessories. The store will also do make-up application for events.

Don't miss the superb skin-care products made on-site from local tropical plants by **Ligne de St. Barth** (✉ *Rte. de Saline, Lorient* ☎ *0590/27–82–63*).

FOODSTUFFS

A.M.C (✉ *Quai de la République, Gustavia*) is a bit older than the island's other big supermarket, Match, but able to supply anything you might need for housekeeping in a villa, or for a picnic.

JoJo Supermarché (✉ *Lorient*) is the well-stocked counterpart to Gustavia's large supermarket and gets daily deliveries of bread and fresh produce. Prices are lower here than at the larger markets.

Match (✉ *St-Jean*), a fully stocked supermarket across from the airport, has a wide selection of French cheeses, pâtés, cured meats, produce, fresh bread, wine, and liquor.

Maya's to Go (✉ *Galleries du Commerce, St-Jean* ☎ *0590/29–83–70*) is the place to go for prepared picnics, meals, salads, rotisserie chickens, and more from the kitchens of the popular restaurant.

For exotic groceries or picnic fixings, stop by St. Barth's gourmet *traiteur* (take-out eatery) **La Rotisserie** (⊠ *Rue du Roi Oscar II, Gustavia* ☎ *0590/27–63–13* ⊠ *Centre Vaval, St-Jean* ☎ *0590/29–75–69*) for salads, prepared meats, groceries from Fauchon, and Iranian caviar.

HANDICRAFTS

Call the tourist office, which can provide information about the studios of island artists Christian Bretoneiche, Robert Danet, Nathalie Daniel, Patricia Guyot, Rose Lemen, Aline de Lurin, and Marion Vinot.

Chez Pompi (⊠ *Route de Toiny* ☎ *0590/27–75–67*) is a cottage whose first room is a gallery for the naive paintings of Pompi (also known as Louis Ledée).

Couleurs Provence (⊠ *St-Jean* ☎ *0590/52–48–51*) stocks beautiful, handcrafted French-made items like jacquard table linens in brilliant colors; decorative tableware, including trays in which dried flowers and herbs are suspended; and the home fragrance line by L'Occitane.

Look for unusual jewelry, including original designs and modern baubles by Tamara Comolli at **Fabienne Miot** (⊠ *Rue de la République, Gustavia* ☎ *0590/27–73–13*).

JEWELRY

Bijoux de la Mer (⊠ *Rue de la Républic, Gustavia* ☎ *590/52–37–68*) carries beautiful and artistic jewelry made of South Sea pearls in wonderful hues strung in clusters on leather to wrap around the neck or arms.

Carat (⊠ *Quai de la République, Gustavia*) has Chaumet and a large selection of Breitling watches.

For fine jewelry, visit **Cartier** (⊠ *Quai de la République, Gustavia*).

A good selection of watches, including Patek Phillippe and Chanel, can be found at **Diamond Genesis** (⊠ *Rue Général-de-Gaulle, Gustavia*).

Next door to Cartier, **Donna del Sol** (⊠ *Quai de la République, Gustavia*) carries beautiful Tahitian pearl pieces, and baubles in multicolor diamonds.

Sindbad (⊠ *Carré d'Or, Gustavia* ☎ *0590/27–52–29*) is a tiny shop with funky, unique couture fashion jewelry by Gaz Bijou of St-Tropez, crystal collars for your pampered pooch, chunky ebony pendants on silk cord, and other reasonably priced, up-to-the-minute styles.

La Cave du Port Franc (✉ *Rue de la République, Gustavia* ☎ *0590/27–65–27*) has a good selection of wine, especially from France.

La Cave de Saint-Barths (✉ *Marigot* ☎ *0590/27–63–21*) has an excellent collection of French vintages stored in temperature-controlled cellars.

Le Comptoir du Cigare (✉ *La Carré d'Or, Gustavia* ☎ *0590/27–50–62*), run by Jannick and Patrick Gerthofer, is a top purveyor of cigars. The walk-in humidor has an extraordinary selection. Try the Cubans while you are on the island, and take home the Davidoffs. Refills can be shipped stateside. Be sure to try on the genuine Panama hats.

Couleur des Isles Cuban Cigar (✉ *Rue Général-de-Gaulle, Gustavia* ☎ *0590/27–79–60*) has many rare varieties of smokeables and good souvenir T-shirts, too.

At **M'Bolo** (✉ *Rue Général-de-Gaulle, Gustavia* ☎ *0590/27–90–54*), be sure to sample the various varieties of infused rums, including lemongrass, ginger, and, of course, the island favorite, vanilla. Bring home some in the beautiful hand-blown bottles.

4

Anguilla

WORD OF MOUTH

"There are 35 white sand beaches around the island, many with very calm waters. If the water is "wavy" at one beach simply drive to one of the beaches on the opposite side of the island for calm waters."

—RoamsAround

Updated
by Elise
Meyer

PEACE, PAMPERING, GREAT FOOD, AND a wonderful local music scene are among the star attractions on Anguilla (pronounced ang-*gwill*-a). Beach lovers may become giddy when they first spot the island from the air; its blindingly white sand and lustrous blue-and-aquamarine waters are intoxicating. And, if you like sophisticated cuisine served in casually elegant open-air settings, this may be your culinary Shangri-la.

HISTORY AND CULTURE

The island's name, a reflection of its shape, is most likely a derivative of *anguille,* which is French for "eel." (French explorer Pierre Laudonnaire is credited with having given the island this name when he sailed past it in 1556.) In 1631 the Dutch built a fort here, but so far no one has been able to locate its site. English settlers from St. Kitts colonized the island in 1650, with plans to cultivate tobacco and, later, cotton and then sugar. But the thin soil and scarce water doomed these enterprises to fail. Except for a brief period of independence, when it broke from its association with St. Kitts and Nevis in the 1960s, Anguilla has remained a British colony ever since.

From the early 1800s various island federations were formed and disbanded, with Anguilla all the while simmering over its subordinate status and enforced union with St. Kitts. Anguillians twice petitioned for direct rule from Britain and twice were ignored. In 1967, when St. Kitts, Nevis, and Anguilla became an associated state, the mouse roared; citizens kicked out St. Kitts's policemen, held a self-rule referendum, and for two years conducted their own affairs. To what *Time* magazine called "a cascade of laughter around the world," a British "peacekeeping force" of 100 paratroopers from the Elite Red Devil unit parachuted onto the island, squelching Anguilla's designs for autonomy but helping a team of royal engineers stationed there to improve the port and build roads and schools. Today Anguilla elects a House of Assembly and its own leader to handle internal affairs, while a British governor is responsible for public service, the police, the judiciary, and external affairs.

The territory of Anguilla includes a few islets (or cays, pronounced *keys*), such as Scrub Island, Dog Island, Prickly Pear Cay, Sandy Island, and Sombrero Island. The 16,000 or so residents are predominantly of African descent, but there are also many of Irish background, whose ancestors

TOP REASONS TO GO

■ Anguilla is known far and wide for its beautiful, powdery soft beaches. Miles of brilliant beach ensure that you have a quality spot to lounge.

■ Though nothing comes cheap because of the island's isolation and size (virtually everything has to be imported), the dining scene offers everything from top-price gourmet dining to delicious casual food.

■ Anguilla is certainly not a nightlife-heavy destination,

but if you like to party, don't plan on going to bed early; a funky late-night local music scene features reggae and string bands.

■ Excellent luxury resorts, including the famed Cap Juluca and the Cuisinart resorts, coddle you in comfort.

■ Although Anguilla is known for its luxury establishments, there are also a few relative bargains if you look hard enough.

4

came over from St. Kitts in the 1600s. Historically, because the limestone land was unfit for agriculture, attempts at enslavement never lasted long; consequently, Anguilla doesn't bear the scars of slavery found on so many other Caribbean islands. Instead, Anguillians became experts at making a living from the sea and are known for their boatbuilding and fishing skills. Tourism is the stable economy's growth industry, but the government carefully regulates expansion to protect the island's natural resources and beauty. New hotels are small, select, and casino-free; Anguilla emphasizes its high-quality service, serene surroundings, and friendly people.

EXPLORING ANGUILLA

Exploring on Anguilla is mostly about checking out the spectacular beaches and resorts. The island has only a few roads; but they have been improving significantly in recent years, and the lack of adequate signage is being addressed. Locals are happy to provide directions, but using the readily available tourist map is the best idea. Visit the Anguilla Tourist Board (*see* ⇨ *Visitor Information in Travel Smart*), centrally located on Coronation Avenue in The Valley.

Restaurants	Hotels
Blanchard's, **17**	Allamanda, **3**
da'Vida, **9**	Altamer, **11**
English Rose, **7**	Anguilla Great House, **6**
Geraud's Patisserie, **2**	Arawak Beach Inn, **5**
Hibernia, **12**	Cap Juluca, **10**
KoalKeel, **8**	Carimar Beach Club, **16**
Luna Rosa, **4**	Covecastles, **12**
Madeariman Reef, **10**	CuisinArt, **7**
Mango's, **15**	Frangipani Beach Club, **1**
Michel Rostang, **18**	Indigo Reef, **13**
Picante, **14**	Kú, **2**
Roy's Bayside Grill, **5**	Malliouhana, **17**
Smokey's, **13**	Paradise Cove, **8**
Straw Hat, **6**	Serenity Cottages, **4**
Tasty's, **3**	Sheriva, **9**
Trattoria Tramonto, **16**	Sirena, **15**
Veya, **1**	The Viceroy, **14**
Zara's, **11**	

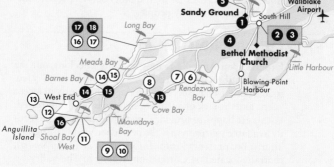

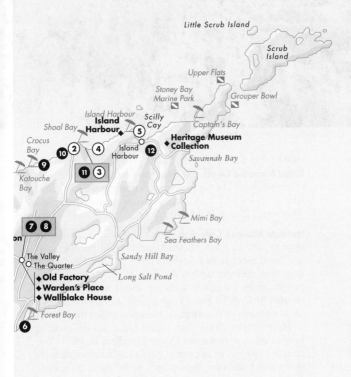

Anguilla

Little Scrub Island

Scrub Island

Upper Flats

Stoney Bay
Marine Park

Grouper Bowl

Island Harbour   Scilly
                        Cay
Shoal Bay   **Island
               Harbour**   Captain's Bay

Crocus
Bay   **Heritage Museum
                               Collection**

9   **10** **2** **4**   Island
                                Harbour   Savannah Bay

Katouche
Bay   **11** **3**

                                Mimi Bay

7 **8**   Sea Feathers Bay

on   The Valley   Sandy Hill Bay
            The Quarter
            ◆ **Old Factory**   Long Salt Pond
            ◆ **Warden's Place**
            ◆ **Wallblake House**

            Forest Bay

6

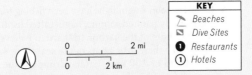

KEY
⚓ Beaches
◩ Dive Sites
● Restaurants
① Hotels

0   2 mi

0   2 km

Cacti growing on one of Anguilla's scrub-covered coral flats

WHAT TO SEE

Bethel Methodist Church. Not far from Sandy Ground, this charming little church is an excellent example of skillful island stonework. It also has some colorful stained-glass windows. ⊠ *South Hill* ☎ *No phone.*

Heritage Museum Collection. Don't miss this remarkable opportunity to learn about Anguilla. Old photographs and local records and artifacts trace the island's history over four millennia, from the days of the Arawaks. The tiny museum (complete with gift shop) is painstakingly curated by Colville Petty. High points include the historical documents of the Anguilla Revolution and the albums of photographs chronicling island life, from devastating hurricanes to a visit from Queen Elizabeth in 1964. You can see examples of ancient pottery shards and stone tools along with fascinating photographs of the island in the early 20th century—many depicting the heaping and exporting of salt and the christening of schooners—and a complete set of beautiful postage stamps issued by Anguilla since 1967. ⊠ *East End at Pond Ground* ☎ *264/497–4092* 🖃 *$5* ⊘ *Mon.–Sat. 10–5.*

★ **Island Harbour.** Anguillians have been fishing for centuries in the brightly painted, simple, handcrafted fishing boats that line the shore of the harbor. It's hard to believe, but skillful pilots take these little boats out to sea as far as 50 mi or 60 mi (80 km or 100 km). Late afternoon is the best time to see the day's catch. Hail the free boat to Gorgeous Scilly Cay, a classic little restaurant offering sublime lobster and Eudoxie Wallace's knockout rum punches on Wednesday, Friday, and Sunday.

Old Factory. For many years the cotton grown on Anguilla and exported to England was ginned in this beautiful historic building, now home of the Anguilla Tourist Office. Some of the original ginning machinery is intact and on display. ⊠ *The Valley* ☎ *264/497–2759* ⌨ *Free* ☉ *Weekdays 10–noon and 1–4.*

Old Prison. The ruins of this historic jail on Anguilla's highest point—213 feet above sea level—offer outstanding views. ⊠ *Valley Rd. at Crocus Hill.*

WORD OF MOUTH. "Anguillians have a lot of pride and don't tolerate rudeness or patronizing attitudes, but when treated respectfully are very friendly and will gladly show off their home. There are areas for hiking (Katouche Bay among others) and lots to explore. The former Chief Minister gives a bird watching tour!" —Beachykeen.

Sandy Ground. Almost everyone who comes to Anguilla stops by this central beach, home to several popular open-air bars and restaurants, as well as boat-rental operations. You can also tour the Pyrat rum factory, also in Sandy Ground. Finally, this is where you catch the ferry for tiny Sandy Island, just 2 mi (3 km) offshore.

Wallblake House. The only surviving plantation house in Anguilla, Wallblake House was built in 1787 by Will Blake (Wallblake is probably a corruption of his name) and has recently been thoroughly and thoughtfully restored. The place is associated with many a tale involving murder, high living, and the French invasion in 1796. On the grounds are an ancient vaulted stone cistern and an outbuilding called the Bakery (which wasn't used for making bread at all but for baking turkeys and hams). Tours are usually at 10 AM and 2 PM. ⊠ *Wallblake Rd., The Valley* ☎ *264/497–6613* ⌨ *Free* ☉ *Mon., Wed., and Fri.*

Warden's Place. This former sugar-plantation great house was built in the 1790s and is a fine example of island architecture. It now houses KoalKeel restaurant and a sumptuous bakery upstairs. But for many years it served as the residence of the island's chief administrator, who also doubled as the only medical practitioner. Across the street you can see the oldest dwelling on the island, originally built as slave housing. ⊠ *The Valley*.

WHERE TO EAT

Despite its small size, Anguilla has nearly 70 restaurants ranging from stylish temples of haute cuisine to classic, barefoot beachfront grills, roadside BBQ stands, food carts, and casual cafés. Many have breeze-swept terraces, where you can dine under the stars. Call ahead—in winter to make a reservation and in late summer and fall to confirm that the place you've chosen is open. Anguillian restaurant meals are leisurely events, and service is often at a relaxed pace, so settle in and enjoy. Most restaurant owners are actively and conspicuously present, especially at dinner. It's a special treat to take the time to get to know them a bit when they stop by your table to make sure that you are enjoying your meal.

WHAT TO WEAR

During the day, casual clothes are widely accepted: shorts will be fine, but don't wear bathing suits and cover-ups unless you're at a beach bar. In the evening, shorts are okay at the extremely casual eateries. Elsewhere, women wear sundresses or nice casual slacks; men will be fine in short-sleeved shirts and casual pants. Some hotel restaurants are slightly more formal, but that just means long pants for men.

WHAT IT COSTS IN DOLLARS				
¢	$	$$	$$$	$$$$
RESTAURANTS				
under $8	$8–$12	$12–$20	$20–$30	Over $30

Restaurant prices are per person for a main course at dinner and do not include taxes or service charges.

RECOMMENDED RESTAURANTS

★ Fodor'sChoice ✕ **Blanchard's.** *American.* This absolutely delight-
$$$$ ful restaurant, a mecca for foodies, is considered one of the best in the Caribbean. Proprietors Bob and Melinda Blanchard moved to Anguilla from Vermont in 1994 to fulfill their culinary dreams. A festive atmosphere pervades

Best Bets for Anguilla Dining

With the many restaurants to choose from, how will you decide where to eat? Fodor's writers and editors have selected their favorite restaurants in the Best Bets lists below. The Fodor's Choice properties represent the "best of the best." Find specific details about a restaurant in the full reviews.

★ **Fodor's** Choice

Blanchard's, Hibernia, KoalKeel,

Straw Hat, Veya

Best Budget Eats: English Rose, Geraud's Patisserie, Picante

Best for Families: da'Vida, Picante, Smokey's

Most Romantic: Hibernia, Luna Rosa, Michel Rostang at Malliouhana, Veya

Best for Local Cuisine: Roy's Bayside Grille, Smokey's, Tasty's

4

the handsome, airy white room, which is accented with floor-to-ceiling teal-blue shutters to let in the breezes, and colorful artwork by the Blanchards' son Jesse on the walls. A masterful combination of creative cuisine, an upscale atmosphere, attentive service, and an excellent wine cellar (including a selection of aged spirits) pleases the star-studded crowd. The nuanced contemporary menu is ever changing but always delightful; house classics like corn chowder, lobster cakes, and a Caribbean sampler are crowd pleasers. For dessert, you'll remember concoctions like the key lime "pie-in-a-glass" or the justly famous "cracked coconut" long after your suntan has faded. A recent addition is a three-course prix-fixe menu that includes many of the signature dishes and is a bargain at $45. ⊠ *Box 898, Meads Bay* ☎ *264/497–6100* ⚑ *Reservations essential* ☰ *AE, MC, V* ⊘ *Closed Sun. in Aug. Closed Sept. No lunch.*

$$$ ╳ **da'Vida.** *Caribbean.* Sometimes you really can have it all. Right on exquisite Crocus Bay, this resort cum restaurant cum club is a place where you could spend the whole day dining, drinking, and lounging under umbrellas on the comfortable chairs. There are kayaks and snorkeling equipment for rent, not to mention two boutiques. You can picnic at the Beach Grill (burgers, hotdogs, wraps, salads) or head inside the main building for contemporary choices like dumplings, soups, pastas, and pizzas. Lunch starts at 11, and then you can get tapas and sunset drinks from about 3. At dinner, the stylish and relaxed wood interior (built by craftsmen from St. Vincent) is accented by candlelight. On the menu are such dishes as tasty seared snapper with

gingered kale, coconut-crusted scallops, and Angus steaks. On Fridays there's afternoon tea at 4. At night, there's often good live music. Owners David and Vida Lloyd, brother and sister, who also operate Lloyd's Guest House, grew up right here, and they have taken pains to get it all just right. ⊠ *Box 52, Crocus Bay* ☎ *264/498–5433* ⊕ *www.davida anguilla.com* ⊟ *AE, D, MC,V.*

$$ ✕ **English Rose.** *Caribbean.* Lunchtime finds this neighborhood hangout packed with locals: cops flirting with sassy waitresses, entrepreneurs brokering deals with politicos, schoolgirls in lime-green outfits doing their homework. The decor is not much to speak of, but this is a great place to eavesdrop or people-watch while enjoying island-tinged specialties like beer-battered shrimp, jerk chicken Caesar salad, snapper creole, and buffalo wings. There is karaoke on Friday. ⊠ *Main St., The Valley* ☎ *264/497–5353* ⊟ *MC, V* ⊙ *Closed Sun.*

$$ ✕ **Geraud's Patisserie.** *French.* A stunning array of absolutely delicious French pastries and breads—and universal favorites like cookies, brownies, and muffins—are produced by Le Cordon Bleu dynamo Geraud Lavest in this tiny, well-located shop. Come in the early morning for cappuccino and croissants, and pick up fixings for a wonderful lunch later (or choose from among the list of tempting daily lunch specials). Geraud also does a lively offsite catering business, from intimate villa and yacht dinners to weddings. ⊠ *South Hill Plaza* ☎ *264/497–5559* ⊟ *AE, MC, V* ⊙ *No dinner.*

★   Fodor'sChoice ✕ **Hibernia.** *Asian.* Some of the island's most
$$$$ creative dishes are served in this wood-beam cottage restaurant–art gallery overlooking the water at the far eastern end of Anguilla. Unorthodox yet delectable culinary pairings—inspired by chef-owners Raoul Rodriguez and Mary Pat's annual travels to the Far East—include Asian mushroom soup topped with cream of cauliflower, duck breast with Chinese plum and five-spice sauce with black-sesame-crusted gnocchi; a crayfish casserole with steamed rice noodles in basil and coconut milk; and roasted lobster, served with Lao purple rice and artichoke hearts filled with spinach and pine nuts in a vanilla-bean sauce. Every visit here is an opportunity to share in Mary Pat and Raoul's passion for life, expressed through the vibrant combination of setting, art, food, unique tableware, beautiful gardens, and thoughtful hospitality. ⊠ *Box 268, Island Harbour* ☎ *264/497–4290* ⊕ *hiberniarestaurant.com* ⊟ *MC, V* ⊙ *Closed mid-Aug.–mid-Oct. Call for seasonal hrs.*

Asian-inspired cuisine at Hibernia restaurant

★ **Fodor's**Choice ✕ **KoalKeel.** *Caribbean.* Dinner at KoalKeel is a unique culinary and historic treat not to be missed on Anguilla. Originally part of a sugar and cotton plantation, the restaurant, with its beautiful dining veranda, is owned and lovingly overseen by Lisa Gumbs, a descendent of the slaves once housed here. A tour of the history-rich buildings is a must. A 200-year-old rock oven is used in the on-site bakery upstairs, and with a day's notice you can enjoy a slow-roasted whole chicken from that oven. It is also used to delightful effect in the East Indies meets West Indies menu, which includes treats like tandoori-spiced lamb, spiced vegetable samosa, and tandoori roasted shrimp spring rolls. Be sure to save room for the incredible desserts. Wine lovers take note of the exceptional 15,000-bottle wine cellar, in an underground cistern. Anguilla's savvy early risers show up here for the fresh French bread, croissants, and *pain au chocolat,* which are sold out by 9 AM. ✉ *Coronation Ave., Box 640, The Valley* ☎ *264/497–2930* ⚑ *Reservations essential* ▤ *AE, MC, V.*

$$$– $$$$

$$$ ✕ **Luna Rosa.** *Italian.* Classic upscale Italian favorites, light and tasty pastas, and luscious vegetables prepared with sensitivity to the importance of authentic ingredients is a

winning formula. The eggplant Parmesan is crisp and light with an intense tomato ragout, and the wild-mushroom risotto is so delicious you may be tempted to lick your plate. The thrilling sea view and charming management are icing on the cake. ⊠ *Lower South Hill* ☎ *264/497–6810* ⌂ *Reservations essential* ⊟ *AE, MC, V* ☉ *Closed Sun.*

$$ ✕ **Madeariman Reef Bar and Restaurant.** *French.* This casual, feet-in-the-sand bistro right on busy, beautiful Shoal Bay is open for breakfast, lunch, and dinner; the soups, salads, and simple grills here are served with a bit of French flair. Come for lunch and stay to lounge on the beach chaises or barhop between here and Uncle Ernie's barbecue next door. ⊠ *Shoal Bay East* ☎ *264/497–5750* ⊟ *AE, MC, V.*

$$$–
$$$$ ✕ **Mango's.** *Seafood.* One meal at Mango's and you'll understand why it's a perennial favorite of repeat visitors to Anguilla. Sparkling-fresh fish specialties have starring roles on the menu here. Light and healthy choices like a spicy grilled whole snapper are deliciously perfect. Save room for dessert—the warm apple tart and the coconut cheesecake are worth the splurge. There's an extensive wine list, and the Cuban cigar humidor is a luxurious touch. ⊠ *Barnes Bay* ☎ *264/497–6479* ⌂ *Reservations essential* ⊟ *AE, MC, V* ☉ *Closed Tues. No lunch.*

$$$$ ✕ **Michel Rostang at Malliouhana.** *French.* Sparkling crystal and fine china, attentive service, a wonderful 25,000-bottle wine cellar, and a spectacularly romantic, open-air room complement exceptional haute cuisine rivaling any in the French West Indies. Consulting chef Michel Rostang, renowned for his exceptional Paris bistros, revamps the menu seasonally, incorporating local ingredients in both classic and contemporary preparations. The dining patio is one of the most sublime spots in the Caribbean, if not the world. The ultimate in hedonism is sipping champagne as the setting sun triggers a laser show over the bay, before repairing to your table. ⊠ *Meads Bay* ☎ *264/497–6111* ⌂ *Reservations essential* ⊟ *AE, D, MC, V* ☉ *Closed Sept. and Oct.*

$$ ✕ **Picante.** *Mexican.* This casual, bright-red roadside Carib-
☼ bean *taquería*, opened by a young California couple, serves huge, tasty burritos with a choice of fillings, fresh warm tortilla chips with first-rate guacamole, seafood enchilada, and tequila-lime chicken grilled under a brick. Passion-fruit Margaritas are a must, and the creamy Mexican chocolate pudding makes a great choice for dessert. Seating is at picnic tables; the friendly proprietors cheerfully supply pillows on request. Reservations are recommended. ⊠ *West End*

Rd., West End ☎*264/498–1616* ═*AE, MC, V* ☉*Closed Tues. No lunch*.

$$$ ✕ **Roy's Bayside Grille.** *Caribbean*. Some of the best grilled ★ lobster on the island is served up here along with burgers, fish-and-chips, and good home-style cooking, Happy hour hops from 4 to 6 every day, because of the good rum concoctions. On Sundays you can get roast beef and Yorkshire pudding, and there is free Wi-Fi. The restaurant is open every day. ✉*Sandy Ground* ☎*264/497–2470* ═*AE, MC, V.*

$$ ✕ **Smokey's.** *Barbecue*. There's no sign, so you'll have to ask ☯ the way to Cove Bay to find this quintessential Anguillian beach barbecue, part of the Gumbs family mini-empire of authentic and delicious eateries. The popular spot is freshly rebuilt after the hurricane in 2008. African-style hot wings, honey-coated smoked ribs, salt-fish cakes, curried chicken roti, and grilled lobsters are paired with local staple side dishes such as spiced-mayonnaise coleslaw, hand-cut sweet-potato strings, and crunchy onion rings. If your idea of the perfect summer lunch is a roadside lobster roll, be sure to try the version here, served on a home-baked roll with a hearty kick of hot sauce. The dinner menu includes crayfish tails and chicken in orange sauce. On Saturday afternoon a popular local band, the Musical Brothers, enlivens the casual, laid-back atmosphere, and on Sunday the restaurant is party-central for locals and visitors alike. ✉ *Cove Rd., Box 31, Cove Bay* ☎*264/497–6582* ═*AE, MC, V* ☉*Closed Mon. and May–Nov.*

★ Fodor'sChoice ✕ **Straw Hat.** *Eclectic*. Since this Anguilla favorite $$$$ moved to the beautiful sands of Meads Bay (at the Frangi-☯ pani) in 2008, its many fans now enjoy lunch and dinner seven days a week on its tropical beachfront patio. Charming owners Peter and Anne Parles, the sophisticated and original food, and friendly service are the main reasons the restaurant has been in business since the late 1990s. The menu features appealing small plates like lobster spring rolls and duck-breast flatbreads, which diners can share; or mix and match for the perfect meal. The curried goat here sets the bar for the island. And "fish of the day" truly means fish caught that day. ✉ *Frangipani Beach Club, Box 1197, Meads Bay* ☎*264/497–8300* ═*AE, D, MC, V.*

$$$ ✕**Tasty's.** *Caribbean*. Once your eyes adjust to the quirky kiwi, lilac, and coral color scheme, you'll find that breakfast, lunch, or dinner at Tasty's is, well, very tasty. It's open all day long, so if you come off a mid-afternoon plane starving, head directly here—it's right near the airport.

Straw Hat's outdoor patio on Meads Bay

Chef-owner Dale Carty trained at Malliouhana, and his careful, confident preparation bears the mark of French culinary training, but the menu is classic Caribbean. It's worth leaving the beach at lunch for the lobster salad here. A velvety pumpkin soup garnished with roasted coconut shards is superb, as are the seared jerk tuna and the garlic-infused marinated conch salad. Yummy desserts end meals on a high note. This is one of the few restaurants that do not allow smoking, so take your Cubans elsewhere for an after-dinner puff. The popular Sunday brunch buffet features island specialties like salt-fish cakes. Dale also cooks lunch at Bankie Banx's Dune Preserve on the white sands of Rendezvous Bay. ⊠ *On main road in South Hill* ☎ *264/497–2737* ⚓ *Reservations essential* ⊟ *AE, MC, V* ⊘ *Closed Thurs.*

$$$ ✕ **Trattoria Tramonto and Oasis Beach Bar.** *Italian.* The island's only beachfront Italian restaurant features a dual (or dueling) serenade of Andrea Bocelli on the sound system and gently lapping waves a few feet away. Chef Valter Belli artfully adapts recipes from his home in Emilia-Romagna. Try the delicate lobster ravioli in truffle-cream sauce, or go for a less Italian option: kangaroo steak. For dessert, don't miss the authentic tiramisu. Though you might wander in here for lunch after a swim, when casual dress is accepted, you'll still be treated to the same impressive menu. You can also choose from a luscious selection of champagne fruit drinks, a small but fairly priced Italian wine list, and homemade

grappa. ⊠ *Shoal Bay West* ☎ *264/497–8819* ⚐ *Reservations essential* ⊟ *MC, V* ☉ *Closed Mon. in Sept.–Oct.*

★ Fodor'sChoice ✕ **Veya.** *Eclectic.* On the suavely minimalist,
$$$$ draped, four-sided veranda, the stylishly appointed tables glow with flickering candlelight (white-matte sea-urchin votive holders made of porcelain). A lively lounge where chic patrons mingle and sip mojitos to the purr of soft jazz anchors the room. Inventive, sophisticated, and downright delicious, Carrie Bogar's "Cuisine of the Sun" features thoughtful but ingenious preparations of first-rate provisions. Ample portions are sharable works of art—sample Moroccan-spiced shrimp "cigars" with roast tomato–apricot chutney or Vietnamese-spiced calamari. Jerk-spiced tuna is served with a rum-coffee glaze on a juicy slab of grilled pineapple with curls of plantain crisps. Dessert is a must. Sublime warm chocolate cake with chili-roasted banana ice cream and caramelized bananas steals the show. Downstairs there is a café that serves breakfast and light lunches like salads and panini, as well as delicious bakery goodies. It opens at 6:30 AM for early risers. ⊠ *Sandy Ground, Box WE 8067,* ☎ *264/498–8392* ⚐ *Reservations essential* ⊟ *AE, MC, V* ☉ *Closed Sun. Closed weekends June, July, Sept., and Oct. Closed Aug. No lunch.*

WORD OF MOUTH. "The best meal we had in Anguilla was [at] Veya, near Sandy Ground. (We also had great dinners at Deon's Overlook, The Barrel Stay, and Zara's." –Callaloo

$$–$$$$ ✕ **Zara's.** *Eclectic.* Chef Shamash Brooks presides at this cozy restaurant with beamed ceilings, terra-cotta floors, and colorful artwork. His kitchen turns out tasty fare that combines Caribbean and Italian flavors with panache (Rasta Pasta is a specialty). Standouts include a velvety pumpkin soup with coconut milk, crunchy calamari, lemon pasta scented with garlic, herbed rack of lamb served with a roasted applesauce, and spicy fish fillet steamed in banana leaf. ⊠ *Allamanda Beach Club, Upper Shoal Bay* ☎ *264/497–3229* ⊟ *AE, D, MC, V* ☉ *No lunch.*

WHERE TO STAY

Tourism on Anguilla is a fairly recent phenomenon—most development didn't begin until the early 1980s, so most hotels and resorts are of relatively recent vintage. The lack of native topography and, indeed, vegetation, and the blindingly white expanses of beach have inspired building designs of some interest; architecture buffs might have fun

DID YOU KNOW?

With almost two miles of powdery white sand, Rendezvous Bay has only three resorts, including the luxurious CuisinArt Resort & Spa.

trying to name some of the most surprising examples. Inspiration largely comes from the Mediterranean: the Greek Islands, Morocco, and Spain, with some Miami-style art deco thrown into the mixture.

Anguilla accommodations basically fall into two categories: grand resorts and luxury resort-villas, or low-key, simple, locally owned inns and small beachfront complexes. The former can be surprisingly expensive, the latter surprisingly reasonable. In the middle are some condo-type options, with full kitchens and multiple bedrooms, which are great for families or for longer stays. At this writing, many properties are in the building, expanding, or planning stages, but current conditions preclude outlining any definite opening dates. Private villa rentals are becoming more common and are increasing in number and quality every season, as development on the island accelerates.

A good phone chat or e-mail exchange with the management of any property is a good idea, as some lodgings don't have in-room TVs, a few have no air-conditioning, and units within the same complex can vary greatly in layout, accessibility, distance to the beach, and view. When calling to reserve a room, ask about special discount packages, especially in spring and summer. Most hotels include continental breakfast in the price, and many have meal-plan options. But before you lock yourself into an expensive meal plan that you may not be able to change, keep in mind that Anguilla is home to dozens of excellent restaurants. All hotels charge a 10% tax, a $1 per-room/per-day tourism marketing levy, and—in most cases—an additional 10% service charge.

VILLAS AND CONDOMINIUM RENTAL AGENCIES

The tourist office publishes an annual *Anguilla Travel Planner* with informative listings of available vacation apartment rentals.

You can contact the **Anguilla Connection** (☎ 264/497–9852 or 800/916–3336 ⊕ *www.luxuryvillas.com*) for condo and villa listings.

Anguilla Luxury Collection (☎ 264/497–6049 ⊕ *www.anguilla luxurycollection.com*) is operated by Sue and Robin Ricketts, longtime Anguilla real estate experts, who manage a collection of first-rate villas. They also manage a range of attractive properties in the Anguilla Affordable Collection linked through the same Web site.

The largest local private villa rental company is **myCaribbean** (☎ *877/471–2733* ⊕ *www.mycaribbean.com*). Gayle Gurvey and her staff manage and rent more than 100 local villas, and have been in business for almost 10 years.

¢	$	$$	$$$	$$$$
WHAT IT COSTS IN DOLLARS				
HOTELS				
under $80	$80–$150	$150–$250	$250–$350	Over $350

Hotel prices are per night for a double room in high season, excluding taxes, service charges, and meal plans.

RECOMMENDED LODGING

$$ ⬚ **Allamanda Beach Club.** *Vacation Rental.* Youthful, active
☼ couples from around the globe happily fill this casual, three-story, white-stucco building hidden in a palm grove just off the beach, opting for location and price over luxury. Units are neat and simply furnished, with tile floors and pastel *matelassé* (heavy cotton) bedspreads; ocean views are best from the top floor. On the ground floor are four apartment suites that are good for families. People return year after year, thanks to the management's dedicated hospitality. The creative restaurant, Zara's (⇨ *above)*, is a popular draw, as is the less expensive Gwen's Reggae Grill, a boisterous and colorful beachside joint with a relaxed, frat-party atmosphere. Look into special summer packages. **Pros:** front row for all Shoal Bay's action; young crowd; good restaurant. **Cons:** location requires a car; rooms are clean, but not at all fancy; beach and pool lounges are aging poorly. ⌂ *Box 662, Upper Shoal Bay Beach AI2640* ☎ *264/497–5217* ⊕ *www. allamanda.ai* ↺ *20 units* ⌂ *In-room: kitchen. In-hotel: 2 restaurants, pool, gym, water sports, Internet terminal* ▭ *AE, D, MC, V* ⊚*EP.*

$$$$ ⬚ **Altamer.** *Vacation Rental.* Architect Myron Goldfinger's geometric symphony of floor-to-ceiling windows, cantilevered walls, and curvaceous floating staircases is fit for any king (or CEO)—as is the price tag that goes along with it. Each of the three multi-bedroom villas here has a distinct decorative theme and must be rented in its entirety; choose from Russian Amethyst, Brazilian Emerald, or African Sapphire. Striking interiors are filled with custom-made and antique pieces—Murano fixtures, Florentine linens, Turkish kilims, Fabergé ornaments, Tsarist silver candelabras. They're also outfitted with the latest gadgetry, from touchpad stereo systems to Wi-Fi. A private butler and eight staff, including a chef, anticipate your every whim. Full conference facilities make this an ideal location for corporate or family retreats of up to 40 people. **Pros:** plenty of space; lots of electronic diversions; great for big groups. **Cons:** a bit out of the way; interiors are starting to show some wear and tear. ⊠ *Shoal Bay West, The Valley* ☎ *264/498–4000* ⊕ *www.altamer.com* ⇘ *3 5-bedroom villas* ☼ *In-room: kitchen, DVD, Wi-Fi. In-hotel: tennis courts, pool, gym, beachfront, water sports, laundry service, Internet terminal* ⊟ *AE, D, DC, MC, V* ☞ *1-week minimum* ⦿ *AI.*

$$$ ☖ **Anguilla Great House Beach Resort.** *Resort.* These traditional West Indian–style bungalows strung along one of Anguilla's longest beaches evoke an old-time Caribbean feel with their cotton-candy colors, and the gentle prices and interconnected rooms appeal to families and groups of friends traveling together. Gingerbread trim frames views of the ocean from charming verandas. Rather basic rooms are decorated with local artwork, mahogany and wicker furnishings, tropical-print fabrics, and ceiling fans; some have hand-painted floral borders. Those numbered 111 to 127 offer beach proximity and the best views; newer units aren't as well situated and lack views, but have television and Internet access. The restaurant serves a mix of West Indian, Italian, and continental cuisines; the bartenders proudly ask you to sample their special concoctions, exemplifying the friendly service. The hotel can arrange in-room massage and other spa treats. **Pros:** real, old-school Caribbean; young crowd; gentle prices. **Cons:** rooms are very simple, and bathrooms are the bare basics. ⊠ *Rendezvous Bay* ☎ *264/497–6061 or 800/583–9247* ⊕ *www.anguillagreathouse.com* ⇘ *31 rooms* ☼ *In-room: refrigerator, Internet (some). In-hotel: restaurant, pool, gym, beachfront, water sports* ⊟ *AE, MC, V* ⦿ *EP.*

$$–$$$ ☖ **Arawak Beach Inn.** *Inn.* These hexagonal two-story villas are a good choice for a funky, budget-friendly, low-key guesthouse experience. The pricier units on the top floors are more spacious and a bit quieter, and enjoy spectacular views of the rocky shores of boat-dotted Island Harbor and beyond to Scilly Key. Rooms are pretty basic, but some are being upgraded at this writing, and some have kitchenettes. Most aren't air-conditioned, and those that are cost more, but the harbor breezes are usually sufficient. The inn's manager, Maria Hawkins, will make you feel like one of

the family by the time you leave. Mix your own drinks at the bar—or, if co-owner Maurice Bonham-Carter is around, have him mix you the island's best Bloody Mary. The Arawak Café, splashed in psychedelic colors, serves special pizzas and lip-smacking Caribbean comfort food. A small private cove with a sandy beach is a five-minute walk away. The common areas have Wi-Fi. **Pros:** funky, casual crowd; friendly owners; gentle rates. **Cons:** not on the beach; isolated location makes a car a must. *⌂ Box 1403, Island Harbour AI2640 ☎264/497–4888, 877/427–2925 reservations ⊕www.arawakbeach.com ⌑17 rooms ⌂ In-room: no a/c (some), safe, kitchen (some), no TV (some), Wi-Fi. In-hotel: restaurant, bar, pool, beachfront, water sports ⊟AE, MC, V ⌖⊖EP.*

★ Fodor'sChoice ⌇ **Cap Juluca.** *Resort.* Sybaritic and serene, this
$$$$ 179-acre resort wraps around breathtaking Maundays Bay.
⌁ The glittering sand is rivaled only by the dramatic, domed, white, Moorish-style villas; caring staff; and first-rate sports facilities (all on-site water sports are included in the rates). A $20-million renovation in the fall of 2008 refreshed and updated the decor, and more upgrades are on the way at this writing. In late 2009, Cap Juluca took over management of the spectacular Greg Norman–designed Temenos golf course. There's lush landscaping and a welcome reorganization of the public spaces, as well as changes in all the restaurants, with a modern but sophisticated garden-to-table approach to the cuisine. Fresh herbs and spices, grown on the premises, are used in the restaurants, and ably utilized by René Bajeux, the award-winning chef of René Bistrot in New Orleans. With a nod to the fragile environment, guests now have private solar-powered golf carts to buzz around the grounds in. Enormous and private, guest rooms are furnished with white organdy beds swathed in yards of netting canopies and Frette linens, big flat-screen TVs, resort-wide Wi-Fi, and new outdoor furniture on the private patios and the beach. The romantic atmosphere makes this resort popular for honeymoons and destination weddings. And for an especially demanding international elite clientele, the four-to-one staff-to-room ratio assures first-rate service. Facilities include a fitness center, an aqua-golf driving range, and an extensive water-sports pavilion. Standard accommodations are well laid out, spacious, and comfortable. Flexible multi-bedroom private villas with beachfront infinity pools are beautifully furnished and include a 24-hour-a-day butler. A variety of spa services can be provided in the privacy of your own accommodations,

and a daily schedule of activities like morning pool-side yoga, beach fitness, or nature walks tempts you to leave your beach chaise. Afternoon tea is served under the dome. **Pros:** golf course; lots of space to stretch out on miles of talcum-soft sand; warm service; romantic atmosphere; all on-site water sports are included, even waterskiing **Cons:** as of this writing, bathrooms are still to be updated. ⌂ *Box 240, Maundays Bay AI2640* ☎ *264/497–6779, 888/858–5822 in U.S.* ⊕ *www.capjuluca.com* ➾ *72 rooms, 7 patio suites, 6 pool villas* ⌃ *In-room: refrigerator, Wi-Fi. In-hotel: 3 restaurants, room service, bar, golf course, tennis courts, pool, gym, spa, beachfront, water sports, children's programs (ages 3–14), Wi-Fi hotspot, laundry service* ⊟ *AE, D, MC, V* ⊙ *CP.*

$$$$ ☎ **Carimar Beach Club.** *Vacation Rental.* This horseshoe of bougainvillea-draped Mediterranean-style buildings on beautiful Meads Bay has the look of a Sun Belt condo. Although only two buildings—No. 1 and No. 6—stand at the water's edge, all have balconies or patios with ocean views. Bright, white, one- and two-bedroom apartments are individually owned and thus reflect their owners' tastes, but most are well appointed, fully equipped, and carefully maintained. The kitchens were all upgraded in 2008. The cordial staff, supreme beachfront location, and several fine restaurants within walking distance make this a good choice if you really don't want to rent a car. If you want a TV you can rent one for $50 a week. **Pros:** tennis courts; easy walk to restaurants and spa; right next door to Malliouhana; laundry facilities. **Cons:** no pool or restaurant; only bedrooms have a/c. ⊠ *Meads Bay* ⌂ *Box 327, The Valley AI2640* ☎ *264/497–6881 or 800/235–8667* ⊕ *www.carimar.com* ➾ *24 apartments* ⌃ *In-room: kitchen, no TV. In-hotel: tennis courts, beachfront, water sports, Internet terminal* ⊟ *AE, MC, V* ⊙ *Closed Sept. and Oct.* ⊙ *EP.*

$$$$ ☎ **Covecastles Villa Resort.** *Vacation Rental.* Though this secluded Myron Goldfinger–designed enclave resembles a series of giant concrete baby carriages from the outside, the airy curves and angles of the skylighted interiors are comfortable, if a little dated, with the sort of oversize wicker furniture, and raw-silk accessories that defined resort-chic in the late 1980s. Louvered Brazilian walnut doors and windows perfectly frame tranquil views of St. Martin. Units are equipped with current amenities like flat-screen TVs and DVD players, but the Formica kitchens and standard-issue bathrooms could stand some upgrading, especially at these prices. The Point, the newest unit, features five large

CuisinArt Resort & Spa

The Viceroy

bedrooms right on the beach and a private pool and hot tub on a broad oceanfront terrace. There is also a fitness facility. At this writing the management is offering 20% off all rates, so be sure to ask if any unpublished discounts are available when you book. **Pros:** secluded large private villas; private beach with reef for snorkeling; great service. **Cons:** beach is small and rocky; located at the far end of the island. ⌂ *Box 248, Shoal Bay West AI2640* ☎ *264/497–6801 or 800/223–1108* ⊕ *www.covecastles.com* ➫ *16 apartments* ⟁ *In-room: DVD, Internet. In-hotel, room service, tennis courts, gym, beachfront, water sports, bicycles, laundry service* ▭ *AE, MC, V* ⏍ *EP.*

★ Fodor'sChoice ☒ **CuisinArt Resort and Spa.** *Resort.* This family-
$$$$ friendly beachfront resort's design—gleaming white-stucco
☻ buildings, blue domes and trim, glass-block walls—blends art deco with a Greek Islands feel. Huge rooms were refurnished and redecorated in 2008, painted in a calming sky blue and fitted with flat-screen TVs. Guests return in droves to enjoy the casual atmosphere, full-service spa, extensive sports facilities, and the fulfill-every-wish concierge crew, who provide everything from vacation-long nannies to local cell phones to dinner reservations. Continuing facility upgrades include a spacious health club with a Technogym system and spa with dozens of personalized treatments. High-season children's programs give parents a chance to enjoy the holiday, too. A hydroponic farm provides ultrafresh organic produce for the two restaurants; tours of the greenhouse, lush tropical gardens, and orchards are fun and engaging. Cooking classes and demonstrations are conducted in the teaching kitchen, and enjoyed at a Chef's Table twice a week. Six private villas opened in 2009. **Pros:** family-friendly; great spa and sports; gorgeous beach and gardens. **Cons:** food service can be slow; pool area is noisy. ⌂ *Box 2000, Rendezvous Bay AI2640* ☎ *264/498–2000 or 800/943–3210* ⊕ *www.cuisinartresort.com* ➫ *93 rooms, 2 penthouses, 6 villas* ⟁ *In-room: safe, refrigerator, Internet. In-hotel: 3 restaurants, bars, tennis courts, pool, gym, spa, beachfront, water sports, bicycles, laundry service* ▭ *AE, D, MC, V* ⏍ *Closed Sept. and Oct.* ⏍ *EP.*

$$$$ ☒ **Frangipani Beach Club.** *Resort.* This flamingo-pink Mediterranean-style complex on the beautiful champagne sands of Meads Bay was redone in 2008, and is under new management as of 2009. The attractive units are nicely decorated and fully equipped, with brand-new kitchens and marble baths. Perfect for independent travelers, the feel here is more condo than resort. Accommodations range from simple rooms to a three-bedroom suite. Larger units have full kitchens and laundry facilities, and are well suited for families and for longer stays. Special packages and rates that include meals and excursions are often offered. Straw Hat restaurant (*see* ⇨ *Where to Eat*), an island favorite, relocated here with the renovation, and serves all day long on a broad patio right on the beach. ■TIP→ **Try to get a room with an ocean view; Nos. 1 to 8 have the best vistas.** **Pros:** great beach; good location for restaurants and resort-hopping; first-rate on-site restaurant; helpful staff. **Cons:** not the greatest pool area. ⌂ *Box 1655, Meads Bay AI2640* ☎ *264/497–6442 or 866/780–5165* ⊕ *www.frangipaniresort.com* ⇨ *18 rooms, 7 suites* ⌂ *In-room: kitchen (some), Internet. In-hotel: restaurant, bar, tennis court, pool, beachfront, water sports, laundry facilities* ⊟ *AE, MC, V* ⏐◎⏐ *EP* ⊗ *Closed Sept. and Oct.*

$$$–
$$$$
☼

⊡ **Indigo Reef.** *Vacation Rental.* If you are looking for the antidote to the big resort developments on the island but still want attractive, modern, private villa accommodations close to the restaurants, resorts, and beautiful beaches of West End, this intimate enclave of eight small villas (one- to four-bedroom) nestled at the tip of the island could be just the thing. Designed and built in 2004 by (architect) Iain and (artist) Aileen Smith, who left Scotland for the Caribbean more than 30 years ago, these individually owned beach cottages, each named for a flower, are private, attractive, well-equipped, reasonably priced, and set in small but exquisite tropical gardens. Some have outdoor showers, and two have private plunge pools. There is a small private beach of the wild and rocky variety that is great for snorkeling, but the stunning sands of Shoal Bay West are a 10-minute walk—and are worth the trouble. A central public area includes a pool, library, and BBQ patio. As with most villas on the island, there is daily maid service. **Pros:** cozy, fresh, and well designed; great for groups traveling together; far from the madding crowd but still on the West End. **Cons:** the beach here is rocky and the water's rough; a/c only in bedrooms; must have car. ⊠ *Indigo Reef, West End* ☎ *264/497–6144* ⊕ *www.indigoreef.com* ⇨ *8 villas* ⌂ *In-room: a/c, kitchen, DVD, Wi-Fi. In-hotel: pools, laundry facilities, laundry service, Wi-Fi hotspot, some pets allowed* ⊟ *MC, V* ⏐◎⏐ *EP.*

$$$–
$$$$
★
☼

⊡ **Kú.** *Hotel.* This all-suites hotel is modeled on the barefoot chic of Miami's South Beach; the airy white apartments have lime and turquoise decorative accents, glass and chrome furniture, and balconies overlooking the beach or the pool. It's a great choice for young people because of the relaxed attitude and relatively gentle room rates. Plans are underway for upgrades to the property for 2011. The location on 1½-mi-long (2½-km-long) Shoal Bay Beach, with its string of lively beach grills and dive shops, is a winner. The open-air restaurant hops at breakfast, lunch, and dinner with omelets, salads, pizza, grilled seafood, and burgers and the famous fish-and-chips of Chef Deon. The 70-foot-long beachside bar serves up snacks and frosty drinks as well as such entertainments as live music and karaoke, but Shoal Bay regulars know that the spectacular sunsets are reason enough to hang till dark. Top off the whole package with a St. Barth–style beachwear boutique (ZaZaa) and a minimarket to provision your unit's kitchen. **Pros:** beautiful beach with tropical sunsets; the convenience of apartment living; several walkable dining options; good beds with nice linens. **Cons:** bathrooms are small and older; decor is pleasant but not luxurious. ⌂ *Box 51, Shoal Bay East AI2640* ☎ *264/497–2011 or 800/869–5827* ⊕ *www. kuanguilla.com* ⊸ *27 suites* ⌂ *In-room: kitchen, Internet. In-hotel: restaurant, bar, pool, gym, spa, beachfront, water sports* ⊟ *AE, MC, V* ⦿ *EP.*

$$$$ 🖵 **Malliouhana Hotel and Spa.** *Resort.* European refinement ⌚ in a tranquil beach setting, attentive service, fine dining, and a plethora of activities keep the international clientele returning, despite nearly universal agreement that a general refurbishment is overdue. The restaurant has been newly refurbished for 2010, and the redesigned gardens are lovely; a new resort manager will, we hope, bring further much-needed updates and upgrades. The oversized rooms have high ceilings, large balconies, and marble baths, although the decor is rather dated. Some suites even have private hot tubs; one has a private swimming pool. Extensive facilities allow you to be as active—or sedentary—as you wish: spend your days snorkeling, waterskiing, or fishing, or just relax at the spa or take a leisurely stroll along mile-long Meads Bay. Malliouhana is family-friendly. Kids enjoy a beachside pirate-ship playground, playroom, and separate dining facilities. However, only the one-bedroom suites have TVs, except on request. Summer packages offer two rooms for the price of one. **Pros:** huge rooms; stellar dining on a beautiful terrace over the sea; caring service. **Cons:** the beach drops off at the edge, and the water can be rough; dated decor; shabby outdoor furniture. ⌂ *Box 173, Meads Bay AI2640* ☎ *264/497–6011 or 800/835–0796* ⊕ *www. malliouhana.com* ⊸ *34 rooms, 6 junior suites, 13 suites*

⛱ *In-room: safe, refrigerator, no TV (some). In-hotel: 2 restaurants, room service, bars, tennis courts, pools, gym, spa, beachfront, water sports, laundry service, Internet terminal* ▭ *AE, MC, V* ⊘ *Closed Sept. and Oct.* ⓄⅠ *EP.*

$$$–
$$$$
★
☾
🍴 **Paradise Cove.** *Vacation Rental.* This simple complex of reasonably priced one- and two-bedroom apartments compensates for its location away from the beach with two whirlpools, a large pool, and tranquil tropical gardens where you can pluck fresh guavas for breakfast. The beautiful Cove and Rendezvous bays are just a few minutes' stroll away. Spotless units are appointed with somewhat generic white rattan and natural wicker furniture, gleaming white-tile floors, large kitchens, and soft floral or pastel fabrics ranging from mint to mango. Second-floor units have high-beamed ceilings. Maid service and private cooks are available. Very reasonable seven-night packages include a car. **Pros:** reasonable rates; great pool; lovely gardens. **Cons:** a bit far from the beach; decor is bland. ✉ *Box 135, The Cove AI2640* ☎ *264/497–6959 or 264/497–6603* ⊕ *www.paradise.ai* ⮑ *12 studio suites, 17 1- and 2-bedroom apartments* ⛱ *In-room: kitchen (some), Wi-Fi. In-hotel: restaurant, bar, pools, gym, laundry facilities, laundry service, Internet terminal* ▭ *AE, MC, V* ⓄⅠ *EP.*

$$–$$$
☾
🍴 **Serenity Cottages.** *Vacation Rental.* Despite the name of this property, it comprises not cottages but rather large, fully equipped, and relatively affordable one- and two-bedroom apartments (and studios created from lock-outs) in a small complex at the farthest end of glorious Shoal Bay Beach. The restaurant is on a breezy veranda near the beach. Guests gather on mismatched Adirondack-type chairs for sundowner cocktails. But there isn't much attention from staff, so stay here only if you are self-sufficient. **Pros:** big apartments; quiet end of beach; snorkeling right outside the door. **Cons:** no pool, generic decor; more condo than hotel in terms of staff; location at the end of Shoal Bay pretty much requires a car and some extra time to drive to the West End. ✉ *Upper Bay, Shoal Bay East* ☎ *264/497–3328* ⊕ *www.serenity.ai* ⮑ *2 1-bedroom suites, 8 2-bedroom apartments* ⛱ *In-room: kitchen. In-hotel: restaurant, bar, beachfront, Internet terminal* ▭ *AE, MC, V* ⊘ *Closed Sept.* ⓄⅠ *EP.*

$$$$
★
☾
🍴 **Sheriva.** *Hotel.* This intimate, luxury-villa hotel opened in 2006, offering a glimpse into the future of Anguilla's high-end lodgings. Three cavernous private villas containing a total of 20 guest rooms and 7 private swimming pools overlook a broad swath of turquoise sea. The villas can be divided into one- to seven-bedroom residences, completely

outfitted with all kinds of amenities: fully-equipped offices, exercise rooms, multiple plasma TVs, video libraries, and poker tables. Besides these perks, you have a concierge, a private chef to prepare your meals (these cost extra), and an attentive housekeeping staff that even does your laundry. Private golf carts shuttle Sheriva guests to nearby Cap Juluca for beach, tennis, spa, and restaurants, with signing privileges. **Pros:** incredible staff to fulfill every wish; all the comforts of home and more; good value for large family groups. **Cons:** not on the beach; you risk being spoiled for life by the staff's attentions. ✉ *Maundays Bay Rd., West End* ☎ *264/498–9898* ⊕ *www.sheriva.com* ➭ *20 rooms* ☖ *In-room: kitchen, DVD, Wi-Fi. In-hotel: pools, laundry service* ▤ *AE, MC, V* ⫼⦿⫼ *EP.*

$–$$$$ ⟟ **Sirena.** *Hotel.* Young management and a hip, modern look please new and repeat visitors to this low-key resort overlooking Meads Bay. Although small, the standard rooms have fresh white paint, flat-screen TVs, comfy beds, and contemporary touches of Asian decor. Budget-conscious travelers appreciate the garden suites and larger villas, which have full kitchens. Junior suites have kitchenettes, big granite bathrooms, and whirlpool baths. The restaurant is a gathering spot for guests, many of whom choose a meal plan that includes breakfast and dinner or, for more flexibility, purchase meal vouchers for a part of their stay. Though the five-minute walk to the beach is not the prettiest, you'll find thatched umbrellas and chaises when you get there. **Pros:** modern, clean, and well equipped; good value; nice high-tech amenities. **Cons:** long walk to the beach with many stairs; services and facilities are basic. ⌖ *Box 200, Meads Bay AI2640* ☎ *264/497–6827 or 877/647–4736* ⊕ *www.sirenaresort.com* ➭ *4 villas* ☖ *In-room: safe, kitchen (some), no TV, Wi-Fi. In-hotel: restaurant, bar, pools, diving, bicycles, laundry service* ▤ *AE, D, MC, V* ⫼⦿⫼ *CP.*

★ Fodor'sChoice   ⟟ **The Viceroy.** *Resort.* Set on a promontory
$$$$ over 3,200 feet of the gorgeous pearly sand on Meads
☺   Bay, Kelly Wurstler's haute-hip showpiece will wow the chic international-sophisticate set, especially those lucky enough to stay in one of the spacious two- to five-bedroom villas, complete with private infinity pools and hot tubs, indoor-outdoor showers, electronics galore, and a gourmet/professional kitchen stuffed with high-end equipment. But even the standard rooms (studios and one-bedroom suites) are grand and brimming with glamorous luxuries. There is a full spa, gym, and yoga center, a camplike kid's program, tons of activities, and five restaurants ranging from

beach barbecue to a banquet. The warm but professional management keeps everything as cool and suave as the fashionable guests. If you want a funky, toes-in-the sand and piña colada-with-umbrella escape, look elsewhere, but nothing currently on Anguilla can compare with the Viceroy's posh style. **Pros:** state-of-the-art luxury; cutting-edge contemporary design; flexible, spacious rooms. **Cons:** international rather than Caribbean in feel; very large resort; kind of a see-and-be-seen scene; there is still some construction going on.

✉ *Barnes Bay, Box 8028, West End* ☎ *264/497–7000, 866/270-7798 in the U.S.* ⊕ *www.viceroyhotelsandresorts. com* ⇨ *163 suites, 3 villas* ⚓ *In-room: safe, kitchen (some), refrigerator (some), DVD, Wi-Fi. In-hotel: 5 restaurants, room service, bars, tennis courts, pools, gym, spa, beachfront, diving, water sports, bicycles, children's programs (ages 2–12), laundry facilities, laundry service, Internet terminal, Wi-Fi hotspot, some pets allowed* ⊟ *AE, MC, V* ☉ *Closed Sept.* ⊚ *CP.*

BEACHES

You can always tell a true beach fanatic: say "Anguilla" and watch for signs of ecstasy. They say there are 33 beaches on the island's 34 square miles; we say, "Who's counting? Pack the sunscreen!"

Renowned for their beauty, Anguilla's 30-plus dazzling white-sand beaches are renowned. You can find long, deserted stretches for sunset walks, or beaches lined with lively bars and restaurants— all surrounded by crystal clear warm waters of turquoise. Depending on the season and the seas, there are areas where swimming is not recommended, including Captain's Bay and Katouche Bay, due to strong westerly currents and potentially dangerous undertows. Note that the topless bathing common on some of the French islands is strictly forbidden here. ⚠ As anywhere, exercise caution in remote locations, and never swim alone, and do not leave personal property in parked cars—theft can be a problem, especially at Little Bay.

NORTHEAST COAST

Captain's Bay. On the north coast just before the eastern tip of the island, this quarter-mile stretch of perfect white sand is bounded on the left by a rocky shoreline where Atlantic waves crash. If you make the tough, four-wheel-drive-only trip along the dirt road that leads to the northeastern end of the island toward Junk's Hole, you'll be rewarded with peaceful isolation. The surf here slaps the sands with a vengeance, and the undertow is strong—so wading is the safest water sport. And if you are lucky, you might spot dolphins right off the shore.

Island Harbour. These mostly calm waters are surrounded by a slender beach. For centuries Anguillians have ventured from these sands in colorful handmade fishing boats. Its not much of a beach for swimming or lounging, but there are a couple of restaurants (Hibernia, Arawak Café, Côtée Mer, and Smitty's), and this is the departure point for the three-minute boat ride to Scilly Cay, where a thatched beach bar serves seafood. Just hail the restaurant's free boat and plan to spend most of the day (the all-inclusive lunch starts at $40 and is worth the price—Wednesday, Friday, and Sunday only). Be sure to pack a mask and snorkel, because there is a reef right off the beach.

NORTHWEST COAST

Barnes Bay. Between Meads Bay and West End Bay, this little cove is a good spot for windsurfing and snorkeling, but at this writing the beach still hasn't recovered from Hurricane Omar in 2008. Public access is on the road to Mango's restaurant and Caribella resort.

Little Bay. Little Bay is on the north coast between Crocus Bay and Shoal Bay, not far from the Valley. Sheer cliffs lined with agave and creeping vines rise behind a small gray-sand beach, usually accessible only by water (it's a favored spot for snorkeling and night dives). The easiest way to get here is a five-minute boat ride from Crocus Bay (about $10 round-trip). The young and agile can clamber down the cliffs by rope to explore the caves and surrounding reef; this is the only way to access the beach from the road, and is not recommended for inexperienced climbers. Do not leave personal items in cars parked here, because theft can be a problem.

Road Bay (*Sandy Ground*). The big pier here is where the cargo ships dock, but so do some pretty sweet yachts, sailboats, and fishing boats. The brown-sugar sand is home to terrific restaurants that hop from day through dawn, including Veya, Roy's Bayside Grille, Ripples, Barrel Stay, the Pumphouse, and Elvis' quintessential beach bar. There are all kinds of boat charters available here. The snorkeling isn't very good, but the sunset vistas are glorious, especially with a rum punch in your hand.

Shoal Bay, considered by many to be the most beautiful beach on Anguilla

Sandy Island. A popular day-trip for Anguilla visitors, tiny Sandy Island shelters a pretty lagoon, nestled in coral reefs about 2 mi from Road Bay. Most of the operators in Sandy Ground can bring you here.

★ **Fodor's Choice Shoal Bay.** Anchored by sea grape and coconut trees, the 2-mi powdered-sugar strand at Shoal Bay (not to be confused with Shoal Bay West at the other end of the island)—is universally considered one of the world's prettiest beaches. You can park free at any of the restaurants, including Elodia's, Ernies, or Gwen's Reggae Grill, most of which either rent or provide chairs and umbrellas for patrons for about $20 a day per person. There is plenty of room to stretch out in relative privacy, or you can bar-hop, take a ride on Junior's Glass Bottom Boat, or arrange a wreck dive at PADI-certified Shoal Bay Scuba near Kú, where ZaZaa, the island's chic-est boutique will satisfy fans of St. Barth shopping. The relatively broad beach has shallow water that is usually gentle, making this a great family beach; a coral reef not far from the shore is a wonderful snorkeling spot. Sunsets over the water are spectacular. You can even enjoy a beachside massage at Malakh, a little spa near Madeariman's.

SOUTHEAST COAST

Sandy Hill. You can park anywhere along the dirt road to Sea Feathers Bay to visit this popular fishing center. What's good for the fishermen is also good for snorkelers. But the beach here is not much of a lounging spot. The sand is too narrow and rocky for that. However, it's a great place to buy lobsters and fish fresh out of the water in the afternoon.

SOUTHWEST COAST

★ Fodor'sChoice **Cove Bay.** Follow the signs to Smokey's at the end of Cove Road, and you will find water that is brilliantly blue and sand that is as soft as sifted flour. It's just as spectacular as its neighbors Rendezvous Bay and Maundays Bay. You can walk here from Cap Juluca for a change of pace, or you can arrange a horseback ride along the beach. Weekend barbecues with terrific local bands at Smokey's are an Anguillian "must."

★ Fodor'sChoice **Maundays Bay.** The dazzling, mile-long platinum-white beach is especially great for swimming and long beach walks. It's no wonder that Cap Juluca, one of Anguilla's premier resorts, chose this as its location. Public parking is straight ahead at the end of the road near Cap Juluca's Pimms restaurant. You can have lunch or dinner at Cap Juluca (just be prepared for the cost), and if you dine, you can also rent chaises and umbrellas from the resort for the day. Depending on the season, you can book a massage in one of the beachside tents.

Rendezvous Bay. Follow the signs to Anguilla Great House for public parking at this broad swath of pearl-white sand that is some 1½ mi long. The beach is lapped by calm, bluer-than-blue water and a postcard-worthy view of St. Martin. The expansive crescent is home to three resorts; stop in for a drink or a meal at one of the hotels, or rent a chair and umbrella at one of the kiosks. Don't miss the day-long party at the tree-house Dune Preserve, where Bankie Banx, Anguilla's most famous musician, presides and where Dale Carty (of Tasty's fame) cooks delicious barbecue and fixes great salads.

Shoal Bay West. This glittering bay bordered by mangroves and sea grapes is a lovely place to spend the day. This mile-long sweep of sand is home to the architecturally dazzling Covecastles and Altamer villas. The tranquillity is sublime, with coral reefs for snorkeling not too far from shore. Punctuate your day with a meal at beachside Trattoria Tramonto. Reach the beach by taking the main road to the West End and bearing to the left at the fork, then continue to the end. Note that similarly named Shoal Bay is a separate beach on a different part of the island.

SPORTS AND ACTIVITIES

Anguilla's expanding sports options are enhanced by its beautiful first golf course, designed by Greg Norman to accentuate the natural terrain and maximize the stunning ocean views over Rendezvous Bay. Players say the par-72, Troon-managed course is reminiscent of Pebble Beach. Personal experience says: bring a lot of golf balls! The Anguilla Tennis Academy, designed by noted architect Myron Goldfinger, operates in the Blowing Point area. The 1,000-seat stadium, equipped with pro shop and seven lighted courts, was created to attract major international matches and to provide a first-class playing option to tourists and locals.

BOATING AND SAILING

Anguilla is the perfect place to try all kinds of water sports. The major resorts offer complimentary Windsurfers, paddleboats, and water skis to their guests.

Island Yacht Charters (✉ *Sandy Ground* ☎ *264/497–3743 or 264/235–6555*) rents the 35-foot, teak *Pirate* powerboat

A Day at the Boat Races

CLOSE UP

If you want a different kind of trip to Anguilla, try for a visit during Carnival, which starts on the first Monday in August and continues for about 10 days. Colorful parades, beauty pageants, music, delicious food, arts-and-crafts shows, fireworks, and nonstop partying are just the beginning. The music starts at sunrise jam sessions—as early as 4 AM—and continues well into the night. The high point? The boat races. They are the national passion and the official national sport of Anguilla.

Anguillians from around the world return home to race old-fashioned, made-on-the-island wooden boats that have been in use on the island since the early 1800s. Similar to some of today's fastest sailboats, these are 15 to 28 feet in length and sport only a mainsail and jib on a single 25-foot mast. The sailboats have no deck, so heavy bags of sand, boulders, and sometimes even people are used as ballast. As the boats reach the finish line, the ballast—including some of the sailors—gets thrown into the water in a furious effort to win the race. Spectators line the beaches and follow the boats on foot, by car, and by even more boats. You'll have almost as much fun watching the fans as the races.

and the 30-foot Beneteau *Eros* sailboat and organizes snorkeling, sightseeing, and fishing expeditions.

If your hotel lacks facilities, you can get in gear at **Sandy Island Enterprises** (⊠ *Sandy Ground* ☎ *264/476–6534*), which rents Sunfish and Windsurfers and arranges fishing charters.

DIVING

Sunken wrecks; a long barrier reef; terrain encompassing walls, canyons, and hulking boulders; varied marine life, including greenback turtles and nurse sharks; and exceptionally clear water—all of these make for excellent diving. Prickly Pear Cay is a favorite spot. **Stoney Bay Marine Park,** off the northeast end of Anguilla, showcases the late-18th-century *El Buen Consejo*, a 960-ton Spanish galleon that sank here in 1772. Other good dive sites include **Grouper Bowl,** with exceptional hard-coral formations; **Ram's Head,** with caves, chutes, and tunnels; and **Upper Flats,** where you are sure to see stingrays.

DID YOU KNOW?

Fishermen in Anguilla often fish for albacore tuna, wahoo, barracuda, and kingfish in local waters.

Anguillian Divers (✉ *Meads Bay* ☎ *264/497–4750* ⊕ *anguilliandiver.com*) is a full-service dive operator with a PADI five-star training center.

Shoal Bay Scuba and Watersports (☎ *264/497–4371* ⊕ *www.shoalbayscuba.com*) is in beautiful Shoal Bay. Single-tank dives start at $50, two-tank dives, $80. Daily snorkel trips at 1 PM are $25 per person.

FISHING

Albacore, wahoo, marlin, barracuda, and kingfish are among the fish angled after off Anguilla's shores. You can strike up a conversation with almost any fisherman you see on the beach, and chances are, you'll be a welcome addition on his next excursion. If you'd rather make more formal arrangements, **Johnno's Beach Stop** (☎ *264/497–2728*) in Sandy Ground has a boat and can help you plan a trip.

GOLF

Temenos Golf Club (*Long Bay* ☎ *264/498–5602*), the 7,200-yard, $50-million wonder designed by superstar Greg Norman, has 13 of its 18 holes directly on the water. Now managed by Cap Juluca, the course features sweeping sea vistas and an ecologically responsible watering system of ponds and lagoons that snake through the grounds. Players thrill to the spectacular vistas of St. Maarten and blue sea at the tee box of the 390-yard starting hole. The fairway descends over 40 feet to a narrow, two-tiered green sitting precariously on the edge of a saltwater lagoon. This first hole has been called "the Caribbean's answer to the 18th at Pebble Beach." At this writing, the greens fee for a round of 18 holes during peak times is $225 per person. Discounted greens fees will be offered for twilight tee times.

GUIDED TOURS

A round-the-island tour by taxi takes about 2½ hours and costs $55 for one or two people, $5 for each additional passenger.

Bennie's Tours (✉ *Blowing Point* ☎ *264/497–2788*) is one of the island's more reliable tour operators.

Malliouhana Travel & Tours (✉ *The Quarter* ☎ *264/497–2431*) will create personalized package tours of the island.

The **Old Valley Tour** (☎264/497–2263), created by longtime resident Frank Costin, ambles up Crocus Hill, a treasure trove of Anguilla's best-preserved historic edifices, including Ebenezer's Methodist Church (the island's oldest), the Warden's Place, and typical turn-of-the-20th-century cottages (most housing galleries). The tour is by appointment only, and offers a fascinating insight into Anguillian architecture, past and present.

Sir Emile Gumbs (☎264/497–2759 *or 800/553–4939 for Anguilla Tourist Office, 264/497–2711 direct to Sir Emile*), the island's former chief minister, offers a guided tour of the Sandy Ground area. This tour, which highlights historic and ecological sites, is on Tuesday at 10 AM. The $20 fee benefits the Anguilla Archaeological Historical Society. Gumbs also organizes bird-watching expeditions that show you everything from frigate birds to turtle doves. You can book the tour through the Anguilla Tourist Office or through Sir Emile directly.

HORSEBACK RIDING

The scenic Gibbons nature trails, along with any of the island's miles of beaches, are perfect places to ride, even for the novice. Ride English- or Western-style or take lessons at **El Rancho Del Blues** (☎264/497–6334). The stable is near Anguilla Gases, across from Bennie's Tours on the Blowing Point Road. Prices start at $25 to $35 per hour ($50 for two-hour rides).

Seaside Stables (✉ *Paradise Dr., Cove Bay* ☎264/497–3667 ⊕ *www.seaside-stables-anguilla.com*), located in Cove Bay, offers rides and instruction, if a sunset gallop (or slow clomp) has always been your fantasy. Private rides at any time of the day are about $75, and prior experience is not required. They have English saddles, as well as some Western and Australian.

SEA EXCURSIONS

A number of boating options are available for airport transfers, day trips to offshore cays or neighboring islands, night trips to St. Martin, or just whipping through the waves en route to a picnic spot.

Chocolat (✉ *Sandy Ground* ☎264/497–3394) is a 35-foot catamaran available for private charter or scheduled excursions to nearby cays. Captain Rollins is a knowledgeable,

Little Bay, on Anguilla's northwest shore

affable guide. Rates for day sails with lunch are about $80 per person.

Funtime Charters (✉ *The Cove* ☎ *264/497–6511*) operates five powerboats ranging in size from 32 to 38 feet.

For an underwater peek without getting wet, catch a ride ($20 per person) on **Junior's Glass Bottom Boat** (✉ *Sandy Ground* ☎ *264/235–1008* ⊕ *www.junior.ai*). Snorkel trips and instruction are available, too.

No Fear Sea Tours (✉ *The Cove* ☎ *264/235–6354*) has three 32-foot speedboats and a 19-foot ski boat.

Picnic, swimming, and diving excursions to Prickly Pear Cay, Sandy Island, and Scilly Cay are available through **Sandy Island Enterprises** (☎ *264/476–6534*).

NIGHTLIFE

In late February or early March, reggae star and impresario Bankie Banx stages Moonsplash, a three-day music festival that showcases local and imported talent around the nights of the full moon. At the end of July is the International Arts Festival, which hosts artists from around the world. BET (Black Entertainment Television) sponsors the Tranquility Jazz Festival in November, attracting major musicians such as Michel Camilo, James Moody, Bobby Watson, and Dee Dee Bridgewater.

Most hotels and many restaurants offer live entertainment in high season and on weekends, ranging from pianists and jazz combos to traditional steel and calypso bands. Check the local tourist magazines and newspaper for listings. Friday and Saturday, Sandy Ground is the hot spot; Wednesday and Sunday the action shifts to Shoal Bay East.

The nightlife scene here runs late into the night—the action doesn't really start until after 11 PM. If you do not rent a car, be aware that taxis are not readily available at night. If you plan to take a taxi back to your hotel or villa at the end of the night, be sure to make arrangements in advance with the driver who brings you or with your hotel concierge.

The funky **Dune Preserve** (⊠ *Rendezvous Bay* ☎ *264/497–6219*) is the driftwood-fabricated home of Bankie Banx, Anguilla's famous reggae star. He performs here weekends and during the full moon. Kevin Bacon also plays here when he's on the island. There's a dance floor and a beach bar, and sometimes you can find a sunset beach barbecue in progress. In high season there's a $15 cover charge.

★ Fodor'sChoice **Elvis' Beach Bar** (⊠ *Sandy Ground* ☎ *264/772–0637*) is the perfect locale (it's actually a boat) to hear great music and sip the best rum punch on earth. The bar is open every day but Tuesday, and there's live music on Wednesday through Sunday nights during the high season—as well as food until 1 AM. Check to see if there's a full-moon LunaSea party. You won't be disappointed.

★ Things are lively at **Johnno's Beach Stop** (⊠ *Sandy Ground* ☎ *264/497–2728*), with live music and alfresco dancing every night and on Sunday afternoon, when just about everybody drops by. This is *the* classic Caribbean beach bar, attracting a funky eclectic mix, from locals to movie stars.

★ At the **Pumphouse** (⊠ *Sandy Ground* ☎ *264/497–5154*), in the old rock-salt factory, you can find live music most nights—plus surprisingly good pub grub, celebrities like Bruce Willis and Charlie Sheen, and a mini-museum of artifacts and equipment from 19th-century salt factories. There's calypso-soca on Thursday; it's open from noon until 3 AM daily, except Sunday.

SHOPPING

Anguilla is by no means a shopping destination. In fact, if your suitcase is lost, you will be hard-pressed to secure even the basics on-island. If you're a hard-core shopping enthusiast, a day trip to nearby St. Martin will satisfy. Well-heeled visitors sometimes organize boat or plane charters through their hotel concierge for daylong shopping excursions to St. Barth. The island's tourist publication, *What We Do in Anguilla,* has shopping tips and is available free at the airport and in shops. Pyrat rums—golden elixirs blending up to nine aged and flavored spirits—are a local specialty available at the Anguilla Rums distillery and several local shops. For upscale designer sportswear, check out the small boutiques in hotels (some are branches of larger stores in Marigot on St. Martin). Outstanding local artists sell their work in galleries, which often arrange studio tours (you can also check with the Anguilla Tourist Office).

CLOTHING

Boutique at Malliouhana (⊠ *Malliouhana, Meads Bay* ☎ *264/497–6111*) specializes in such upscale designer specialties as jewelry by Oro De Sol, luxurious swim fashion by Manuel Canovas and La Perla, and Robert La Roche sunglasses.

Boutique Blu (⊠ *CuisinArt Resort and Spa, Rendezvous Bay* ☎ *264/498–2000*) carries custom designs by the renowned jewelers Alberto e Lina, as well as Helen Kaminski accessories and more brand-name merchandise.

Caribbean Fancy (⊠ *West End* ☎ *264/497–3133*) sells Ta-Tee's line of crinkle-cotton resort wear, plus books, spices, perfumes, wines, and gift items.

Caribbean Silkscreen (⊠ *South Hill* ☎ *264/497–2272*) creates designs and prints them on golf shirts, hats, sweatshirts, and jackets.

Irie Life (⊠ *South Hill* ☎ *264/497–6526*) sells vividly hued beach and resort wear and flip-flops.

Head to **Why Knot** (⊠ *West End Rd., West End, between Cheddie's Carving Studio and the Shell gas station* ☎ *264/772–7685*) for Fabiana's jewel-color cotton tie-able garments, and the beads and sandals that perfectly accessorize them. If the road sign says KNOT TODAY come back later.

Sue Ricketts, the First Lady of Anguilla marketing, opened the fun **ZaZaa** (⊠ *Kú Resort, Shoal Bay* ☎ *264/235–8878* *anguillaluxurycollection.com*) boutique at Kú on Shoal Bay. It offers Anguillian crafts as well as wonderful ethnic jewelry and beachwear from around the globe, like sexy Brazilian bikinis and chic St. Barth goodies. There are beach sundries and souvenirs as well. Another location is in South Hill Plaza.

HANDICRAFTS

Anguilla Arts and Crafts Center (✉ *Brooks Building, The Valley* ☎ *264/729–4825*) carries island crafts, including textiles and ceramics. Of particular interest are unique ceramics by Otavia Fleming, lovely spotted glaze items with adorable lizards climbing on them. Look for special exhibits and performances—ranging from puppetry to folk dance—sponsored by the Anguilla National Creative Arts Alliance.

Cheddie's Carving Studios (✉ *West End Rd., The Cove* ☎ *264/497–6027*) showcases Cheddie Richardson's fanciful wood carvings and coral and stone sculptures.

Devonish Art Gallery (✉ *West End Rd., George Hill* ☎ *264/497–2949*) purveys the wood, stone, and clay creations of Courtney Devonish, an internationally known potter and sculptor, plus creations by his wife, Carolle, a bead artist. Also available are works by other Caribbean artists and regional antique maps.

★ **Hibernia Restaurant and Gallery** (✉ *Island Harbour* ☎ *264/497– 4290*) has striking pieces culled from the owners' travels, from contemporary Eastern European artworks to traditional Indo-Chinese crafts.

★ **Savannah Gallery** (✉ *Coronation St., Lower Valley* ☎ *264/497– 2263* ⊕ *www.savannahgallery.com*) specializes in works by local Anguillian artists as well as other Caribbean and Central American art, including oil paintings by Marge Morani. You'll also find works by artists of the renowned Haitian St. Soleil school, as well as Guatemalan textiles, Mexican pottery, and brightly painted metal work.

★ The peripatetic proprietors of **World Arts Gallery** (✉ *Cove Rd., West End* ☎ *264/497–5950 or 264/497–2767*), Nik and Christy Douglas, display a veritable United Nations of antiquities: exquisite Indonesian ikat hangings to Thai teak furnishings, Aboriginal didgeridoos to Dogon tribal masks, Yuan Dynasty jade pottery to Uzbeki rugs. There is also handcrafted jewelry and handbags.

Travel Smart St. Maarten, St. Barth, and Anguilla

WORD OF MOUTH

"Philipsburg is lined with a boardwalk now. There are restaurants and water sports all along it. . . . The whole boardwalk is packed when there are cruise ships in."

—Barbara 1

GETTING HERE AND AROUND

St. Maarten/St. Martin, St. Barthélemy, and Anguilla are part of a cluster of islands in the Lesser Antilles that are fairly close together. In fact, the islands are linked by both frequent ferries and small-plane flights. St. Maarten/St. Martin, which has the only international airport among the three, is the international flight hub. Most travelers, regardless of which island they plan to visit, land in St. Maarten/St. Martin and make their way to their final destination.

■ AIR TRAVEL

ANGUILLA

American Eagle flies daily from San Juan. TransAnguilla Airways offers daily flights from Antigua, St. Thomas, and St. Kitts and provides air-taxi service on request from neighboring islands. Windward Islands Airways (Winair) flies several times a day from St. Maarten. Anguilla Air Services is a reliable charter operation that flies to any Caribbean destination and runs day trips between Anguilla and St. Barth at the reasonable round-trip rate of $175 per person (four-person minimum). LIAT comes in from Antigua, Nevis, St. Kitts, St. Thomas, and Tortola. Note that LIAT requires all passengers to reconfirm 72 hours in advance, to avoid cancellation of their reservations.

The departure tax is $20, payable in cash at the airport.

Local Airline Contacts
American Eagle (☎ 264/497–3500). **Anguilla Air Services** (☎ 264/498–5922 ⊕ www.anguillaairservices.com). **TransAnguilla Airways** (☎ 264/497–8690). **LIAT** (☎ 264/497–5002). **Winair** (☎ 264/497–2748 ⊕ www.fly-winair.com).

AIRPORTS

Wallblake Airport is the hub on Anguilla.

Airport Contacts **Wallblake Airport** (☎ 264/497–2719).

GROUND TRANSPORTATION

A taxi ride to the Sandy Ground area runs $7 to $10; to West End resorts it's $16 to $22.

ST. BARTHÉLEMY

There are no direct flights to St. Barth from the U.S. Most North Americans fly first into St. Maarten's Queen Juliana International Airport, from which the island is 10 minutes by air. Flights are scheduled several times a day from 7:30 AM to 5:30 PM on Winair. Anguilla Air Services is an excellent charter company that flies to any Caribbean destination and runs day trips between Anguilla and St. Barth, at the very reasonable rate of $175 per person (four-person minimum). St. Barth Commuter is a small, private charter company that can also arrange service. Tradewind Aviation offers charters and regularly scheduled, daily nonstop Premium service from San

Juan, Puerto Rico. Flights are timed conveniently to meet early flights from the United States.

You must confirm your return interisland flight, even during off-peak seasons, or you may very well lose your reservation. Be certain to leave ample time between your scheduled flight and your connection in St. Maarten—three hours is the minimum recommended. Do not be upset if your luggage has not made the trip with you. It frequently will arrive on a later flight, and your hotel will send a porter to receive it; villa-rental companies may also help you retrieve luggage from the airport, but you may have to beg. It's a good idea to pack a change of clothes, required medicines, and a bathing suit in your carry-on—or better yet, pack very light and don't check baggage at all.

Local Airline Contacts **Anguilla Air Services** (☎ *264/498–5922* ⊕ *www.anguillaairservices.com*). **St. Barth Commuter** (☎ *0590/27–54–54* ⊕ *www.stbarthcommuter.com*). **Tradewind Aviation** (☎ *800/376–7922* ⊕ *www.tradewindaviation. com*). **Winair** (☎ *0590/27–61–01* or *800/634–4907* ⊕ *www.fly-winair. com*).

AIRPORTS

Airport Contacts**Aéroport de St-Jean** (☎ *0590/27–75–81*).

GROUND TRANSPORTATION

Some hotels (and even some villa management companies) provide airport transfers, because often guests rent their cars directly from the hotel or villa manager. Other-

wise, all the car-rental companies on the island are represented at the airport, and there are also taxis.

ST. MAARTEN/ST. MARTIN

Many major airlines offer nonstop service from the U.S. Air Caraïbes, Caribbean Airlines, Dutch Antilles Express, Insel, LIAT, and Winair (Windward Islands Airways) offer service from other islands in the Caribbean. Windward Express Airways offers charter flights to St. Maarten.

Local Airline Contacts **Air Caraïbes** (☎ *590/546–7663* ⊕ *www.air caraibes.com*). **American Airlines** (☎ *599/545–2040* ⊕ *www.aa.com*). **Caribbean Airlines** (☎ *599/546–7610* ⊕ *www.caribbean-airlines.com*). **Continental Airlines** (☎ *599/546–7671* ⊕ *www.continental.com*). **Delta Airlines** (☎ *599/546–7615* ⊕ *www. delta.com*). **Dutch Antilles Express** (☎ *599/546–7842* ⊕ *www.flydae. com*). **Insel Air** (☎ *599/546–7690* ⊕ *www.fly-inselair.com*). **JetBlue** (☎ *599/546–7664* or *599/546–7663* ⊕ *www.jetblue.com*). **LIAT** (☎ *599/546–7677* ⊕ *www.liatairline. com*). **Spirit Airlines** (☎ *599/546–7621* ⊕ *www.spiritair.com*). **St. Barths Commuter** (☎ *599/546–7698* ⊕ *www.stbarthcommuter. com*). **United** (☎ *599/546–7664* ⊕ *www.united.com*). **US Airways** (☎ *599/546–7683* ⊕ *www.usairways. com*). **Winair** (☎ *599/546–7690* ⊕ *www.fly-winair.com*). **Windward Express Airways** (☎ *599/545–2001* ⊕ *www.windwardexpress.com*).

AIRPORTS

Aéroport de L'Espérance, on the French side, is small and handles only island-hoppers. Jumbo jets fly into Princess Juliana International Airport, on the Dutch side.

Airport Contacts **Aéroport de L'Espérance** (*SFG* ✉ *Rte. l'Espérance, Grand Case* ☎ *590/87-53-03*). **Princess Juliana International Airport** (*SXM* ☎ *599/546-7542* ⊕ *www.pjiae.com*).

GROUND TRANSPORTATION

Taxis offer fixed fares from the airport. There is a government-sponsored taxi dispatcher. Posted fares are for one or two people; add $5 for each additional person, $1 to $2 per bag, $1 for a box or bundle. It costs about $18 from the airport to Phillipsburg or Marigot, and about $30 to Dawn Beach. Most visitors to St. Maarten/St. Martin rent a car, and there are agencies both at the airport and nearby; if you have rented a car, you will probably meet your company's representative at the airport and will be brought to the rental office if it is off-site.

■ BIKE AND MOPED TRAVEL

ST. BARTHÉLEMY

Several companies rent motorbikes, scooters, mopeds, and mountain bikes. Motorbikes go for about $30 per day and require a $100 deposit. Helmets are required. Scooter and motorbike rental places are located mostly along rue de France in Gustavia and around the airport in St-Jean. They tend to shift locations slightly.

Scooter Rental Contacts **Barthloc Rental** (✉ *Rue de France, Gustavia* ☎ *0590/27-52-81*). **Chez Béranger** (✉ *Rue de France, Gustavia*

☎ *0590/27-89-00*). **Ets Denis Dufau** (✉ *St-Jean* ☎ *0590/27-70-59*).

ST. MAARTEN/ST. MARTIN

Though traffic can be heavy, speeds are generally slow, so a moped can be a good way to get around. Parking is easy, filling the tank is affordable, and you've got that sea breeze to keep you cool. Scooters rent for as low as €25 per day and motorbikes for €37 a day at Eugene Moto, on the French side. If you're in the mood for a more substantial bike, contact the Harley-Davidson dealer, on the Dutch side, where you can rent a big hog for $150 a day or $900 per week.

Scooter Rental Contacts **Eugene Moto** (✉ *Sandy Ground Rd., Sandy Ground* ☎ *590/87-13-97*). **Harley-Davidson** (✉ *71 Union Rd., Cole Bay* ☎ *599/544-2704* ⊕ *www. h-dstmartin.com*).

■ BOAT AND FERRY TRAVEL

ANGUILLA

Ferries run frequently between Anguilla and St. Martin. Boats leave from Blowing Point on Anguilla approximately every half hour from 7:30 AM to 6:15 PM and from Marigot on St. Martin every 45 minutes from 8 AM to 7 PM. There are no evening ferries. You pay a $5 departure tax before boarding, in addition to the $15 one-way fare. On very windy days the 20-minute trip can be bouncy, so bring medication if you suffer from motion sickness. An information booth outside the customs shed in Blowing Point is usually open daily from 8:30 AM to 5 PM.

For schedule information and info on special boat charters, contact Link Ferries. Bear in mind that on your return you will still have to transfer by taxi from the Marigot ferry terminal to the airport, a trip that can take up to 45 minutes with traffic. The larger resort hotels offer escorted private transfers by speedboat, to and from a dock right at the airport, at a cost of about $75 per person. If you need this service, mention it to your reservations representative, who will make the arrangements.

In addition to scheduled public service, private ferry companies, including Shauna, run six or more round-trips a day, conveniently timed for major flights from Blowing Point to the airport in St. Maarten. On the St Maarten side they will bring you right to the terminal in a van, or you can just walk across the parking lot. These trips are $35 one-way or $60 round-trip (cash only). Shauna also can arrange charters.

Ferry Contacts Anguilla Ferries (☎ No phone ⊕ www.anguillaferry. com). **Link Ferries** (☎ 264/497–2231 ⊕ www.link.ai). **Shauna Ferries** (☎ 264/772–2031).

ST. BARTHÉLEMY

All ferry services to and from St. Barth come into and go out of the ferry terminal at Quai de la République in Gustavia

The *Voyager II* offers daily service from Marigot and Oyster Bay to St. Barth. The cost for the 75-minute ride is €67 from Oyster Pond and €93 from Marigot, round-trip. The price includes an open bar, tasty snacks, and port fees; children under 12 travel for about half-price. It takes about 40 minutes to get to St. Barth from the Dutch side, about half an hour longer from Marigot.

Great Bay Express runs several round-trips a day from Bobby's Marina in St. Maarten, one in the morning and a return in the evening, so you can have a full day on the island. You can enjoy the 45-minute ride on an outside deck or in the air-conditioned inside cabin. It costs €55 if reserved in advance, or €60 for same-day departures.

Private boat charters are also available, but they are very expensive. Master Ski Pilou is one of the companies that offer the service.

Ferry Contacts Voyager (☎ 0590/87–10–68 ⊕ www.voy12. com). **Great Bay Express Ferry** (☎ 590/52–45–06 lsbh.ferry@orange. fr). **Master Ski Pilou** (☎ 0590/27–91–79 ⊕ www.st-barths.com/ master-ski-pilou).

ST. MAARTEN/ST. MARTIN

In addition to Anguilla and St. Barth, Saba is served by ferries from St. Maarten/St. Martin. The *Dawn II* sails Tuesday, Thursday, and Saturday to Saba. The round-trip fare is $90. High-speed passenger ferries *Edge I* and *Edge II* motor from Simpson Bay's Pelican Marina to Saba on Wednesday through Sunday in just an hour ($100 round-trip plus $12 port tax).

Ferry Contacts Dawn II (☎ 599/416–2299 ⊕ www.sabac transport.com). **Edge I** and **Edge II**

(☎ 599/544–2640 or 599/544–2631 ⊕ www.stmaarten-activities.com).

■ CAR TRAVEL

ANGUILLA

Although most of the rental cars on-island have the driver's side on the left as in North America, Anguillian roads are like those in the United Kingdom—driving is on the left side of the road. It's easy to get the hang of, but the roads can be rough, so be cautious, and observe the 30 mph speed limit. Roundabouts are probably the biggest driving obstacle for most. As you approach, give way to the vehicle on your right; once you're in the rotary you have the right of way.

A temporary Anguilla driver's license is required—you can get into real trouble if you're caught driving without one. You get it for $20 (good for three months) at any of the car-rental agencies at the time you pick up your car; you'll also need your valid driver's license from home. Rental rates are about $45 to $55 per day, plus insurance.

Car-Rental Contacts **Apex/Avis** (✉ Airport Rd. ☎ 264/497–2642). **Triple K Car Rental/Hertz** (✉ Airport Rd. ☎ 264/497–5934).

ST. BARTHÉLEMY

Most travelers to St. Barth rent a car.

You'll find major rental agencies at the airport. You must have a valid driver's license and be 25 or older to rent, and in high season there may be a three-day minimum. During peak periods, such as Christ-mas week and February, be sure to arrange for your car rental ahead of time. When you make your hotel reservations, ask if the hotel has its own cars available to rent; some hotels provide 24-hour emergency road service—something most rental companies don't offer. If there are only two of you, think about renting a Smart car. Tiny but powerful on the hills, it's a blast to buzz around in, and also a lot easier to park than larger cars.

Roads are sometimes unmarked, so get a map and look for signs pointing to a destination. These will be nailed to posts at all crossroads. Roads are narrow and sometimes very steep, so check the brakes and gears of your rental car before you drive away, and make a careful inventory of the existing dents and scrapes on the vehicle. Maximum speed on the island is 30 mph (50 kph). Driving is on the right, as in the United States and Europe, and cars have their steering wheels on the left. Parking is an additional challenge.

There are two gas stations on the island, one near the airport and one in Lorient. They aren't open after 5 PM or on Sunday, but you can use the one near the airport at any time with some credit cards, including Visa. Considering the short distances, a full tank of gas should last you most of a week.

Car-Rental Contacts **Avis** (☎ 0590/27–71–43). **Budget** (☎ 0590/27–66–30). **Europcar** (☎ 0590/27–74–34 ⊕ www.st-barths. com/europcar/index.html). **Gumbs** (☎ 0590/27–75–32). **Gust Smart**

of St-Barth (☎ 0690/41–66–72).
Hertz (☎ 0590/27–71–14). **Turbe**
(☎ 0590/27–71–42 ⊕ www.saint-barths.com/turbecarrental/).

ST. MAARTEN/ST. MARTIN

Most people rent a car so they can more easily reach both sides of the island and interesting beaches. Depending on the time of year, a subcompact car will cost between $20 and $60 a day with unlimited mileage. You can rent a car on the French side, but this rarely makes sense for Americans because of the unfavorable exchange rates.

Driving is on the right, as in the United States and Europe, and cars have their steering wheels on the left. Most roads are paved and in generally good condition. However, they can be crowded, especially when the cruise ships are in port. Be alert for potholes and speed bumps, as well as the island tradition of stopping in the middle of the road to chat with a friend or yield to someone entering traffic. Few roads are identified by name or number, but most have signs indicating the destination. International symbols are used.

Car-Rental Contacts **Avis**
(☎ 599/545–2847 or 590/0690–634–947). **Budget** (☎ 599/545–4030 or 599/55–40–30). **Dollar/ Thrifty Car Rental** (☎ 599/545–2393). **Empress Rental a Car** (☎ 599/545–2067). **Golfe Car Rental** (☎ 0590/51–94–81) ⊕ www.golfecarrental.com). **Hertz** (☎ 599/545–4541).

■ TAXI TRAVEL

ANGUILLA

Taxis are fairly expensive, so if you plan to explore the island's many beaches and restaurants, it may be more cost-effective to rent a car. Taxi rates are regulated by the government, and there are fixed fares from point to point, which are listed in brochures the drivers should have handy and are also published in the local guide, *What We Do in Anguilla*. Taxis are $24 from the airport or $22 from the Blowing Point Ferry to West End hotels. Posted rates are for one or two people; each additional passenger adds $4 to the total and there is sometimes a charge for luggage. You can also hire a taxi by the hourly rate of $25. Surcharges of $2–$5 apply to trips after 6 PM. You'll always find taxis at the Blowing Point Ferry landing and at the airport. You'll need to call them to pick you up from hotels and restaurants, and arrange ahead with the driver who took you if you need a taxi late at night from one of the nightclubs or bars.

Taxi Contacts **Airport Taxi Stand** (☎ 264/235–3828). **Blowing Point Ferry Taxi Stand** (☎ 264/497–6089).

ST. BARTHÉLEMY

Taxis are expensive and not particularly easy to arrange, especially in the evening. There's a taxi station at the airport and another in Gustavia; from elsewhere you must contact a dispatcher in Gustavia or St-Jean. Technically, there's a flat rate for rides up to five-minutes long. Each additional three minutes is an additional amount. In reality, however, cabbies usually name a fixed rate—and will not budge. Fares are 50% higher from 8 PM to 6 AM and on Sunday and holidays. If you go out to dinner by taxi, let the restaurant know if you will be needing a taxi at the end of the meal, and they will call one for you.

Taxi Contacts **Gustavia taxi dispatcher** (☎ 0590/27–66–31). **St-Jean taxi dispatcher** (☎ 0590/27–75–81).

ST. MAARTEN/ST. MARTIN
There is a government-sponsored taxi dispatcher at the airport and at the harbor. Posted fares are for one or two people; add $5 for each additional person, $1 to $2 per bag, $1 for a box or bundle. It costs about $18 from the airport to Phillipsburg or Marigot, and about $30 to Dawn Beach. After 10 PM

fares go up 25%, and after midnight 50%. Licensed drivers can be identified by the TAXI license plate on the Dutch side, and the window sticker on the French.

You can hail cabs on the street or call the taxi dispatch to have one sent for you. You can arrange with the driver who brought you to pick you up at your restaurant when you are ready. On the French side of the island, the minimum rate for a taxi is $4, $2 for each additional passenger. There's a taxi service at the Marigot port near the tourist information bureau. Fixed fares apply from Juliana International Airport and the Marigot ferry to the various hotels around the island.

Taxi Contacts **Airport Taxi Dispatch** (☎ 9247). **Phillipsburg dispatch** (☎ 599/543–7815, 599/543–7814, or 590/542–2359).

ESSENTIALS

■ ACCOMMODATIONS

St. Maarten/St. Martin has the widest array of accommodations of any of the three islands, with a range of large resort hotels, small resorts, time-shares, condos, private villas, and small B&Bs scattered across the island. Most of the larger resorts are concentrated in Dutch St. Maarten. Visitors find a wide range of choices in many different price ranges.

Anguilla has several large luxury resorts, a few smaller resorts and guesthouses, and a rather large mix of private condos and villas. Lodging on Anguilla is generally fairly expensive, but there are a few more modestly priced choices.

The vast majority of accommodations on St. Barth are in private villas in a wide variety of levels of luxury and price; villas are often priced in U.S. dollars. The island's small luxury hotels are exceedingly expensive, made more so for Americans because prices are in euros. A few modest and moderately priced hotels do exist on the island, but there's nothing on St. Barth that could be described as cheap, though there are now a few simple guest houses and inns that offer acceptable accommodations for what in St. Barth is a bargain price (under € 100 per night in some cases).

■TIP➔ Assume that hotels operate on the European Plan (**EP**, no meals) unless we specify that they use the Breakfast Plan (**BP**, with full breakfast), Continental Plan (**CP**, continental breakfast), Full American Plan (**FAP**, all meals), or Modified American Plan (**MAP**, breakfast and dinner), or are **all-inclusive** (**AI**, all meals and most activities).

■ COMMUNICATIONS

INTERNET

ANGUILLA

In Anguilla, Internet access is common at hotels, but Internet cafés are not. Many hotels offer only Wi-Fi access, so you may need to bring your own laptop to stay connected.

ST. BARTHÉLEMY

Most hotels provide Internet and e-mail access for guests at the front desk, if not right in the room, and you can easily connect your laptop to the Wi-Fi that is common. If you have a Wi-Fi-equipped laptop, there are hotspots at the port area, the Guanahani, and in the parking lot of the Oasis Shopping Center in Lorient; service is provided by Antilles Référencement, an excellent computer shop that can set you up with a temporary Internet account or provide other computer support.

Internet Cafés **Antilles Référencement** (✉ *Oasis Shopping Centre, Lorient* ☎ *0590/52–07–22*). **France Télécom** (✉ *Espace Neptune, St-Jean* ☎ *0590/27–67–00*).

ST. MAARTEN/ST. MARTIN

Many hotels offer Internet service—some complimentary and some for a fee. There are cybercafés scattered throughout the island and free Wi-Fi hotspots (look for signs) at Bubble Tea (in the McDonald's building) and at Pineapple Pete in the Simpson Bay area. There is quite good free Wi-Fi coverage in many of the main areas of the French side, and DVPro2000 in Grand Case (next to Bounty Bakery) sells access cards for paid Wi-Fi service.

Internet Cafés **Bubble Tea Café** (✉ *12 Airport Rd., Simpson Bay*). **Cyber Link** (✉ *53 Front St., Philipsburg*). **DVPro2000** (✉ *1 rue Franklin Laurence, Grand Case*). **Pineapple Pete** (✉ *Airport Rd., Simpson Bay* ☎ *599/544–6030*).

TELEPHONES

ANGUILLA

To make a local call, dial the seven-digit number. Most hotels will arrange with a local provider for a cell phone to use during your stay. Try to get a prepaid, local one for the best rates. Some GSM international cell phones will work, some won't; check with your service before you leave. Hotels usually add a hefty surcharge to all calls.

LIME, the phone company, formerly called Cable & Wireless is open weekdays 8–6, Saturday 9–1, and Sunday 10–2. Here you can rent a cell phone for use during your stay. Or ask your hotel to arrange it for you. Inside the departure lounge at the Blowing Point Ferry dock and at the airport there's an AT&T USADirect access phone for collect or credit-card calls to the United States.

To call Anguilla from the United States, dial 1 plus the area code 264, then the local seven-digit number. From the United Kingdom dial 001 and then the area code and the number. From Australia and New Zealand dial 0011, then 1, then the area code and the number.

To call the United States and Canada, dial 1, the area code, and the seven-digit number. For other international calls, dial 011, the country code, and the local number. The country code for the United Kingdom is 44, Australia is 61, and New Zealand is 64.

Telephone Contacts **LIME** (✉ *Wallblake Rd.* ⊕ *www.time4lime.com*).

ST. BARTHÉLEMY

AT&T services are available. Public telephones do not accept coins; they accept *télécartes,* prepaid calling cards that you can buy at the gas station next to the airport and at post offices in Lorient, St-Jean, and Gustavia. Making an international call using a télécarte is much less expensive than making it through your hotel.

To activate your cell phone for local use, visit St. Barth Eléctronique across from the airport. You can also buy an inexpensive cell phone with prepaid minutes for as little as €50, including some initial airtime. Consider getting an unlocked mobile phone if you travel frequently; that way you can just switch SIM cards in and out wherever you are and take advantage of cheaper rates from the local carrier. Many hotels will rent you a local-service cell phone; ask the manager or concierge.

The country code for St. Barth is 590. Thus, to call St. Barth from the U.S., dial 011 + 590 + 590 and the local six-digit number. Some cell phones use the prefix 690, in which case you would dial 590 + 690. For calls on St. Barth, you must dial 0590 plus the six-digit local number; for St. Martin dial just the six-digit number for the French side, for the Dutch side (St. Maarten) dial 00–599–54 plus the five-digit number, but remember that this is an international call and will be billed accordingly. To call the United States from St. Barth, dial 001 plus the area code plus the local seven-digit number.

Telephone Contacts **France Télécom** (⊠ Espace Neptune, St-Jean ☎ 0590/27–67–00). **St. Barth Eléctronique** (⊠ St-Jean ☎ 0590/27–50–50).

ST. MAARTEN/ST. MARTIN

Calling from one side of the island to another is an international call. (Because of this, many businesses will have numbers on each side for their customers.) To phone from the Dutch side to the French, you first must dial 00–590–590 for local numbers, or 00–590–690 for cell phones, then the six-digit local number. To call from the French side to the Dutch, dial 00–599, then the seven-digit local number. To call a local number on the French side, dial 0590 plus the six-digit number. On the Dutch side, just dial the seven-digit number with no prefix.

For calls to the Dutch side from the United States, dial 011–599 plus the seven digit local number; for the French side, 011–590–590 plus the six-digit local number. At the Landsradio in Philipsburg, there are facilities for overseas calls and a USADirect phone, where you're directly in touch with an operator who will accept collect or credit-card calls. To call direct with an AT&T credit card or operator, dial 001–800/872–2881. On the French side, AT&T can be accessed by calling 080–099–00–11. If you need to use public phones, go to the special desk at Marigot's post office and buy a *télécarte* (phone card). There's a public phone at the tourist office in Marigot where you can make credit-card calls: the operator takes your card number (any major card) and assigns you a PIN, which you then use to charge calls to your card.

It's not a bad idea to get a local cell phone to use while on the island. Any of the local carriers—and most hotel concierges—can arrange a pre-paid rental phone for your use while you are on the island for $15 to $20 a week plus time (about 30¢ minute for outgoing calls, incoming calls are free). If you will mostly be on the French Side, get a French phone. Skype is a terrific option for laptop users.

■ ELECTRICITY

Generally, the Dutch St. Maarten and Anguilla operate on 110 volts AC (60-cycle) and have outlets that accept flat-prong plugs—the same as in North America. You will need neither an adaptor nor a transformer on these islands.

French St. Martin and St. Barth operate on 220 volts AC (60-cycle), with round-prong plugs, as in Europe; you need an adapter and sometimes a converter for North American appliances. The French outlets have a safety mechanism—equal pressure must be applied to both prongs of the plug to connect to the socket. Most hotels have hair dryers, so you should not need to bring one (but ask your hotel to be sure), and some hotels have shaver outlets in the bathroom that accept North American electrical plugs.

■ EMERGENCIES

ANGUILLA

As in the United States, dial 911 in any emergency.

ST. BARTHÉLEMY
Emergency Services **Ambulance and Fire** (☎ 0590/27–62–31). **Police** (☎ 17 or 0590/27–66–66).

ST. MAARTEN/ST. MARTIN
Emergency Services **Dutch-side emergencies** (☎ 911 or 599/542–2222). **French-side emergencies** (☎ 17 or 590/52–25–52). **Ambulance or fire emergencies Dutch side** (☎ 120; 130 for ambulances; 599/542–2111). **Ambulance or fire emergencies French side** (☎ 18; 590/87–95–01 in Grand Case; 590/87–50–08 in La Savanne). **Police emergencies Dutch side** (☎ 599/542–2222). **Police emergencies French side** (☎ 17; 590/87–88–35 in Marigot; 590/87–19–76).

■ HEALTH

An increase in dengue fever has been reported across the Caribbean since early 2007. While Puerto Rico, Martinique, and Guadeloupe have been the islands most heavily affected, instances have been reported in other parts of the Caribbean as well, including St. Barth. Since there are no effective vaccines to prevent dengue fever, visitors to the region should protect themselves with mosquito repellent (particularly repellant containing DEET, which has been deemed the most effective) and keep arms and legs covered at sunset, when mosquitoes are particularly active.

There are no particular problems regarding food and water safety in St. Maarten/St. Martin, Anguilla, or St. Barth. If you have an especially sensitive stomach, you may wish to drink only bottled water; also be sure that food has been thoroughly cooked and is served to you fresh and hot. Peel fruit. If you have problems, mild cases of traveler's diarrhea may respond to Pepto-Bismol. Generally, Imodium (known generically as loperamide) just makes things worse, but it may be necessary if you have persistent problems. Be sure to drink plenty of fluids; if you can't keep fluids down, seek medical help immediately.

MEDICAL INSURANCE AND ASSISTANCE

Consider buying trip insurance with medical-only coverage. Neither Medicare nor some private insurers cover medical expenses anywhere outside of the United States. Medical-only policies typically reimburse you for medical care (excluding that related to pre-existing conditions) and hospitalization abroad, and provide for evacuation. You still have to pay the bills and await reimbursement from the insurer, though.

Another option is to sign up with a medical-evacuation assistance company. A membership in one of these companies gets you doctor referrals, emergency evacuation or repatriation, 24-hour hotlines for medical consultation, and other assistance. International SOS Assistance Emergency and AirMed International provide evacuation services and medical referrals. MedjetAssist offers medical evacuation.

Medical Assistance Companies
AirMed International (⊕ www.airmed.com). **International SOS Assistance Emergency** (⊕ www.intsos.com). **MedjetAssist** (⊕ www.medjetassist.com).

Medical-Only Insurers In-ternational Medical Group (☎ 800/628–4664 ⊕ www.imglobal.com). **International SOS** (⊕ www.internationalsos.com). **Wallach & Company** (☎ 800/237–6615 or 540/687–3166 ⊕ www.wallach.com).

■ MAIL

ANGUILLA

Airmail postcards and letters cost EC$1.50 (for the first ½ ounce) to the United States, Canada, and the United Kingdom. The only post office is in the Valley; it's open weekdays 8 to 4:45.When writing to the island, you don't need a postal code; just include the name of the establishment, address (location or post-office box), and "Anguilla, British West Indies." There's a FedEx office near the airport. It's open weekdays 8 to 5 and Saturday 9 to 1.

ST. BARTHÉLEMY

Mail is slow. Correspondence between the United States and the island can take up to three weeks to arrive. The main post office is in Gustavia; in season it's open daily 7:30–3, (except for Wednesday and Saturday, when it closes at noon), but smaller post offices are in St-Jean and Lorient. These are open a few hours each morning. When writing to an establishment on St. Barth, be sure to include "French West Indies" at the end of the address. Because of the slow mail service, faxes are widely used.

ST. MAARTEN/ST. MARTIN

The main Dutch-side post office is on Walter Nisbeth Road in Philipsburg. There's a branch at Simpson Bay on Airport Road. The main post office on the French side is in Marigot, on rue de la Liberté. Letters from the Dutch side to North America and Europe cost ANG2.85; postcards to all destinations are ANG1.65. From the French side, letters up to 20 grams and postcards are €1 to North America. When writing to Dutch St. Maarten, call it "Sint Maarten" and make sure to add "Netherlands Antilles" to the address. When writing to the French side, the proper spelling is "St. Martin," and you add "French West Indies" to the address. Postal codes are used only on the French side.

■ MONEY

Prices throughout this guide are given for adults. Substantially reduced fees are almost always available for children, students, and senior citizens. Throughout this guide, the following abbreviations are used: **AE**, American Express; **D**, Discover; **DC**, Diners Club; **MC**, MasterCard; and **V**, Visa.

ANGUILLA

The legal tender on Anguilla is the Eastern Caribbean (EC) dollar, but U.S. dollars are widely accepted. (You'll often get change in EC dollars, though.) ATMs dispense American and Eastern Caribbean dollars. Credit cards are usually accepted. Be sure to carry lots of small bills; change for a $20 bill is often difficult to obtain.

ST. BARTHÉLEMY

The euro is the official currency on St. Barth; however, U.S. dollars are accepted in almost all shops and in many restaurants, though you will probably receive euros in change. The exchange rate for using dollars may or may not be favorable, so if you have access to euros, ask about exchange before you pay. Banks and ATMs are well located throughout the island, so getting money is rarely a problem, though they dispense only euros. Credit cards are accepted at most shops, hotels, and restaurants.

ST. MAARTEN/ST. MARTIN

Legal tender in Dutch St. Maarten is the Netherlands Antilles florin (guilder), written NAf or ANG, though U.S. dollars are universally accepted, and you may not see a single local note during your stay (gas prices are in florins, but the stations happily accept U.S. currency). The official currency in French St. Martin is the euro, and prices are usually displayed in euros (though some may be displayed in dollars); even then, the U.S. dollar is almost universally accepted on the French side, often at a favorable exchange rate. ATMs on the French side dispense only euros, while those on the Dutch side usually dispense dollars or florins.

■ PASSPORTS

A valid passport and a return or ongoing ticket is required for travel to Anguilla, St. Barthélemy, and St. Maarten/St. Martin. There are no border controls whatsoever between the Dutch and French sides of St. Maarten/St. Martin.

■ SAFETY

ANGUILLA

Anguilla is a quiet, relatively safe island, but crime has been on the rise, and there's no sense in tempting fate by leaving your valuables unattended in your hotel room, on the beach, or in your car. Avoid remote beaches, and lock your car, hotel room, and villa. Most hotel rooms are equipped with a safe for stashing your valuables.

ST. BARTHÉLEMY

There's relatively little crime on St. Barth. Visitors can travel anywhere on the island with confidence. Most hotel rooms have mini safes for your valuables. As anywhere, don't tempt loss by leaving cameras, laptops, or jewelry out in plain sight in your hotel room or villa. Don't walk barefoot at night. There are venomous centipedes that can inflict a remarkably painful sting.

ST. MAARTEN/ST. MARTIN

Petty crime can be a problem on both sides of the island (though less so on the French side than on the Dutch side), and robberies (including armed robberies) have been on the upswing during 2009. Always lock your valuables and travel documents in your room safe or your hotel's front-desk safe. Don't ever leave anything in the car, even in the glove compartment. When driving, keep your seatbelt on and the car doors locked. Never leave anything unattended at the beach. Despite the romantic imagery of the Caribbean, it's not good policy to take long walks along the beach at night. You should be on guard even during the day. Don't flash cash or jewelry, carry your handbag securely and zipped, and park in the busier areas of parking lots in towns and at beaches. Other suggestions include carrying only your driver's license and a photocopy of your passport with you for identification, leaving the original in your hotel safe. In general, use the same caution here as you would use at home.

■ TAXES AND SERVICE CHARGES

ANGUILLA

The departure tax is $20 for adults and $10 for children, payable in cash, at the airport or $5, payable in cash, at the Blowing Point Ferry Terminal. A 10% accommodations tax is added to hotel bills along with a $1 per night marketing tax, along with whatever service charge the hotel adds.

ST. BARTHÉLEMY

The island charges a $5 departure tax when your next stop is another French island, $10 if you're off to anywhere else. This is payable in cash only, dollars or euros, at the airport. At this writing, some hotels have added an additional 10% service charge to bills, though most include it in their tariffs. There is a 10% room tax on hotels and villa rentals.

ST. MAARTEN/ST. MARTIN

Departure tax from Juliana Airport is $10 to destinations within the Netherlands Antilles and $30 to all other destinations. This tax is included in the cost of many airline tickets, so check with your airline. If not included, the tariff must be paid in cash (dollars, euros, or local currency) before you get on your plane. There is no departure tax for "in transit" passengers who arrive by plane and depart within 24 hours. It will cost you €3 (usually included in the ticket price) to depart by plane from L'Espérance Airport and $5 (the rate can change) by ferry to Anguilla from Marigot's pier.

Hotels on the Dutch side add a 15% service charge to the bill as well as a 5% government tax, for a total of 20%. Some hotels include it in the rates, so be sure to ask. Hotels on the French side add 10% to 15% for service and a *taxe de séjour*; the amount of this visitor tax differs from hotel to hotel, but it is generally 5% above the cost of the room.

■ **TIME**

St. Maarten, Anguilla, and St. Barth are in the Atlantic Standard Time zone, which is one hour later than Eastern Standard and four hours earlier than GMT. Caribbean islands don't observe daylight saving time, so during the period when it's in effect, Atlantic Standard and Eastern Standard are the same.

■ **TIPPING**

ANGUILLA

A 10% to 15% service charge is added to all hotel bills, though it doesn't always go to staff.

It's usually expected that you will tip more—$5 per person per day for the housekeeping staff, $20 for a helpful concierge, and

$10 per day for the group to beach attendants. It's not uncommon to tip more generously, particularly at higher-end resorts during high season.

Many restaurants include a service charge of 10% to 15% on the bill; it's your choice to tip more if you feel the service is deserving. If there's no surcharge, tip about 15%. If you have taken most meals at your hotel's dining room, approximately $100 per week can be handed to the restaurant manager in an envelope to be divided among the staff.

Taxi drivers should receive 10% of the fare.

ST. BARTHÉLEMY

Restaurants include a 15% service charge in their published prices, but it's common French practice to leave 5% to 10% *pourboire* (a tip; literally, "for a drink")— in cash, even if you have paid by credit card. When your credit-card receipt is presented to be signed, the tip space should be blank— just draw a line through it—or you could end up paying a 30% service charge. Most taxi drivers don't expect a tip. Tip massage therapists at spas or hotels 10%; additional gratuities for services you arrange to your hotel or villa are at your discretion, but always appreciated.

ST. MAARTEN/ST. MARTIN

Seemingly without consistency, service charges of 10% to 15% may be added to hotel and restaurant bills. If you are unsure, be sure to ask whether a tip is included; on the French side, it is customary. On top of the included service (*service compris*), it is usual to leave an extra 5%–10% *in cash* for the server. Taxi drivers, porters, chambermaids, and restaurant waitstaff depend on tips. The guideline is 10% to 15% for waitstaff and cabbies, $1 per bag for porters, and $2 to $5 per night per guest for chambermaids.

■ TRIP INSURANCE

Comprehensive travel policies typically cover trip-cancellation and interruption, letting you cancel or cut your trip short because of a personal emergency, illness, or, in some cases, acts of terrorism in your destination. Such policies also cover evacuation and medical care. Some also cover you for trip delays because of bad weather or mechanical problems as well as for lost or delayed baggage. Another type of coverage to look for is financial default—that is, when your trip is disrupted because a tour operator, airline, or cruise line goes out of business. Generally you must buy this when you book your trip or shortly thereafter, and it's only available to you if your operator isn't on a list of excluded companies.

At the very least, consider buying medical-only coverage. Neither Medicare nor some private insurers cover medical expenses anywhere outside of the United States (including time aboard a cruise ship, even if it leaves from a U.S. port). Medical-only policies typically reimburse you for medical care (excluding that related to preexisting conditions) and hospi-

talization abroad, and provide for evacuation. You still have to pay the bills and await reimbursement from the insurer, though.

Another option is to sign up with a medical-evacuation assistance company. A membership in one of these companies gets you doctor referrals, emergency evacuation or repatriation, 24-hour hotlines for medical consultation, and other assistance. International SOS Assistance Emergency and AirMed International provide evacuation services and medical referrals. MedjetAssist offers medical evacuation. *For contact information on these services, see* ⇨ *Health, above.*

Expect comprehensive travel insurance policies to cost about 4% to 8% of the total price of your trip (it's more like 8%–12% if you're over age 70). A medical-only policy may or may not be cheaper than a comprehensive policy. Always read the fine print of your policy to make sure that you are covered for the risks that are of most concern to you. Compare several policies to make sure you're getting the best price and range of coverage available.

■TIP➔ OK. You know you can save a bundle on trips to warm-weather destinations by traveling in rainy season. But there's also a chance that a severe storm will disrupt your plans. The solution? Look for hotels and resorts that offer storm/hurricane guarantees. Although they rarely allow refunds, most guarantees do let you rebook later if a storm strikes.

Insurance Comparison Sites
Insure My Trip.com (☎ 800/487–4722 ⊕ www.insuremytrip.com). **Square Mouth.com** (☎ 800/240–0369 or 727/490–5803 ⊕ www.squaremouth.com).

Comprehensive Travel Insurers
Access America (☎ 866/729–6021 ⊕ www.accessamerica.com). **AIG Travel Guard** (☎ 800/826–4919 ⊕ www.travelguard.com). **CSA Travel Protection** (☎ 800/873–9855 ⊕ www.csatravelprotection.com). **HTH Worldwide** (☎ 610/254–8700 ⊕ www.hthworldwide.com). **Travelex Insurance** (☎ 888/228–9792 ⊕ www.travelex-insurance.com). **Travel Insured International** (☎ 800/243–3174 ⊕ www.travelinsured.com).

■ VISITOR INFORMATION

ANGUILLA

The Anguilla Tourist Office can provide up-to-the-minute information about attractions, events, and tours.

In Anguilla **Anguilla Tourist Office** (✉ Coronation Ave., The Valley ☎ 264/497–2759; 800/553–4939 from U.S. ⊕ www.anguilla-vacation.com).

ST. BARTHÉLEMY

A daily news sheet called *News* lists local happenings like special dinners or music and is available at markets and newsstands.

Also, the free weekly *Journal de Saint-Barth*—mostly in French—is useful for current events. The small *Ti Gourmet Saint-Barth* is a free pocket-size guidebook that's invaluable for addresses and telephone numbers of restaurants and services. Look for the annual *Saint-Barth Tables* for full restaurant menus. Its counterpart, *Saint-Barth Leisures*, contains current information about sports, spas, nightlife, and the arts.

Before You Leave **French Government Tourist Office** (☎ 900/990–0040 charges a fee ⊕ www.franceguide.com).

In St. Barth **Office du Tourisme** (✉ Quai Général-de-Gaulle ☎ 0590/27–87–27 www.saintbarth-tourisme.com) is an invaluable source for any reliable up-to-the-minute information you may need.

ST. MAARTEN/ST. MARTIN
Before You Leave **St. Maarten Tourist Office** (Dutch side only; ⊕ www.st-maarten.com). **St. Martin Office of Tourism** (French side only; ⊕ www.st-martin.org).

In St. Maarten/St. Martin **Dutch-side Tourist Information Bureau** (✉ Vineyard Park Bldg., 33 W.G. Buncamper Rd., Philipsburg ☎ 599/542–2337). **French-side Office de Tourisme** (✉ Rte. de Sandy Ground, near Marina de la Port-Royale, Marigot ☎ 590/87–57–21).

INDEX

PHOTO CREDITS

Fodor's InFocus

ST. MAARTEN, ST. BARTH & ANGUILLA

2nd Edition

Fodor's Travel Publications New York, Toronto, London, Sydney, Auckland

www.fodors.com